Ecology and Socialism

Chris Williams

HAYMARKET BOOKS
CHICAGO, ILLINOIS

Published in 2010 by Haymarket Books
P.O. Box 180165
Chicago, IL 60618
773-583-7884
www.haymarketbooks.org

ISBN 978-1-60846-091-5

Cover design by Amy Balkin
Cover photograph of protesters marching through the streets
of Copenhagen on the last day of the UN Climate Summit,
December 18, 2009. AP/Polfoto, Jens Dige

This book has been published with the generous support
of Lannan Foundation and the Wallace Global Fund.

Library of Congress Cataloging-in-Publication Data
is available.

Printed in Canada by union labor on recycled paper containing
100 percent post-consumer waste in accordance with the guidelines
of the Green Press Initiative, www.greenpressinitiative.org.

2 4 6 8 10 9 7 5 3 1

Contents

Introduction

"The American way of life is non-negotiable."
 —George H.W. Bush, Rio de Janeiro Earth Summit, 1992

"America is addicted to oil."
 —George W. Bush, State of the Union Address, 2008

"The world's energy system is at a crossroads. Current global trends in energy supply and consumption are patently unsustainable—environmentally, economically, socially."
 —International Energy Agency, World Energy Outlook, Executive Summary, November 2008

There is a giant death sentence hanging over much of our world. The once majestic polar bear, reduced to starvation due to dwindling sea ice in the Arctic, is only the latest forlorn poster child for the coming global ecocide that human civilization is visiting upon the earth. With rates of extinction running at a hundred to a thousand times the geological statistical norm, it is a species sadly far from alone. Thousands of species sit on Extinction Death Row awaiting the coup de grace, to be administered by a mutually reinforcing set of human-induced conditions.

At the forefront of these conditions rank habitat destruction and rapid, human-induced climate change. The human species seems well on the way to creating the Sixth Great Extinction as we exterminate other species faster than they can be classified; scientists estimate that we have classified less than 10 percent of all the species on earth. According to the International Union for the Conservation of Nature (IUCN), the world's largest coalition of environmental organizations, of the nearly 50,000 on its red list of endangered species up to 17,000 face the prospect of immediate extinction. If nothing is done, the IUCN predicts the demise over the course of the twenty-first century of 50 percent of amphibians, 70 percent of botanic life, 37 percent of freshwater fish, 28 percent of reptilians, 21 percent of mammals, and 12 percent of all birds.[1]

Species extinction is natural and nothing new; 99.999 percent of all species that have ever existed have become extinct. Sentient life, as represented by humans, is one outcome of this turnover. Over a period spanning millions of years, from our immediate bipedal forebears, Homo sapiens have evolved on a planet of stunning biodiversity, breathtaking vistas, and awe-inspiring feats of evolutionary development as biotic and abiotic factors have intertwined in a spectacular and ever-changing dance of mesmerizing beauty.[2] However, we live within a social system intent on hacking, burning, and destroying the biosphere in a time period measured in mere hundreds. It is a social system predicated on endless expansion; one that sickeningly combines historic and gargantuan amounts of wealth alongside oceans of poverty and mountains of waste.

It is no exaggeration to state that without swift, dramatic and profound changes to societal priorities, including a fundamental reorientation away from fossil-fuel-based energy and profit-driven capitalist economic growth, the generation growing up today will be, in all likelihood, the last to know climate stability. Nor is it wild-eyed doom-mongering to argue that if humanity continues on its present course, effecting only minor technological changes over the next ten to twenty years, civilization on anything like the current scale cannot be sustained. Capitalist society threatens the breakdown of the basic biogeochemical cycles of the biosphere as we have come to know them.

We are hurtling toward a series of ecological tipping points beyond which we will lose our ability to preserve a stable climate. Indeed, according to research published in 2009 in the journal *Ecology and Society,* we have already gone beyond three of nine planetary boundaries. A group of internationally renowned environmental and earth-systems scientists delineated nine "planetary life support systems" that were critical to human survival, and the processes that put them under stress: climate change, ocean acidification, stratospheric ozone depletion, interference with global phosphorus and nitrogen cycles, rate of biodiversity loss, global freshwater use, land-system change, aerosol loading, and chemical pollution. While stressing that these are only rough estimates that need refining, the group quantified where we are in relation to keeping within boundaries in order to avoid "irreversible and abrupt environmental change." By their calculations we have already surpassed boundaries for the nitrogen cycle, rate of biodiversity loss, and climate change. This doesn't mean we can't reverse them, but points to the extreme urgency of lowering the disruption that we are causing in these three sectors and making sure we do not pass through any of the other boundaries.[3]

A world economic system predicated on relentless growth, devouring increasing amounts of raw materials and energy and spewing out ever-larger amounts of toxic waste products, has produced a whole series of environmental threats: species extinction, air and water pollution, genetically modified organisms, desertification, deforestation, soil depletion, and the ever-present possibility of nuclear warfare,[4] to name only a few.[5] However, as it intersects with all other threats, and furthermore has a tendency to aggravate them, the most urgent and all-encompassing of these is global climate change.[6]

Among the problems scientists say climate change will bring over the next hundred years: rising sea levels submerging island and coastal areas, crop failures, droughts and floods, ocean acidification leading to the death of coral reefs, more extreme and frequent hurricanes, as well as a 20 to 50 percent reduction in planetary species. Indeed, even the most recent scientific estimates seem to be underrating the pace of change.[7] Worldwide CO_2 emissions rose faster between 2000 and 2004 than in the worst-case scenario reported by the United Nations (UN) in the middle of 2007.[8] And, despite all the rhetoric about implementing more benign and less polluting energy technologies and the hype about the 1997 Kyoto Protocol—the summit of world leaders that made a commitment to reduce greenhouse gasses—CO_2 emissions rose faster in the first years of the twenty-first century (3.1 percent per year) than they did in the 1990s (1.1 percent).[9] This means that even some of the more alarming predictions about the effects of climate change may actually be underestimates.

A case in point: in November 2008, the International Energy Authority released their World Energy Outlook report saying that without significant policy changes, the world could be on track for new global mean temperature rise to an apocalyptic 6.0°C higher than today.[10] The Massachusetts Institute of Technology (MIT) released a follow-up report to predictions on global climate made in 2003. Their new report, released in January 2009, revised their earlier prediction of an average global temperature rise from 2.4°C to 5.1°C.[11]

But perhaps 2°C, or even 5°C, doesn't seem like much, after all people experience much larger seasonal and even daily temperature fluctuations than this. Johann Hari, columnist for the *Independent* (London) newspaper has put those numbers into useful perspective:

> The world's climate scientists have shown that man-made global warming must not exceed 2°C. When you hear this, a natural reaction is—that's not much; how bad can it be if we overshoot? If I go out for a picnic and the temperature rises or falls by 2°C, I don't much notice. But this is the wrong analogy. If your body temperature rises by 2°C, you become feverish and feeble. If it doesn't go back down again, you die. The climate isn't like a picnic; it's more like your body.[12]

Solving the problem of global warming requires understanding the relationship between capitalism and the environment, examining the solutions on offer within the framework of the system, and determining whether those solutions are up to the task of preventing a runaway greenhouse effect. The world system of capitalism has been, and will continue to be, largely impotent in the face of climate change, not because there are evil, uneducated, backward individuals in power—though this is arguably true in many cases—but because capitalism's own social relations prevent effective solutions from being realized. The blind, unplanned drive to accumulate that is the hallmark of capitalist production—the profit motive—has created the problem of climate change, not individuals' profligate natures or overpopulation. The economic system needs to be transformed or we will surely be eking out a living on a much less hospitable planet.

This is not a common approach to the question. On one side, corporations and governments that have a direct interest in maintaining the current social setup and the prevailing power relations argue for nonsystem threatening solutions. Hence the push by governing elites for market-based mechanisms such as cap and trade. On the other side, many environmental organizations and ecologically concerned individuals focus on efforts to combat global warming via individual responsibility, changing personal lifestyles, consuming less, or population reduction. There is more than just overlap here; both approaches allow the system to clamber off the hook of responsibility.

It is rarely acknowledged that capitalism itself might be the problem. Rather, two kinds of growth are blamed—either economic or population. From this flows the following conclusion: we can continue with a market-based system as long as there are "limits to growth" placed on national economies and populations, perhaps with some regulatory restrictions alongside technological breakthroughs.

To retain the system more or less untouched, capitalists and their paid advocates are forced to argue that "sustainable development" is possible; many corporations and governments have substantial sustainable development departments, statements, and growth targets to promote just that. There is much seemingly heartfelt talk of the concept of "corporate social responsibility" (CSR). On the other side, many environmental groups argue for restrictions on population, air travel or general consumption, and a change in personal lifestyles. Some of these proposals do involve curbing industrial growth and regulating the activities of corporations—and deserve examination. For example, many consumer goods, as well as packaging, are superfluous, as is much of business travel; short-haul flights could be better switched to trains without any loss of comfort (in fact quite the opposite). Many proposals, however, involve encouraging ordinary people—who are already facing cuts in their living standards—to further tighten their belts or to spend time and money most of us don't have to make a series of changes in our lifestyles while the life-destroying chaos of the market system rages around us unabated.

An oft-repeated mantra is that the developing world cannot have the same standard of living as the developed if we are to make any progress in slowing down environmental degradation. This statement rests on the patently false assumption that everyone in the Global South has one standard of living (very low) and everyone in the North another (very high). The truth is that while absolute poverty is much more serious and widespread in the South, and consumer goods are much less widely available, every country is divided into a tiny minority of rich and the vast majority of the less well-off and poor who actually do all the work.

It is true that less developed countries of the South cannot emulate the consumer lifestyles and type of development of the North to which everyone, without a hint of irony, North and South, is nevertheless constantly taught to aspire. Further capitalist development of the North is quite enough to wreck the planet on its own; were the people of the southern hemisphere to join in and catch up, we would need the equivalent of five planets.[13] The problem, this book will argue, is not economic growth per se or population growth, but profit-driven, unplanned growth that in many cases is either socially useless or actively detrimental to humans and the biosphere—the kind of growth that has brought us to the brink of social and ecological disaster. Development and growth must be fundamentally redefined to prioritize real human and ecological needs rather than the priorities of profit and the market.

Currently, development means more roads, more industry, more waste, more commodification of everything; in short: more profits. Development and progress are equated with capitalist modernity; "underdevelopment" or "less developed" with a lack of it. Modernization in turn is about increased technology and urbanization in the service of providing goods for a market to be bought and sold, alongside "market democracy" to be accomplished via social and economic mobility and facilitated by education. Any aspects of "pre-modern" society such as traditional forms of knowledge, farming methods, collectivities or alternative kinship or organizational models are denigrated and actively uprooted. The only collective that is recognized and validated is that of the nation-state.

Development needs to be about the enhancement of human life and culture in the context of co-evolution with nature that will require nothing less than a social, economic, political and cultural revolution. Important aspects of this will be technological, but the key dynamic is mass democratic decision-making based on the needs of the producers in conjunction with a long-term commitment to sustainable ecological living. As Vandana Shiva, the Indian physicist and world-renowned environmental activist and author, has argued—in strong echoes of Marx—while it's true that we need a change in our energy systems, this must be accompanied by a far more significant paradigm shift from:

- A reductionist to a holistic worldview based on inter-connections
- A mechanistic, industrial paradigm to an ecological one
- A consumerist definition of being human to one that recognizes us as conservers of the earth's finite resources and co-creators of wealth with nature[14]

Much of the environmental movement in the North is consumed by arguing for ordinary people to make sacrifices in order to save the planet. They then wonder why more people aren't on the demonstrations against global warming and why the movement isn't more diverse. For those millions out of work in the North, the millions on part-time work and mired in debt, the millions losing their homes to foreclosure and the hundreds of thousands of already homeless or the forty-five million North Americans made sick each year from contaminated food and water,[15] this argument rings particularly hollow. In reality the argument about sacrifice speaks to and for a very narrow segment of middle-class opinion formers. If we are to make environmental arguments meaningful to the vast majority of people in the developed world, let alone the Global South, the argument must focus on justice, jobs, equality, and improving the quality of life, not the need for more sacrifice. In other words, environmental activism must be about socio-ecological justice the world over.

Not only are some of the solutions proposed by the mainstream environmental movement misguided, but there is often an enormous chasm between the problems environmentalists describe and the solutions many of them propose. While there are many examples, Al Gore's Oscar-winning documentary, *An Inconvenient Truth*, is a prime case in point. After predicting planet-gone-wild climate gyrations from the continued unsustainable production of greenhouse gases, Gore tells us to consume a bit less stuff, change our lightbulbs, make sure our car tires are properly inflated, and bike to work. The gap between ends and means is so absurd as to be laughable. More insidiously, in a move of political jujitsu, the film shifts the weight of change from corporate polluters to individuals.

Chapter one will demarcate the main contours of global warming and climate change and what the near- and longer-term future will potentially hold in store. Subsequent chapters will take up what can still be done to avert a calamitous and irreversible journey into global climate instability. Some prominent environmentalists, such as James Lovelock, author of *The Gaia Hypothesis* and *The Revenge of Gaia*, argue that it is already too late to make significant changes.[16] Indeed, Lovelock now argues that people are "too stupid" to make the necessary changes as we are not sufficiently evolved. In an interview in March 2010, he goes on to say that one of the major impediments to effective action is "modern democracy" and what is required is more authoritarian rule by a select few as democracy needs to be put on hold in order to deal with climate change.[17] Lovelock thus lays the blame entirely on ordinary people as if we are the ones really in charge of making the economic decisions that got us to this point.

Others, including myself, believe that there is still time to avoid planetary meltdown. However, we are at such a precipitous point, having done essentially nothing for so long, that swift, decisive action that ultimately challenges the continuance of the system itself is required. This cannot mean replacing oil, coal, and natural gas with nuclear energy, which has its own potentially catastrophic environmental problems and is in any case an expensive alternative that would take too long to implement. Nor can we accept the Pentagon's apocalyptic vision of Fortress United States vs. the Rest of the World.[18]

Neo-Malthusian arguments about population are resurfacing with a vengeance as explanations for the recent global food crisis and, even more so, amongst people genuinely concerned by the ongoing and indeed accelerating destabilization of planetary ecosystems. Population growth is inversely related to economic development and reductions in poverty levels; the higher the standard of living, the lower the rate of population growth.[19] Chapter two takes up the argument about population by digging into the question of whether there is enough food to feed everyone, and argues that 6.7 billion people can live on the planet without irreparably degrading it and depleting resources at unsustainable rates.

The real question is: Would there be enough resources for *all* 6.7 billion people to have a decent standard of living that is at the same time environmentally sustainable if we got rid of unequal classes by eradicating the profit motive that currently drives production? What if instead, production and distribution of goods and services were democratically planned using more environmentally benign technologies? One objective of the book is to sketch out an affirmative answer to those questions.

If the debacle at the climate summit in Copenhagen in December 2009 teaches us nothing else, it is this: world leaders are utterly incapable of negotiating real solutions to climate change. They are wired into the system of profit and competitive national development that brooks no alternative. Hence they suggest, after suitable prodding from their corporate sponsors and notwithstanding their lofty rhetoric, solutions that pose the least interference with business as usual; indeed, obscenely, allow for some of the biggest polluters to make even larger profits.

For example, it is impossible to maintain that cap and trade, the main negotiating plank pushed by conference attendees from the industrialized countries, is the most efficient method of reducing greenhouse gas emissions. Conversely, cap and trade can easily be explained as the most efficient method for continuing with a high-carbon, business-as-usual future that perversely rewards some of the most polluting entities on the planet and simultaneously justifies atmospheric pollution. Chapters three and four expose the many false solutions to climate change and make the case as to why there can be no such thing as sustainable or "environmentally friendly" capitalism.

There is no time to waste, and so building a movement to fight for real reforms within the structure of capitalism is absolutely essential. It is imperative that we slow down the rate of climate change as quickly as possible by moving to less carbon-intensive energy alternatives and by taking energy conservation seriously. This means building the broadest possible movement arguing for increasing public investment in wind farms, solar arrays, and public transport together with strong government-mandated energy efficiency and conservation measures and a robust jobs program to go with it. We need to fight for real change in the here and now and make the pressure on our elected representatives from a broad-based movement against environmental destruction more politically damaging to ignore than the pressure from the corporations. Chapter five will outline what such a socio-ecological justice movement should argue for right now and provide arguments for how it is a practical alternative to a fossil-fuel-driven corporate agricultural and industrial system determined to cling to profits come what may. While we are constantly told there's no money for hospitals, schools, or "saving the environment," the multitrillion dollar global bailout of the banking system, centered in the United States, has shown people otherwise. To paraphrase author and activist Jonathan Neale, if the planet were a bank, governments would already have found the money; vast sums would be conjured up in a matter of days.[20]

Chapter six examines the legacy of Marxist analysis and its continued relevance to ecological questions. It seeks to unearth the significant contributions Marx, Engels, and subsequent Marxists have made to ecological thought in the belief that a Marxist framework allows for the most coherent and useful modality for understanding the roots of the ecological crisis and plotting a way out of it. Marxism posits a dialectical interaction and an essential unity between society and nature that eludes mainstream capitalist and much radical Green thought. The dualism inherent to both, that nature is separate and opposite to society—either to be exploited for the benefit of humans or protected from them—is overcome by the holism central to Marxist historical materialism.

The economic crisis that began in 2008, as seemingly stable economies unraveled across the globe and corporations collapsed under the weight of their own feckless gambling, has caused a profound ideological crisis of capitalist legitimacy. The ideological paradigm that has reigned supreme for thirty years—that the market knows best—has been exposed as the mirage it always was. This paradigm, that, to use Margaret Thatcher's infamous phrase, "there is no alternative" to neoliberal privatization and market flexibility, alongside unrelenting hostility to governments having some responsibility for collective social provision, lies in tatters after the near-collapse of the system and its stabilization only through a massive, internationally coordinated government bailout. The notion of attaining social progress through individualized aspirations for self-advancement has been shattered on the rock of reality. Not since the 1960s have so many people begun to question the prevailing view of what is "normal" or "natural" in society and whether perhaps, after all, another world is possible.

The economic crisis has reawakened interest in investigating what socialism has to offer as an alternative world model and guide to action. The economic crisis broke out alongside the ecological crisis and both can trace their ancestry to the remorseless drive to accumulate characteristic of capitalism. Stating that capitalism must therefore be abolished and replaced with a democratic system of the "associated producers" (i.e., workers) no longer seems so outlandish a proposition to be dismissed as utopian dreaming by unreconstructed socialists still living in the late nineteenth century. Rather it evinces interest, conversation, and dialogue about what that might mean and look like, or how it might be achieved. Chapters seven and eight outline some of the ways in which more fundamental change will have to be envisioned.

Our society is unrecognizable from fifty years ago, let alone one hundred. Imagine what we could do if we the people had the power to decide what it would look like fifty years from now. This book represents the beginning of a discussion of that vision—a contribution to the discussion of real solutions to climate change and ecological degradation and how they could be implemented via collective action for social equality and justice.

CHAPTER ONE

The Science of Climate Change

"Many of the new climates will include combinations of temperature, precipitation, seasonality, and day length that do not currently exist anywhere on Earth...Something will live in these non-analogue climates, but it is difficult to guess what."
—Chris D. Thomas, *Climate Change and Biodiversity*, 2005

"There is a strategy to single out individuals, tarnish them and try to bring the whole of the science into disrepute."
—Ben Santer, prominent climate scientist commenting on climate denial strategy, November 2006[1]

"Even given the uncertainties of the geological record, it is difficult to state this point strongly enough: human releases of carbon dioxide are almost certainly happening faster than any natural carbon releases since the beginning of life on earth...*It can hardly be a surprise either that the climate is changing rapidly: what* would *be a surprise were if everything continued as normal."*
—Mark Lynas, author,
Six Degrees: Our Future on a Hotter Planet[2]

While there remain unreconstructed and powerful climate change deniers, the overwhelming scientific consensus has become harder and harder to ignore, as have new and unusual weather patterns and warming trends. To name only a small number, over the past few years major reports in *Time* magazine, the *Economist,* and the *Nation* have outlined the threats associated with climate change.[3] Even the Pentagon has gotten in on the action; its 2003 report, *An Abrupt Climate Change Scenario and Its Implications for United States National Security*, foresees a fortress America with walls erected against a rising tide of Latin American migrants fleeing ecological disaster and stepped up policing of what it predicts will be a more war-prone world:

> The United States and Australia are likely to build defensive fortresses around their countries because they have the resources and reserves to achieve self-sufficiency...Borders will be strengthened around the country to hold back unwanted starving immigrants from the Caribbean islands (an especially severe problem), Mexico, and South America. Energy supply will be shored up through expensive (economically, politically, and morally) alternatives such as nuclear, renewables, hydrogen, and Middle Eastern contracts...Tension between the U.S. and Mexico rise as the U.S. reneges on the 1944 treaty that guarantees water flow from the Colorado River...Yet, even in this continuous state of emergency the U.S. will be positioned well compared to others. The intractable problem facing the nation will be calming the mounting military tension around the world.[4]

Several of the major corporations previously pumping enormous funds into organizations intent on denying climate change, such as the environmentally friendly sounding Global Climate Coalition,[5] have to some extent switched their millions to campaigns designed to "greenwash" even the most polluting industries.

In a tactical shift—borne of experience combating the environmental movement's demands for government regulation in the 1970s and witnessing Philip Morris's eventual failed efforts to deny the deleterious health effects of tobacco—many corporations have switched from a policy of outright denial to one of convincing us that they, too, can be green. However, this tactic goes on in parallel with continued efforts to sow doubt in the public mind and undermine any momentum for real change in energy production.

To take one example, in response to public criticism and too harsh a public spotlight, ExxonMobil sought to burnish its public image and along with other corporations left the Global Climate Coalition in 2002 when it became too embarrassing, publishing on its website its devotion to corporate responsibility. However, a report by the Union of Concerned Scientists released in 2007 detailed the more recent activities of ExxonMobil that allowed the corporation to continue its activities behind the scenes. ExxonMobil set up, funded, and ran a highly successful disinformation campaign through a series of front organizations and individuals based on the tobacco lobby's campaign to undermine the connection between smoking and negative health effects. According to the report, ExxonMobil has:

- *Manufactured uncertainty* by raising doubts about even the most indisputable scientific evidence
- Adopted a strategy of *information laundering* by using seemingly independent front organizations to publicly further its desired message and thereby

confuse the public

- *Promoted scientific spokespeople* who misrepresent peer-reviewed scientific findings or cherry-pick facts in their attempts to persuade the media and the public that there is still serious debate among scientists that burning fossil fuels has contributed to global warming and that human-caused warming will have serious consequences
- *Attempted to shift the focus* away from meaningful action on global warming with misleading charges about the need for "sound science"[6]

Such was the effectiveness of the ExxonMobil campaign that the British Royal Society, the oldest scientific academy in the world, in 2006 took the unprecedented step of writing to ExxonMobil asking them to desist in their efforts to undermine climate change science.[7] Generally speaking, corporations play both games. They attempt to water down or otherwise alter any potential legislation that they see as hostile to their ability to make money through a veritable army of lobbyists and right-wing or conservative think tanks. Simultaneously they crow about their green credentials and newfound concern for the environment.

The destructive power of the climate change lobbyists has become a disturbingly serious business in its own right. Since 2003, the number of climate change lobbyists has risen by more than 400 percent, from 525 in 2003 to 2,349 in 2009. That's a somewhat mind-boggling five lobbyists for every single member of Congress.

It's not possible to understand the well-orchestrated and successful "swift-boating" of such well-established science that has consumed the media pre- and post-Copenhagen without acknowledging the role of corporate finance, which has allowed conservative think tanks and foundations to spend millions getting the message out that climate change science is not to be trusted.[8]

As a case in point, a March 2010 report by Greenpeace details the activities of U.S. corporate giant Koch Industries. Though most people have probably never heard of Koch, it is the second-largest privately held corporation in the United States after the huge food-processing conglomerate Cargill. It has oil and related business of $100 billion per year and seventy thousand employees operating in sixty countries. The Koch brothers who own the business are the joint ninth richest Americans and nineteenth richest in the world.[9] Between 2005 and 2008, Koch ploughed $25 million into climate opposition groups, outdoing ExxonMobil nearly three to one. It gave money to thirty-five different groups hostile to climate science. Some of the high-profile organizations that Koch gave money to, all of whom have strong public stances attacking climate science, the need to do something about global warming, or the need to change energy policy are: The Heritage Foundation, Americans for Prosperity, the Cato Institute, the Manhattan Institute, the Foundation for Research on Economics and the Environment, Institute for Humane Studies, and the American Council on Science and Health (which claims that reducing greenhouse gases would have detrimental health effects).[10] For those who want to delve deeper into the murky waters of corporate irresponsibility, the extent to which climate change denial has been a fully fledged and rapidly expanding business for years is well documented in James Hoggan's book *Climate Cover-Up*.[11]

It would be hard to find a more pro-business bill than the Waxman-Markey ACES Bill, which passed the House of Representatives in the summer of 2009. It gives billions of dollars in handouts to fossil fuel companies and practically a license to print money from carbon offsets and credits. Despite the pro-business slant of the legislation, some corporate entities and Republicans were nevertheless outraged at the idea of any restrictions placed on their right to freely pollute.

But the lobbyists' efforts at subverting the democratic process couldn't be as effective as they so clearly are without reaching the ear of an already receptive audience in Washington.

Millions of people around the world have seen Al Gore's Oscar-winning documentary, *An Inconvenient Truth,* and been shocked by the climate demons called forth by humanity's reckless and relentless burning of fossil fuels. Yet trying to pick apart all the controversies swirling around this science-based yet highly political debate is complicated enough without having to put up with the shameless self-promotion of Al Gore as the latter-day reincarnation of Rachel Carson or the corporate media taking climate denial arguments on face value as a legitimate counterargument to those of the scientists.[12]

Basics of Global Warming Science

It is important to state from the outset that without global warming the earth would not have been able to evolve complex life—it would be far too cold and prone to wild swings in temperature. The atmosphere acts as a blanket that keeps the earth at an average temperature of 15°C. Without this insulating layer, heat from the sun would simply bounce off the surface of the earth and immediately re-radiate to space.

This atmospheric insulating blanket wrapped around the earth regulates global temperature and makes life possible. In the current context, however, an increase in average global temperatures is being caused by an increase in atmospheric concentrations of one gas in particular: carbon dioxide. Though water, natural gas (methane), and a few other compounds also contribute, CO_2 is the most significant because of its longevity in the atmosphere (around one hundred years) and because we are augmenting its increased atmospheric concentration by burning fossil fuels and cutting down forests. Methane is twenty times more powerful as a greenhouse gas, and there are significant and extremely serious threats from the possibility of hundreds of millions of tons of it being released from Siberian permafrost and underwater deposits, but it has a much shorter atmospheric lifetime due to its higher reactivity.

Carbon dioxide is the gas that animals breathe out as a waste product of respiration and plants absorb in order to grow. It exists as a very small percentage of the air—0.03 percent. However, when it comes to absorbing infrared radiation (heat energy) reflected from the surface of the earth and preventing it from escaping back out to space, this particular molecule is so effective that even small percentage changes in atmospheric concentration have large effects.[13] What is commonly known as the greenhouse effect is CO_2 performing the same function as the glass of a greenhouse by trapping heat inside earth's atmosphere, the process that is leading to global warming and global climate change.

The greenhouse effect is not to be confused with the hole discovered in the ozone layer in the upper atmosphere that became big news in the 1980s. Ozone (O_3) is concentrated in an upper layer of the atmosphere and is responsible for blocking damaging ultraviolet radiation from the sun from reaching the earth's surface. The ozone layer was found to be degraded by chemical compounds called CFCs (chlorofluorocarbons), which destroy ozone and were being producing in large quantities for use as refrigerants and propellants for aerosols. Two massive, seasonally fluctuating holes in this protective layer over the Arctic and Antarctic were confirmed by scientific observation in the 1980s. Professor Paul Crutzen, a world-renowned atmospheric chemist, posited a link between ozone depletion and industrialized manufacturing processes in the 1970s and eventually won the Nobel Prize for Chemistry in 1995 for his work in this area. His research, along with growing concerns about the impact of the hole getting even bigger, led to the international treaty known as the Montreal Protocol, which came into effect in 1989 and sought to phase out the use of CFCs. While some of the causes of the ozone hole are similar and CFCs are partially responsible for trapping heat, the hole in the ozone is not causally linked to global climate change.

Carbon dioxide is generated whenever a substance containing the element carbon is burned. We react some carbon-containing compound with oxygen (i.e., burn it) in order to release the large amounts of energy stored in the chemical bonds. In the process, one of the guaranteed waste products of this process is the colorless, odorless, and poisonous gas carbon dioxide. Eighty percent of the energy generated on the planet—mostly for the production of electricity—and virtually all the fuel used for land, air, or sea transportation (98 percent) depends on the burning of one or another of three types of carbon-containing substances: coal, oil, or natural gas.

These three substances are collectively known as fossil fuels due to their common origin. Fossil fuels are the partially decomposed remains of plants and animals that have been cooked at high temperature and pressure in the earth's crust and accumulated over tens of millions of years. By tapping these vast deposits of buried energy we are drawing down the earth's balance of concentrated energy accrued over many millions of years. This is what makes fossil fuels an essentially finite, nonrenewable source of energy.

While the developed world has gone through two energy transitions from wood to coal and from coal to oil, much of the world's poor, in excess of two billion people, depend for their heating, lighting, and cooking on another carbon-containing compound: biomass in the form of wood, animal dung, or other plant material.

Another 17 percent of our energy is generated from nuclear power, with the remainder, 3 to 4 percent, coming from renewable sources, mostly in the form of hydroelectric dams. Transportation accounts for more than 25 percent of global energy demand. Industrial processes count for a third of energy consumption.[14] Heating and cooling of buildings in the North and deforestation in the South are among the other major contributors.

Evidence for Global Warming

To the extent that a debate around global warming existed among scientists, that debate has now definitively closed. The evidence is overwhelming and incontrovertible. The most recent summary report for policy makers by the Inter-Governmental Panel on Climate Change (IPCC), released in November 2007, begins thus: "Warming of the climate system is unequivocal, as is now evident from observations of increases in global average air and ocean temperatures, widespread melting of snow and ice, and rising global average sea level."[15]

The report goes on to document that eleven of the last twelve years (1995 to 2006) have been in the top twelve warmest since accurate temperature recording began in 1850. From 1961 to 1990, sea levels rose 1.8 mm/yr while since 1993 that rate has increased to 3.1 mm/yr. Satellite data going back to 1978 show annual Arctic sea ice has decreased by 2.7 percent per decade (and three times that percentage in the summer months). In the language of a scientific paper, the IPCC goes on to document other changes: it is "very likely" (90 to 95 percent certain) that, over the last fifty years, cold days, cold nights, and frosts have become less frequent, with the converse true for hot days and nights. It is "likely" (66 to 90 percent certain) that heat waves have become more frequent and that the intensity of tropical cyclones in the North Atlantic has increased since 1970. Average northern hemisphere temperatures are "very likely" higher than any other fifty-year period in the last 500 years and "likely" higher than any period in the last 1,300 years.

All these alterations in climate are leading to other changes: changes in spring runoff from glaciers affecting water availability, earlier springs, and shifts in migratory patterns and ranges to higher latitudes or altitudes for plants and animals. Because the planet is an interconnected whole, climate change negatively impacts sea life as the oceans warm and become more acidic (CO_2 is an acidic compound), leads to an increase in forest fires and agricultural and other pests, and precipitates changes to the geographical spread of disease vectors such as malaria-carrying mosquitoes.

The IPCC report is the fourth compiled by more than two thousand of the foremost scientists investigating climate change; the first was published in 1990. Each study has been more definitive than the last. These reports have been criticized in the past because they are produced by consensus and have to be supported by all the governments that have signed on to the IPCC process. This means that they can hardly be taken as the wild-eyed musings of some fringe scientist with an ideological anticapitalist grudge, nor can they be simply dismissed as the work of a group self-serving people on the lookout for more research funding.

Some argue that warming patterns are not due primarily to anthropogenic (human) sources, but are the result of natural changes in the orbit of the earth and the cycles of the sun. It is true that, in the 4.5 billion years that the earth has been around, the earth's climate has gone through some extremely dramatic climatic changes. In fact, the climate stability of the last 12,000 years, enabling the prediction of annual weather patterns and a shift to farming concomitant with the rise of civilization since the last ice age, is more of an anomaly than the norm.[16] However—and the IPCC report is quite definitive on this—left to nature, the sum of solar and volcanic activity over the last fifty years would "likely" have produced cooling. So the warming that has occurred can only be laid at the door of greenhouse gas emissions that result from human activity.

Since 1750, levels of CO_2 in the atmosphere have grown from 280 parts per million (ppm) to today's level of 387 ppm, with an increase of 70 percent between 1970 and 2004, precisely mirroring the vast global economic expansion that occurred during those years.[17]

CO_2 and CH_4 concentrations in the atmosphere are now *higher than at any time in the last 650,000 years.*[18] In the last 250 years 1,100 billion tons of CO_2 have been released into the atmosphere through industrial processes, mostly due to the burning of fossil fuels. *Half* of these emissions occurred after the mid-1970s.[19] As the CO_2 that we put into the air is from partly decomposed organic matter laid down millions of years ago, using radiological dating, it is possible to distinguish between CO_2 put into the atmosphere by us and the CO_2 that cycles through from natural causes. The evidence is unequivocal that industrial processes are responsible for the resulting increase.

How Bad Can It Get?

Scientists predict that global greenhouse gas emissions will continue to increase over the next few decades by 25 to 90 percent. The range of possibilities depends on the extent to which governments adopt "lower carbon" programs. As the graphic below illustrates, based on available data and likely changes to the current global energy mix, the authoritative U.S. Energy Information Agency projections predict continued growth in CO_2 emissions by fuel type to 2030, rather than their decline. While the bulk of this increase will come from non-OECD (Organization of Economic Cooperation and Development) countries, per capita, they will remain far lower emissions than the OECD per capita average.

Climate scientists project a warming of 0.2°C/decade for various possible scenarios and state that even if emissions had been stabilized at 2000 levels (which they were not), a warming of 0.1°C/decade would still occur. The 2007 report goes on to state:

> Sea level rise under warming is inevitable. Thermal expansion would continue for many centuries after GHG concentrations have stabilized, for any of the stabilization assessed, causing an eventual sea level rise much larger than projected for the 21st century. The eventual contributions from Greenland ice sheet loss could be several meters, and larger than from thermal expansion, should warming in excess of 1.9–4.6°C above pre-industrial levels be sustained over many centuries. The long time scales of thermal expansion and ice sheet response to warming imply that stabilization of GHG concentrations at or above present levels would not stabilize sea level for many centuries.[20]

In other words, regardless of what we do now, the world is locked into a warming of between 1.5 and 2.0°C by 2050, a date that is within the lifetime of 70 percent of the people currently living on the planet. We can no longer avoid increasing CO_2 concentrations, nor can we prevent the CO_2 already in the atmosphere from setting in motion much slower changes, such as thermal expansion of the oceans, which will continue for hundreds of years. However, if we continue on our present path of increasing rather than reducing emissions of greenhouse gases, primarily CO_2, a much larger temperature increase is the almost certain outcome. If we go above a 2°C average temperature rise—which will absolutely happen without radical economic and social changes in the next decade or so—future scenarios for the environmental consequences become increasingly apocalyptic. They are outlined very clearly in Mark Lynas's *Six Degrees: Our Fu-*

ture on a Hotter Planet, a book that is notable as a popular science book because it takes its data entirely from peer-reviewed scientific journals.[21]

It's important to state that the increase of average global temperatures is a trend, not an absolute. This means two things: first, that there is no relentless march to higher temperatures every year (some temporary cooling is predicted for the next twenty years or so), and second, that not everywhere on the planet will experience heating equally. Some areas, such as the Arctic, are predicted to be worst affected due to positive feedback loops, and could see a rise of 6°C even if the rest of the planet only sees two; other regions will see increased rainfall and floods rather than drought. A large part of the problem will be that yearly weather patterns will become unpredictable, making agriculture—the basis of human sustenance—increasingly difficult to plan.

Now that we are already at a CO_2 concentration of almost 400ppm, what is urgently required is that we stay below 450ppm and as quickly as possible reduce that back to 350ppm in order to limit warming to 2°C. We need to actually reduce CO_2 in the atmosphere to 350ppm as highlighted by the environmental activist Bill McKibben with his organization, 350.org. Once we go above 450ppm much historical evidence, as well as recent research, points to the possibility of an unstoppable increase in global temperatures that would eventually make human civilization virtually untenable across large swathes of the planet.[22] As this will occur simultaneously with the decline of traditional energy resources and water shortages, the potential for warfare between nuclear-armed states is terrifyingly real.

If two degrees of warming is indeed a planetary "critical

threshold," then once we have passed it, we head inexorably for three degrees of warming, then four, five, and six. What would a world five to six degrees warmer look like? A glance back millions of years, to when crocodiles flourished in what is now Canada, gives us some idea. The Amazon will have disappeared and turned into a desert. The collapse of the Greenland ice sheet and the Antarctic ice shelf will produce sea-level rises of 25 meters, inundating coastal cities and placing large areas of land far underwater. Coral reefs will be dead from ocean acidification. Fish stocks will plunge due to acidity and decreased dissolved oxygen as oceans warm. Searing heat, the extreme violence of "hypercanes" caused by warmer oceans and greater kinetic energy in the atmosphere, and flash flooding will make growing crops impossible across large areas of formerly fertile continents. Southern Europe, the Southwestern U.S., and Central America, along with Central Asia and Africa and almost the whole of Australia will become desert. Humans will be constrained to "zones of habitability" near the poles to escape the twin extremes of drought and flood.

All these changes will occur far too rapidly to allow for adaptation on the part of upwards of 50–60 percent of plant and animal species, which will cease to exist. The level of mass extinction could rival the climate-change-induced Permian-Triassic (P-T) mass extinction of 251 million years ago, which saw planetary life hanging by a thread as 95 percent of all species, plant and animal became extinct; it took 50 million years for the earth to return to its pre P-T level of biodiversity. Human population will drop by the billions even as mass migrations and civilizational breakdown become continuous features of life for those who survive. More worrisome still—if that's possible—is that, while in the past such "rapid" climate swings generally occurred over thousands or hundreds of years, continuing on our present course could produce a similar swing in a matter of decades.[23]

CHAPTER TWO

Is Population the Problem?

*"The idea that developing countries should feed themselves
is an anachronism from a bygone era. They could better
ensure their food security by relying on U.S. agricultural
products, which are available, in most cases at lower cost."*
  —John Block, U.S. Agriculture Secretary, Uruguay Round
                          of trade negotiations, 1986[1]

*"The biggest threat to global stability is the potential for
food crises in poor countries to cause government collapse. Those crises are brought on by ever worsening environmental degradation."*
                                          —Lester Brown

The second of the above quotes begins the article titled,
"Could Food Shortages Bring Down Civilization?" in the May
2009 edition of the magazine *Scientific American*.[2] Lester
Brown is no fringe character; he has won numerous environmental awards and authored more than fifty books addressing various aspects of the environmental crisis. Until 2000 he
was president of the Worldwatch Institute, which publishes
the influential and authoritative *State of the World* annual reports as well as the annual publication *Vital Signs*. A major

preoccupation of Brown for more than three decades has been the idea that the world is perennially on the brink of running out of food because increases in human population are outstripping food supply. Now he is equally concerned that overpopulation is a major driver of ecological devastation. While Brown has been a resource-depletion doomsayer for decades, he is echoed by many others.

A growing number of liberal writers and publications have raised the specter of growing population as an unpleasant yet necessary topic of conversation as it relates to environmental degradation. Johann Hari, writer for the *Independent,* who has written some excellent pieces on climate change, posed the question in one of his 2008 columns, "Are There Just Too Many People in the World?"

While noting that Malthusian predictions have consistently been wrong and often used as arguments against the poor, he nevertheless concludes that, "After studying the evidence, I am left in a position I didn't expect. Yes, the argument about overpopulation is distasteful, often discussed inappropriately, and far from being a panacea-solution—but it can't be dismissed entirely. It will be easier for 6 billion people to cope on a heaving, boiling planet than for nine or 10 billion."[3] An editorial in the *Guardian* newspaper from March of 2009, entitled "The Malthusian Question," even while rejecting the more outrageous population-reduction arguments and overt Malthusianism of organizations such as the Optimum Population Trust, confirms in alarmist terms the relevance of population-based arguments to environmental decay:

> Yet human numbers continue to swell, at more than 9,000 an hour, 80 million a year, a rate that threatens a doubling in less than 50 years. Land for cultivation is dwindling. Wind

and rain erode fertile soils. Water supplies are increasingly precarious. Once-fertile regions are threatened with sterility. The yield from the oceans has begun to fall. To make matters potentially worse, human numbers threaten the survival of other species of plant and animal. Humans depend not just on what they can extract from the soil, but what they can grow in it, and this yield is driven by an intricate ecological network of organisms. Even at the most conservative estimate, other species are being extinguished at 100 to 1,000 times the background rate observable in the fossil record.[4]

It is clear that population is reemerging as a major question for the environmental movement. Any book talking about solutions to environmental degradation must therefore address the issue in a forthright manner. The argument that overpopulation is the cause of poverty has been around since before Marx's time, when Thomas Malthus addressed it in a series of influential essays (hence these arguments have come to be known as "Malthusian"). Therefore, going back to examine some of the arguments made by Marx and Engels will be instructive for examining today's situation. More recently, it's not just poverty that is blamed on overpopulation, but ecological breakdown as well.

In relation to the argument about population growth, the fundamental questions that need to be answered are twofold: first, does population growth explain food shortages and second, can population growth explain environmental degradation. Whether population growth is outpacing food production and so causing widespread famine or running up against the "natural" ecological limits of the earth are critical ones to answer for three interrelated reasons.

First, many people committed to fighting for a better world answer these questions with an unequivocal yes. It seems commonsense that more people must mean more resource use, therefore fewer resources for everyone and concomitantly greater demands placed on ecological limits.

Second, if the answer is yes, all of us committed to fighting for a more humane world need to adopt radically different emphases for our activism. If population growth is the main danger, then the solution is to pour resources and activism into tackling it as the single most important task to avoid many millions more people descending into starvation and unleashing further environmental damage on the planet.

This leads to the third important reason for taking up the question of population: by arguing that population growth is the main cause of mass starvation and environmental ruin we play into the hands of ruling elites who want to blame the victims; logic that has historically led to some highly unsavory arguments and policy decisions.

The Return of Malthus

The notion that population growth is the foremost cause of environmental degradation and societal destabilization is raised in the summer 2009 issue of *Scientific American*'s publication, *Earth 3.0—Solutions for Sustainable Progress*. The cover article, titled "Population and Sustainability," by Robert Engelman, vice president for programs at the Worldwatch Institute, poses the question: Can we avoid limiting the number of people? It begins:

> In an era of changing climate and sinking economies, Malthusian limits to growth are back—and squeezing us painfully. Whereas *more people* once meant more ingenuity, more talent and more innovation, today it just seems to mean *less for each*.[5] [emphasis in original]

Engelman does not believe that coercive population control methods are necessary, primarily because, as he notes, they haven't worked. Nevertheless, he urges governments, institutions, and people to consider how we can best reduce population growth in order to conserve resources, reduce our ecological footprint, and prevent conflict over worsening environmental conditions.

His solution to this problem, which is the same as Hari's and Brown's, is to ensure women control their lives and bodies through access to reproductive health care, education, and employment opportunities. These measures are to be welcomed and fought for—including in the United States. All empirical evidence points to how socially and financially empowered women, as part of the general economic development of a country that incorporates a robust social safety net, are the key to population stabilization.

But as Frances Moore Lappé notes, the overpopulation-leading-to-hunger argument has it backwards. Higher population growth rates are a product of hunger, not its cause:

> Despite the evidence, many people see high birth rates and hunger in the Global South and arrive at what seems like commonsense: just too many mouths to feed. But scanning the globe, no correlation between people density and undernourishment is to be found. High birth rates are best understood not as a cause of hunger but as a symptom. Along with hunger, they are a symptom of powerlessness, especially of women denied control over their fertility. Mounting evidence from around the world suggests that as people, especially women, gain education and income, fertility rates decline.[6]

Fighting for women's emancipation is a worthy goal in its own right, as is global poverty reduction. The question must be asked: why does women's emancipation have to be linked to population control? This is similar to the way in which fighting climate change is often argued for on the basis of national security—to "reduce our dependence on foreign oil." In this schema, fighting for women's rights or combating climate change are not recommended because they are, in and of themselves, desirable societal aspirations, but rather they conform to other objectives held by ruling elites.

Historical Origins of the Overpopulation Argument

The argument that population always outstrips, or is about to outstrip, food supply has a long and inglorious history stretching back to the late 1700s when world population was a small fraction—around one-twelfth—of what it is today. Thomas Malthus published his first *Essay on the Principle of Population* in 1798, whose arguments were substantially expanded and revised in his more influential *Second Essay,* published in 1803.

Malthus supplied no supportive data for his claim, but this didn't stop him from asserting that population always grows geometrically (i.e. 1, 2, 4, 8, 16, 32… in an exponentially rising curve), whereas the food supply only increases arithmetically (i.e. 1, 2, 3, 4, 5… in a linear relationship). Rather than arguing for the eradication of poverty, Malthus argued against any and all social services to the poor. To provide support of any kind would only encourage the poor and indigent to breed faster, which would keep a constant pressure on food supply and thereby undermine the food required by the middle class and the wealthy. Checks to population growth such as starvation, disease, low wages, and draconian tightening of the English Poor Laws were therefore recommended to ensure a relatively stable working population. To quote a particularly infamous passage from the 1803 edition:

> A man who is born into a world already possessed (i.e., it is already "full"), if he cannot get subsistence from his parents on whom he has a just demand, and if society do not want his labor, has no claim of right to the smallest portion of food, and, in fact, has no business to be where he is. At nature's mighty feast there is no vacant cover for him. She tells him to be gone, and will quickly execute her own orders, if he does not work on the compassion of some of her guests. If these guests get up and make room for him other intruders immediately appear demanding the same favor... The order and harmony of the feast is disturbed, the plenty that before reigned is changed into scarcity...The guests learn too late their error, in counter-acting the strict orders to all intruders, issued by the great mistress of the feast, who, wishing that all her guests should have plenty, and knowing that she could not provide for unlimited numbers, humanely refused to admit fresh comers when her table was already full.[7]

In other words, helping the poor not only hurts *them*, but also threatens to drag the well-fed down to their subsistence level. Under this credo, no sharing is permitted, as it will only generalize starvation to the entire population because there is only so much to go around. Despite his progressive ideas on how to deal with population growth, Engelman explicitly resurrects this argument in his opening sentence quoted above that "*more people* today just seems to mean *less for each*."

Marx and Engels wrote quite extensively about Malthus's thesis because they recognized that, far from representing scientific fact, Malthus was using unsubstantiated class prejudice to blame the poor for being poor. Marx and Engels were scathing in their condemnation of Malthus, whom they considered to be an ideological servant of the ruling class. Blaming the poor for their poverty and finding a "theory" that purported to show that aiding the poor was harmful to society fit perfectly with the needs of capital at the birth of the industrial revolution, when the whip of poverty was useful to dragoon displaced peasants and artisans into factory wage labor. As to Malthus's method, Marx considered his population theory to be both ahistorical and unsupported by facts. As Marx writes in *Grundrisse*,

> Malthus's theory…is significant in two respects: (1) because he gives brutal expression to the brutal viewpoint of capital; (2) because he asserted the fact of overpopulation in all forms of society. Proved it he has not…he regards overpopulation as being of the same kind in all the different historic phases of economic development; does not understand their specific difference…he transforms the historically distinct relations into an abstract numerical relation, which he has fished purely out of thin air, and which rests neither on natural nor on historical laws…overpopulation is likewise a historically determined relation, in no way determined by abstract numbers or by the absolute limit of the productivity of the necessaries of life, but by limits posited rather by specific conditions of production.… How small do the numbers which meant overpopulation for the Athenians appear to us![8]

Marx argues that what level of population is sustainable depends on how people procure their subsistence:

> The overpopulation e.g., among hunting peoples, which shows itself in the warfare between the tribes, proves not that the earth could not support their small numbers, but rather that the condition of their reproduction required a great amount of territory for few people.[9]

There can be no absolute criterion for what constitutes overpopulation if it can exist in societies consisting of thousands of people and those consisting of hundreds of millions. From a Marxist viewpoint therefore, what constitutes overpopulation varies according to the material level of development and operative social relations; both of which are historically determined and therefore must be contextually examined as such. Over the very long term, it has to be recognized that all organisms change their environment in ways that end up detrimental to themselves, not just humans—such is the dialectical contradiction of life. This is one part of the explanation why species are constantly dying out and new ones constantly evolving—there is no such thing as a static and unchanging "environment" to save. To take just one example, without cyanobacteria (blue-green algae) producing oxygen, a gas essentially poisonous to themselves and the other oxygen-intolerant species prevalent three billion years ago, there would have been no transformation to an oxygen-rich atmosphere that allowed for the evolution of animal life.[10]

The modern biological concept of the "carrying capacity" for the earth, K, as it is often presented in connection to humans, has more than an element of Malthusian thought to it. From a biological perspective, carrying capacity is the population of a species that can exist within its ecosystem over a long period of time without degrading it. In other terms, K represents the long-term equilibrium population a particular stable ecosystem will support, wherein birth rates equal death rates. However, applied to humans, it is obvious that as we are the unitary example of a species that can consciously modify its environment, the number of humans a local or global environment can support depends not on some ab-

stract number "fished purely out of thin air," but on the level
of economic development and the social relations of that society. Humans can both grow more food and, given the opportunity, consciously self-limit our reproduction based on rational
economic and social considerations. With specific regard to
humans therefore, putting this into the relevant social and
historical context is the critical point. The shibboleth of absolute overpopulation obscures the more immediate causes of
suffering under capitalism, namely, unemployment. Yet unemployment is not a result of a shortage of means of subsistence (or even of means of production), but as a result of
overproduction. The periodic crises that lead to mass layoffs
are due not to too little, but *too much* being produced in terms
of what can be sold profitably. Malthus, Marx argues,

> relates a specific quantity of people to a specific quantity of
> necessaries. Ricardo [a bourgeois economist of the time]
> immediately and correctly confronted him with the fact that
> the quantity of grain available is completely irrelevant to
> the worker if he has no employment; that it is therefore the
> means of employment and not of subsistence which put
> him in the category of surplus population.[11]

This is clearly shown today when mainstream economists
use the term "effective demand." If people have money to pay
for food, their demand is "effective"; if they are too poor to afford food, then their demand is not effective and they are
"surplus"—they must somehow try to work and survive on
less than $2 a day, as two billion people around the world are
forced to do. This is a fact noted by the UN: "A stubbornly
high share of the world's population remains in absolute
poverty and so lacks the necessary income to translate its
needs into effective demand."[12]

In other words, historically how many humans the earth can support depends primarily on the level of productivity of the existing population and the social relations within which they are embedded. Despite the resurrection of this old argument, which has been continually refuted, statistics show conclusively that carrying capacity is as much socially as it is materially determined from the given level of productive development, not some arbitrary measure of what constitutes "too many" people. Moreover, once class societies come into existence, it is not possible to simplistically extrapolate from the existence of hunger in wildly varying cultures and populations throughout history the common thread of overpopulation as the cause. The existence of hungry people in Malthus's day had nothing to do with the earth not being able to provide for them with the given level of technological development of society; rather they were hungry because they lived in a class-divided society in which the wealth of the few depended on the poorly remunerated labor of the many. It's important to note, as food production has increased, so has health as measured by increases in birth weights, average adult height, etc. Poverty and hunger were a product of social relations, not absolute overpopulation. As will be shown below, the same holds true today.

Neo-Malthusianism with a Green Tinge

In more recent times, overpopulation arguments have been given an ecological hue by some sections of the environmental movement. Most notably, Malthusian arguments connected to environmentalism were resurrected in Garrett Hardin's notorious 1968 essay "The Tragedy of the Commons" published in the prestigious *Science* magazine. In this highly influential essay, again without any empirical data, Hardin, a noted eugenicist,[13] argued that people acting rationally would always denude and degrade their environment—defined as a resource and geographically limited "commons"—to the last piece of arable land or last fish. Hardin describes how "rational" herdsmen in a certain area follow behavior that leads inexorably to overpopulation and environmental degradation:

> Adding together the component partial utilities, the rational herdsman concludes that the only sensible course for him to pursue is to add another animal to his herd. And another.... But this is the conclusion reached by each and every rational herdsman sharing a commons. Therein is the tragedy. Each man is locked into a system that compels him to increase his herd without limit—in a world that is limited. Ruin is the destination toward which all men rush, each pursuing his own best interest in a society that believes in the freedom of the commons. Freedom in a commons brings ruin to all.[14]

Hardin promotes this view of human relations with nature in the same way as Malthus; as a transhistorical fact. Hardin's argument is that the motive for economizing on resource use disappears when everyone can take from a common pool of resources. But it is only "rational" for these herdsmen to keep expanding *if they are operating under capitalist social relations, where land and resources are privately held and exploited for individual gain, rather than shared in common*. It is only rational in a competitive, profit-driven system to fish to the last fish and continually expand one's means of production (in Hardin's example, this is cattle and land). But the problem is not overpopulation; it is that under capitalist social relations people are pushed to rapidly expand production for the market to realize a profit. Entirely missing from Hardin's account is *why* herdsmen would consider it rational to overexploit their local environment. The truth is that this is the very thing that traditional herdsmen and peasants sharing "common" lands historically avoid.[15]

As just one example of how a herding community operates in practice, the Turkana people, before being forced from their land, organized their commons sustainably:

> During the long dry seasons in the far north west of Kenya, the people of the Turkwel River keep themselves alive by feeding their goats on the pods of the acacia trees growing on its banks. Every clump of trees is controlled by a committee of elders, who decide who should be allowed to use them and for how long.
>
> Anyone coming into the area who wants to feed his goats on the pods has to negotiate with the elders. Depending on the size of the pod crop, they will allow him in or tell him to move on. If anyone overexploits the pods or tries to browse his animals without negotiating with the elders first, he will be driven off with sticks: if he does it repeatedly, he may be killed. The acacia woods are a common: a resource owned by many families.[16]

There is a clear difference in motivation between Hardin's capitalist herdsmen and traditional pastoralists or peasants. In a society in which the purpose of production is to procure useful things, the natural qualities of the product, as well as the preservation of the natural prerequisites of production, are the producers' main consideration. While they may take some of their product to market to exchange it for other goods they do not have or cannot manufacture, the overriding purpose of economic activity is to make things that are useful.

Under a system based on production for the market, however, the situation is reversed. Goods are now produced for exchange, independently of whatever useful qualities they may have. They must be useful in some way for someone to buy them, to be sure, but the producer cares not for their use, rather for what exchange value they have—that is, what money can be obtained by their sale. Under fully-developed capitalism, the sole purpose of selling is profit—the expansion of wealth over and above investment. Exchange value comes to dominate use-value, to use Marx's expressions.

Under capitalism, because of the dominance of exchange value over use value, it is rational to continually seek to expand production regardless of the longer-term negative effects that make it logically irrational in relation to human need; indeed it is a requirement that corporations and capitalists do so. What counts as a saleable commodity is not its ultimate usefulness to humanity but how much money can be made from selling it.

The abstraction of exchange value from use value causes broader distortions of rationality that puts capitalism systematically at odds with the environment. One distortion arises from how the exchange value of labor power, also known as wages, can vary a great deal from region to region or country to country. Capital has flowed to China because of its low wage rates, thus setting up an economic routine where goods that could be produced anywhere are produced in China and shipped everywhere. The waste of resources and human effort that goes into this long-distance transport, not to mention the extra pollution of the environment, occurs because "economic rationality" under capitalism is calculated in terms of exchange value and not use value.

A second broad category of harm to the environment arises because private ownership and the drive for profit give capitalists an incentive to "externalize" the environmental costs of any production process. Capitalists contrive to own every tool and every bit of raw material that contributes to making a profitable commodity at the same time that they contrive not to own the waste products of the production process that can't be sold for profit—or to "own" the mess that dumping such waste in the surrounding environment causes. The true environmental costs of capitalist production thus don't show up in a capitalists "bottom line." (We will return to "externalities" again in chapter four with a discussion about carbon-trading schemes.) In *Marx and Nature*, Paul Burkett generalizes points like these by writing, "[H]uman alienation from nature is intrinsic to [exchange] value's formal abstraction from use value."[17]

In spite of capitalism's evident tendency toward environmental destruction, Garrett Hardin's solution to "the tragedy of the commons" was to make the system more capitalistic, arguing that all public land and water should be privatized in order to protect the environment and that coercive restrictions should be placed on the "freedom to breed." In a 1974 paper, Hardin became much more explicit about exactly whose breeding should be restricted. It is only necessary to quote the title of his paper: "Lifeboat Ethics—the Case against Helping the Poor."[18]

According to "lifeboat ethics," there was only so much to go around and some people (the poor) needed to be kept out and their numbers restricted by ending all aid to developing countries in need of food. Paul Ehrlich's similarly influential book, *The Population Bomb*, expanded this line of reasoning, arguing that by the "1970s and 80's hundreds of millions of people are going to starve to death in spite of any crash programs embarked upon now."[19]

Today we again see the resurfacing of arguments about hunger and environmental decay being presented as the result of overpopulation. These arguments come not just from Brown and Engelman, but also from people such as the eminent biologist and natural historian Sir David Attenborough and environmentalist and former director of Friends of the Earth, Jonathan Porritt. Even Cameron Diaz thinks there are too many people on the planet.[20]

Are There Too Many People for the Available Food Supply?

With the summer 2009 cover of *Earth 3.0* depicting a fishbowl teeming with goldfish, the symbolism is hard to miss. For many people, the global food crisis of 2008, which caused huge increases in chronic malnutrition alongside food riots in more than thirty countries, only underlined how there were just too many people and not enough land to feed them. As commonly accepted, maybe Malthusian arguments have been repeatedly and self-evidently wrong in the past, but this time is different—humanity has finally reached, exceeded, or will soon exceed the total number of humans the earth can possibly feed.

Obviously, population is not a completely irrelevant consideration when it comes to food provision and there is an obvious difference in resource use when there are more people. It would be antimaterialist to argue otherwise. But we are not talking about some hypothetical future population number; with almost one billion people suffering chronic malnutrition we are talking about whether or not we have exceeded the capacity of the earth to feed everyone right now.

The reality is that these overpopulation arguments come at a time when enough food is produced globally, according to the UN Food and Agriculture Organization (FAO), to more than feed everyone. At the beginning of the food crisis in 2007, the world's farmers produced 2.13 billion tons of grain, which included record or near record levels of rice, wheat, and corn.[21] According to a World Bank Report, "droughts in Australia and poor crops in the E.U. and Ukraine in 2006 and 2007 were largely offset by good crops and increased exports in other countries and would not, on their own, have had a significant impact on prices. Only a relatively small share of the increase in food production prices (around 15 percent) is due directly to higher energy and fertilizer costs."[22] The FAO's June 2009 Report stated that food stocks are back from their lows of 2008 as a result of a bumper food crop: "With the second-highest recorded cereals crop expected this year and stocks replenished, the world food supply looks less vulnerable to shocks than it was during last year's food crisis."[23] In a quite striking revelation given the extra tens of millions of people thrust into trying to survive starvation in 2008 the report states that "even larger crops than originally forecast" were harvested, making 2008 the highest production year on record: "The increased global production was sufficient to meet demand for food and other uses but also facilitated a replenishment of global reserves to pre-crisis levels. With the new 2009–10 marketing seasons commencing, prospects continue to be positive, as world cereal production is expected to be the second largest ever, after last year's record."[24]

Even at the height of the food crisis of 2008, when the number of seriously malnourished people rose to 963 million, from 923 million in 2007, according to the UN—almost one in every seven people on the planet—there was more than enough food available to give every single person 2,800 kilocalories per day, enough to make every person on the planet overweight. By 2030, with population growth continuing to decline and agricultural output predicted to rise, the UN forecasts enough food will be grown worldwide, despite a global estimated population of 8.3 billion, to give everyone 3,050 kilocalories per day.[25]

Contrary to those who argue population continues to grow exponentially or geometrically, the rate of population growth peaked in the 1960s and has been declining ever since. The rate is set to decline further from the 1.7 percent it has been over the last thirty years to 1.1 percent. World population, rather than increasing exponentially, is predicted to continue to slowly rise through this century before leveling off at around nine billion.[26]

This reduction in growth rate undermines the presumption that human population has reached the earth's carrying capacity. The S-shaped curve of population growth in other species typically climbs because of a rise in births, and levels off because of a rise in deaths. But the human experience, in country after country and worldwide, is that the steep growth of population comes from a decline in death rates, and the leveling off occurs because of a decline in birth rates. Thus, if population alarmists were right that human populations are under pressure because they've reached carrying capacity, then death rates should be rising to meet birth rates—the opposite of what is in fact happening.

This does not mean that there are no local or regional populations that are at carrying capacity, particularly as weather patterns change and multiyear droughts become a regular occurrence in some regions. It also does not answer definitively whether human population as a whole with nine billion people worldwide would exceed the carrying capacity of the earth, since we might not know this until after we've surpassed it. What is definitive is that the earth is now beyond its carrying capacity for capitalist production and further expansion as the elasticity of ecosystems and stable climate is stretched to breaking point.

According to the latest report from the U.S Census Bureau, *An Aging World: 2008*, the fastest growing segment of world population is the over-65 age bracket. For the first time in human history, the over-65 demographic is predicted to outnumber children under five within ten years.[27] By some estimates, population may reach a maximum below nine billion and closer to eight as more countries go through a demographic transition.

There is always going to be time lag between a slowdown in population growth and the point where population reaches its maximum, because it takes some years for humans to grow and procreate. Global fertility peaked in the 1950s with five to six children per female but the percent rate of population growth didn't peak until the late 1960s. In terms of absolute numbers, the number of people added each year peaked in 1987 at eighty-seven million. A bulge in child-bearing-age women takes a while to feed through the system. One graph that population alarmists frequently like to show is how adding each billion to the planet's population has taken a shorter and shorter amount of time as the curve of human population growth versus time becomes almost vertical. While this is initially true as a result of technological, agricultural, and medical improvements, the rate is now definitively slowing and will soon almost certainly reverse itself, as shown by the table below:

TOTAL NUMBER OF PEOPLE (BILLIONS)	TIME TAKEN (YEARS)
1 to 2	130 (1800–1927)
2 to 3	33 (1960)
3 to 4	15 (1975)
4 to 5	12 (1987)
5 to 6	12 (1999)
6 to 7	14? (2013?)
7 to 8	20? (2033?)

It is quite possible that nine or even eight billion will never be reached and population could peak closer to seven billion by 2040. As fertility declines across the world, each succeeding generation of mothers becomes smaller than the last. Because there will be fewer females being born, population decline becomes all but inevitable, to around five billion by 2100. In the interim there will of course be regional imbalances that a rational society would seek to overcome by matching those in need of work with where the work is required.[28]

However, an indication of how the population argument is dominated by conservative thought, which always has more than a shade of racism to it, is that in certain significant sectors of the world population decline is seen as a problem. Rather than viewing considerable decreases in rates of population in some parts of the world as an opportunity to bring young, working-age people in from other parts of the world and ease overcrowding in some of the giant megacities of the South, it is seen along racist lines as a demographic threat.

Of twenty-three European nations, none have rates of fertility at replacement level and many have rates significantly below that. Once a certain level of fertility decline is reached, as mentioned above, it becomes difficult to reverse because the number of women of child-bearing age starts to tail off and everyone gets older. For example, Germany already has twice as many people over forty as it has those under ten. By the end of this century, without large numbers of immigrants, Italy, Spain, and Greece will see population decreases between 74 and 86 percent. That would mean Italy going from a current population of fifty-six million to eight million.[29]

As some of these facts on population decline in the developed world penetrate the minds of conservatives, it sets off alarm bells that focus particularly on fears of a global takeover by countries of the South with high birth rates, particularly in majority Muslim countries as their populations and percentage of young productive workers expand. The cover of the January/February 2010 edition of *Foreign Affairs*, with its headline title: *The New Population Bomb* by Jack Goldstone exemplifies this mode of thinking. While validating UN statistics that global economic output over the next forty years will far surpass global population growth, Goldstone now has security fears about exactly who's doing the multiplying by singling out one religion that has come under relentless attack over the last decade: "Worldwide, of the 48 fastest-growing countries today—those with annual population growth of two percent or more—28 are majority Muslim or have Muslim minorities of 33 percent or more."

The fact that should really be highlighted is what the vast majority of the forty-eight have in common is poverty, much of it induced by Western financial institutions that focus "development" on corporate wealth extraction, production for external markets and debt repayment. One has to feel, in the current political climate, Goldstone, who actually has some fairly sane things to say about facilitating immigration between developed and developing countries, is nevertheless playing into racist paranoia about the supposed inherent anti-Western, antidevelopment bias of Muslims. Furthermore, he essentially accepts the current set of power relations in the world—with a few adjustments to take into account the rise of some developing countries such as China, India, Mexico, Brazil, and South Africa—as more or less immutable. He goes on to write: "It is therefore imperative to improve relations between Muslim and Western societies. This will be difficult given that many Muslims live in poor communities vulnerable to radical appeals and many see the West as antagonistic and militaristic."[30]

What could possibly give them that idea? With the U.S. military occupying Iraq and Afghanistan, feeding high-tech weaponry to Israel to maintain the continued brutal occupation of Palestine, regularly bombing countries like Pakistan, Yemen, and Somalia, facilitating the government onslaught against insurgent groups in Indonesia, helping to ensure that the Mubarak and Saudi dictatorships cling to power with gargantuan arms shipments and military training and saber-rattling against Iran and Syria, there would seem to be a fairly good basis for extreme animosity and seeing the West as "antagonistic and militaristic" from people in those countries, Muslim or not.

If we really want to reverse large sections of the world resenting Western policies and an extremely small minority seeking redress through acts of individual terrorism, the answer is very simple. Rather than blaming a supposedly innately backward religion: withdraw the troops, stop the arms sales to repressive Arab and Israeli governments, cancel all developing-country debt, renounce immigration controls, and provide development assistance based on the needs of the country in question rather than those of the cabal of international financial institutions and multinational corporations.

As a side point, it is noteworthy that in all the debates about curtailing population growth, there is no campaign against the French and Australian governments *paying* women to have a third child in order to avert national population decline or promote population growth, even though both countries have far higher per capita environmental impacts than any developing country. It is also noticeable that these governments would rather pay women to procreate than relax ever-stricter immigration controls and allow in more workers to offset the decline.

The reason that food reserves have declined over the last fifteen years is not because there is not enough land to grow crops for the extra people. The problem comes down once again to social relations. Under neoliberal deregulation, developing countries were pressured by the IMF and the World Bank's Structural Adjustment Programs (SAPs) to move away from food self-sufficiency and assured that the market would take care of any shortfalls. In order to keep up with their debt payments to Western financial institutions, countries of the Global South were told that they had to grow certain crops—ones that earned cash but couldn't be eaten such as coffee and flowers—that held a "comparative advantage" for them on the world market.

This meant that they could drop all their trade barriers and, in theory, still be able to compete on the world market while earning the capital to develop and pay off their debt.

Quite the opposite happened. Local farmers were driven out of business and off the land into burgeoning city slums, land degradation expanded because the crops now being grown were not suited to the soil, and farmers were pushed onto more marginal land, thereby accelerating soil erosion. The farmers who remained were now in debt due to the amounts of fertilizer and pesticide they had to use (and the IMF-forced conditions for the suspension of fertilizer subsidies), and water use for the necessary irrigation of high-water-demand crops shot through the roof. Some of this is documented in the excellent film *Life and Debt*, which focuses on the effects of "free trade" arriving in the Caribbean and the devastating effects on local agricultural production.

Since the 1980s, IMF and World Bank–imposed SAPs have been imposed on ninety developing and transitional economies. It is impossible to explain how the home of corn domestication, Mexico, could have become a net importer of U.S. corn without looking at the role of the coercively imposed SAPs and the North American Free Trade Agreement (NAFTA), which drove fifteen million Mexican farmers from the land.[31]

In a script replayed in country after country, Ghanaian government policies of support for agriculture were reversed in the 1980s, and import tariffs on food were drastically reduced on conditions set by the IMF and World Bank in exchange for development loans. The result was that Ghana, which had sufficient rice output in the 1970s for all its needs, by 2002 was importing 64 percent of its domestic supply as local farmers were unable to compete with subsidized U.S. imports. By 2003, when the U.S. government gave out $1.3 billion in rice subsidies, mostly to large U.S. agribusiness, the United States exported 111,000 tons of rice to Ghana.[32] By

2003, 90 percent of Ghana's local poultry production had been wiped out by poultry imports from the United States, the European Union, and Brazil.[33] The decimation of local food production made Ghana dependent on food aid while subjecting the country's remaining farmers to the vicious gyrations of international food commodity markets, a situation replicated in country after country as indigenous food production is undercut due to Western nations' dumping their highly subsidized agricultural products.[34] Today, Ghana ranks 152 out of 182 in the UN's 2009 Human Development Index.[35]

Without political change, therefore, it is undoubtedly true that there will be more hungry people even if there were no population increase. As FAO assistant director general Hafez Ghanem said in presenting the organization's world hunger report in 2008, "For millions of people in developing countries, eating a minimum amount of food every day to live an active and healthy life is a distant dream. The structural problems of hunger, like the lack of access to land, credit and employment, combined with high food prices remain a dire reality."[36] Taken together, there is neither a shortage of food nor too many mouths to feed; there is merely a shortage of means or will to distribute the food that is already produced to those who need it.

Within individual countries, moreover, there is no direct relationship between population density and malnutrition. Japan is the third most densely populated country on the planet and, unlike Africa, has few natural energy or mineral resources to speak of; yet the Japanese do not suffer from mass starvation. In contrast, Brazil is the fourth largest food exporter, but that doesn't prevent millions of Brazilians from living with food insecurity and malnourishment.

In the United States, enough food is produced for everyone to eat eight full plates of food per day—yet almost *forty million* Americans struggle to put food on the table and are classified as "food insecure."[37] The recent massive increase in allocation of land for the growing of agro-fuel crops, including 30 percent of corn production in the United States going to ethanol manufacture, was, according to a World Bank report leaked to the *Guardian* newspaper, *the* major cause of the spike in food prices in 2008.[38] The other reasons were financial speculation, deliberate reduction of strategic regional and local food stores, and "just-in-time" production.[39]

Even having a job isn't enough to stave off hunger in the world's richest country, as Reuters reported: "'Having a (low wage) job isn't enough anymore. Having two or three jobs isn't enough anymore,' said Marcia Paulson, spokeswoman for Great Plains Food Bank in North Dakota, where nearly half the households receiving food stamp benefits have one or more working adults."[40]

Over the last thirty years the number of hungry people has varied between about one sixth and one seventh of the world population, but in all that time, the growth of food production never fell behind population growth. Population growth, rather than exploding out of control, is slowing as the world goes through a "demographic transition" (i.e., low birth rates come to equilibrate with low death rates). Those regions that are still experiencing high birth rates are precisely those places described in the Frances Moore Lappé quote earlier, in which poverty itself is one of the major causes of population increase.

The policies of neoliberalism are the real root cause of the food crisis, poverty, and hunger. The unremitting capitalist hostility to small farmers must be rolled back by reintroducing state-sponsored farm subsidies at the point of production; instituting massive land reallocation to those that actually farm the land and empowering them to farm it; eliminating "third world" debt and U.S. and EU subsidies to large agribusinesses responsible for food dumping; increasing investment in sustainable agriculture research and restructuring international trade relations and aid to benefit developing countries rather than Western banks and giant corporations such as Cargill and ADM.

Is Ecological Degradation Caused by Overpopulation?

It is undoubtedly true that environmental decline, loss of biodiversity, plunging fish stocks, global climate change, and deforestation continue unabated despite the world being warned of escalating ecological and human damage as far back as 1962 with the publication of Rachel Carson's path-breaking socio-ecological work, *Silent Spring*.[41] It is also true that since that time, world population has more than doubled. It might seem logical, therefore, to put the two together. In one sense, more people do necessarily mean a greater use of resources and a larger encroachment on previously isolated habitats. But, what matters is not so much the number of people as what resources are produced, how those resources are produced, and what they are used for. How else could we explain the fact that population is *falling* in Europe—the EU, even with immigration, is predicted to have at least 50 million fewer people by 2050—while carbon emissions and resource and energy use are nevertheless *rising*? As John Bellamy Foster notes, "Where threats to the integrity of the biosphere as we know it are concerned, it is well to remember that it is not the areas of the world that have the highest rate of population growth but the areas of the world that have the highest accumulation of capital, and where economic and ecological waste has become a way of life, that constitute the greatest danger."[42]

Carson herself was clear that the primary blame for destruction of the natural world lay with the "gods of profit and production" as the world lived "in an era dominated by industry, in which the right to make a dollar at any cost is seldom challenged."[43] Capitalism is a system predicated on continual expansion with an ever-increasing throughput of energy and resources—hence generating ever more, and increasingly toxic, waste. For those corporations that do act to reduce their energy or resource use, the purpose is not to decrease their impact on the environment, however much money they spend touting their newfound green awareness. Rather, the objective is to lower production costs so as to maximize profit in order to reinvest in expansion of production to capture more market share, an activity that regularly leads to an increase in overall throughput.

We see today with the economic crisis that if the economy is not permanently expanding at around 2 to 3 percent, the whole system goes into a tailspin of layoffs, budget cuts, and mass unemployment. This expansion is unrelated to whether population is growing, as is evident in Europe, Russia, and Japan, where economic growth is still required despite falling population numbers. Capitalist crises are not caused by shortages of food or overpopulation. As mentioned earlier, capitalist crises are crises of *overproduction*.

Because of its inherent short-termism, its unrelenting obeisance to the profit motive, and inter-imperial conflict, capitalism, in contrast to all other modes of production, has a

historically unprecedented tendency toward planetary bios-
pheric crisis, regardless of the total number of humans living
on earth. Neoliberal globalization has been the accelerating
force behind the vast economic expansion of the last three
decades that has brought us to the cusp of environmental catastrophe. Rosa Luxemburg comment that ever-expanding
capitalism "ransacks the whole world" is even truer today
than when she wrote it almost one hundred years ago.[44]

Contrary to all claims of capitalist efficiency, the amount of
senseless waste and pollution under capitalism is enormous.
This includes not only the toxic byproducts of the production
process that are routinely dumped into the surrounding environment, but also the production and distribution of useless
products, the preponderance of inefficient transportation systems based on cars rather than effective public transportation
systems, the wasted labor and materials spent on military
spending, the explosion of redundant bureaucracy, and the
creation of mounting piles of garbage as a result of planned
obsolescence and single-use products.

For starters, the world market involves a great deal of socially unnecessary trade. According to the OECD, 60 percent
of world trade is due to *internal transfers* between subsidiaries
of the same multinational corporation. Because of subsidies
and cost of production differences, many goods from one
country are cheaper than the same good produced in another
country, decimating local agriculture and manufacturing as
well as increasing global greenhouse gas emissions by having
container ships plying the seas in ever increasing numbers.
Due to the tax structure, it can often be more profitable to export from your own country than to supply a domestic market, thus requiring imports of goods that the country actually

makes itself. To take just one example, in 1999 Britain exported 111 million liters of milk and 47 million kilograms of butter. In exactly the same period, it imported 173 million liters of milk and an almost identical 49 million kilograms of butter.[45] This should not be taken as a blanket argument against all international trade, merely the useless and superfluous kind that occurs under capitalism because of tax and subsidy structures and political considerations.

According to a recent report, at the various stages of production, transportation, retail and consumption, 50 percent of all food is wasted.[46] As 70 percent of the fresh water used by humans goes to crop irrigation, this corresponds to wasting an enormous quantity of water. In the United States, up to 30 percent of food, worth $48.3 billion, is discarded. This is equivalent to pouring away 40 trillion liters of water; enough to meet the household needs of five hundred million people.[47]

Because industrialized cows are fed a high-protein diet of grain and soya for faster growth to maximize profit, they produce more methane burps—a greenhouse gas twenty times more potent than CO_2—than if they were eating what they were evolutionarily adapted to eat, grass and clover.[10] Nevertheless, such is the overriding drive for profit that rather than switch them back to eating what their bodies can cope with, research is under way to make them more "environmentally friendly" by adding other supplements to their feed such as garlic pills to cut down on their greenhouse gas emissions.

Intensively farmed industrial cows, milked three times daily rather than two, are virtually at the end of their physiological capacity when kept in conditions of maximum productivity: they spend 50 percent of their time inside being force-fed, artificially inseminated, and relentlessly milked. This massive increase in per cow milk productivity breaks the machine-cow down within two to three lactation cycles rather than the nine to ten traditionally raised cows live. European dairy cows are now so genetically different from cows raised for beef that they are unsuitable to be slaughtered for meat. As a result, when a dairy cow gives birth to a male calf, something that occurs almost 50 percent of the time, the calf is considered worthless and is usually destroyed at birth, often to be cannibalistically fed back to the females. Subsidies averaged across all the OECD countries in the year 2000 accounted for half the cost of milk, allowing for large-scale dumping of dairy products in developing countries and immense profits for the large producers and retailers at the expense of small farmers, consumers, the environment, and the cows.[49]

For another example of how degraded our food system has become nutritionally and environmentally, while creating new and more virulent diseases as a result of its being controlled by multinational corporations, one only needs to look at the pork industry.

Smithfield Foods is a notoriously anti-union company convicted on multiple counts of health and safety violations. Its massive lagoons full to overflowing with pig feces have repeatedly burst, inundating surrounding rivers and watercourses with millions of gallons of highly toxic drug-infested fecal matter. The largest spill to date, in 1995, was more than twice as big as the Exxon Valdez oil spill; the toxic brew killed every living creature downriver on its way to the ocean. Smithfield was subject to one of the largest EPA fines in history for thousands of violations, $12.6 million, yet this still only amounted to 0.035 percent of the company's sales. Smithfield slaughters more than 26 million pigs a year that produce enough pig slurry to fill more than 90,000 swimming pools. According to Jeff Tietz, writing in *Rolling Stone*, industrial pig waste "contains a host of other toxic substances: ammonia, methane, hydrogen sulfide, carbon monoxide, cyanide, phosphorous, nitrates and heavy metals. In addition, the waste nurses more than 100 microbial pathogens that can cause illness in humans, including salmonella, cryptosporidium, streptococci and girardia. Each gram of hog shit can contain as much as 100 million fecal coliform bacteria."[50]

As of 2006, Smithfield controlled a quarter of the U.S. hog market, had operating profits of $421 million, and last year a turnover of more than $11 billion. The company has been expanding into Eastern Europe where low wages and fewer environmental restrictions augment its profit margins.[51] According to the *New York Times*, since Smithfield has moved into Eastern Europe, the number of hog farmers in Romania has plunged by 90 percent to 52,100 in 2007 from 477,030 in 2003. This mirrors a long-term drop in hog farmers in the United States, where the number of hog farms dropped 90 percent to 67,000 in 2005 from 667,000 in 1980. It is clear that no worker, North or South, let alone the consumer or the environment, benefits from the corporate control of agriculture.

In western Romania, where Smithfield has numerous large-scale industrial pig farms and is the leading source of air and soil pollution, the company has built enormous metal manure containers to inject the massive amounts of waste it produces into the soil. Because of EU subsidies, Smithfield can afford to export pork scraps as far away as Africa—with all the attendant transportation pollution—and *still* undercut and drive local African pig farmers out of business. In Ivory Coast, fresh local pork sells for $2.50 a kilo, while Smithfield's frozen offal can be had for a mere $1.40.[52] In line with other manufacturers, Smith-field would far rather sell processed products—after "value" has been added—rather than fresh ones, because profits are always higher. This explains the disease-laden shift to high-fat, high-sugar, high-salt nutritionally dubious processed foods prevalent in the West.

Planetary destruction is not limited to land; the oceans too are deteriorating. At current rates of exploitation there will be no wild fish left by 2050. This is not because fish stocks couldn't be regenerated to cope with world demand and fished sustainably. Rather it is due to the hugely destructive, unsustainable and wasteful manner in which fish are caught in order to maximize profit. Huge factory ships do all the processing, freezing, and canning at sea so that they can stay out for weeks at a time. The fine mesh of massive strings of gill nets, which can be left in the water for several weeks, often see *half to three quarters* of their catch unusable by the time the boats return to port. Bottom trawlers with enormous nets that scour the ocean floor typically throw out 20 kilograms of "by-kill" for every kilogram of desired catch. In the process, 55 percent of coral (i.e., fish breeding grounds and coastal defense systems) and 67 percent of sponges are destroyed in a single tow. The sea floor that has been "altered" by U.S. trawlers alone is equal to the surface area of the state of California.[53]

Cod caught off Norway is shipped to China where labor is cheap, only to be turned into filets and shipped back to Norway for sale. Britain imports—and exports—15,000 tons of waffles a year, and exchanges 20 tons of bottled water with Australia.[54] In the United States, the average food product—it's hard to describe much of what we eat today as food—travels a distance of 1,500 miles to get to a grocery store.[55] Eighty percent of fish sold in Europe are caught in non-EU waters because fish stocks in the EU have already gone into precipitous decline. West Africa has become a favorite hunting ground for fleets of European ships out-competing local fishermen, which drives them to privation or piracy. Huge prawn trawlers in this region throw away 10 kilograms of by-catch for every kilogram of prawns.[56]

The capitalist answer to wild fish stock depletion is not to put in place meaningful regulations to rejuvenate stocks but to invent an even more pollution-intensive industry that is nutritionally inferior and leads to a host of negative side-effects: the fish farming industry. Farmed fish have lower levels of omega-3 fatty acids and other compounds connected to improvements in human physical and mental health, produce huge quantities of concentrated fish waste, have to be repeatedly doused with pesticides to prevent outbreaks of disease and to keep parasites in check, and continually escape in large numbers to breed with wild fish where they negatively impact the genetic stock of wild populations.

None of this stupendous waste of resources, with its attendant destruction of ecosystems and voluminous waste production, is related to an increase in the number of people. It is simply the best method of operation for a social system based on profit maximization.

The Importance of "Scarcity" under Capitalism

It should be clear from all of the above examples that it isn't population growth that is causing food scarcity or is primarily responsible for the many accelerating global environmental crises. Even if population growth were to end today, worsening rates of starvation, the growth of slums, and ecosystem collapse would continue more or less undiminished. Food production continues to outstrip population growth, and therefore cannot be considered the cause of hunger.

Clearly, there are very serious planetary problems of soil erosion, overfishing, deforestation, waste disposal, and of course climate change, to name only some, which are putting pressure on the sustainability of food production over the long term. However, these are all inextricably bound to questions of power and a system run in the interest of a small minority where profit continually outweighs issues of hunger, waste, energy use, or environmental destruction. Concentrating on population confuses symptoms with causes while simultaneously validating apologists for the system—and in some cases actively updating and perpetuating Malthusian anti-poor, national-chauvinist, and racist arguments.

Brown, many environmentalists, and others' continual emphasis on population growth dovetails with the ideological needs of the system rather than challenging them and is the principal reason that they receive so much publicity. The people who run the system are perfectly happy to place the blame for hunger and ecological crises on the number of people rather than on capitalism, even when this flies in the face of established fact. The arch-conservative and pro-business magazine the *Economist* has begun to recognize the reality of falling rates of fertility, even for developing countries:

> Something similar is happening in developing countries. Fertility is falling and families are shrinking in places—such as Brazil, Indonesia, and even parts of India—that people think of as teeming with children. As our briefing

shows, the fertility rate of half the world is now 2.1 or less—the magic number that is consistent with a stable population and is usually called "the replacement rate of fertility." Sometime between 2020 and 2050 the world's fertility rate will fall below the global replacement rate.[57]

Nevertheless, many people ignore the facts and remain obsessed with trumpeting a population "explosion." Despite mentioning the statistics on falling rates of fertility below replacement level, the BBC's September 2009 science and technology publication *Focus* features on the front cover an image of the earth with a "Sorry, We're Full" sign hanging on it and a story inside entitled "Population Overload."

A central concept within the ideological armory of capitalism is the idea of scarcity—that there isn't enough to go around. This can justify high prices, budget cuts, wage cuts, unemployment, and all manner of belt-tightening. The reality— that, for example, the "scarcity" of jobs or of food is a product of the economic and social relations of capitalism rather than real shortages—must be buried under the weight of this simple lie.

We are confronted with the idea that there isn't enough food, work, or housing because there is a certain fixed amount of all these things. We then compete in the "free market" where the victory of one person necessarily comes at the expense of someone else. This is the implicit framework that progressives adopt when they acquiesce to the specter of Malthus haunting their thoughts. It accepts the notion that the poor are only consumers, rather than fantastically creative and hard-working producers of wealth, little of which they ever see. Such reasoning is wrong because it is the development of the productive capacity of humankind under capitalism that creates the conditions for ending privation and inequality, as Engels recognized so many years ago:

> It is precisely this industrial revolution which has raised the productive power of human labor to such a high level that— for the first time in the history of humanity—the possibility exists, given a rational division of labor among all, to produce not only enough for the plentiful consumption of all members of society and for an abundant reserve fund, but also to leave each individual sufficient leisure so that what is really worth preserving in historically inherited culture—science, art, human relations—is not only preserved, but converted from a monopoly of the ruling class into the common property of the whole of society, and further developed.[58]

Those committed to fighting for a better world should focus their attention not on curbing population growth, but on the real cause of mass starvation and ecological crises: the capitalist system itself. Doing this necessitates a fight against inequality, exploitation, poverty, environmental degradation, racism, and the oppression of women.

Socially just, sustainable agriculture is not only far less destructive to the environment, but, contrary to common perception, produces higher yields than corporate monocultures.[59] Sustainable agriculture should not be confused with the "organic" lines of produce that are increasingly appearing as part of the selection of goods offered by giant multinational food conglomerates. As corporations have spotted an emerging market for more "natural" food for those who can afford it, they have gobbled up organic farms and businesses and transformed them into "green" arms of their own business.[60] Not only does this allow them to dominate a niche market and make even larger profits from the markup on organic produce, it also deflects attention from their other activities, which continue without change. In the meantime, while they don't use chemicals, large organic farms are still monocultures with very poor working conditions. The notorious multinational corporations Dole and Chiquita for example both have their lines of organic bananas, for which they charge a premium.

In contrast, sustainable agriculture means not only no chemicals but a commitment to multi-cropping, crop rotation and fallow periods, the growing of nitrogen-fixing legumes, and biological forms of pest control. It is not about replicating farming practices from the 1400s but "is a sophisticated combination of old wisdom and modern ecological innovations that help harness the yield-boosting effects of nutrient cycles, beneficial insects, and crop synergies."[61]

To cite just one example of how organic farming does not necessarily lead to precipitous drops in crop yields, though there are many others: "University of California-Davis agricultural scientist Bill Liebhardt found that organic corn yields were 94 percent of conventional yields, organic wheat yields were 97 percent, and organic soybean yields were 94 percent. Organic tomatoes showed no yield difference."[62]

In developing countries, yield difference was in fact positive:

University of Essex researchers Jules Pretty and Rachel Hine looked at over 200 agricultural projects in the developing world that converted to organic and ecological approaches, and found that for all the projects—involving 9 million farms on nearly 30 million hectares—yields increased an average of 93 percent. A seven-year study from Maikaal District in central India involving 1,000 farmers cultivating 3,200 hectares found that average yields for cotton, wheat, chili, and soy were as much as 20 percent higher on the organic farms than on nearby conventionally managed ones.[63]

The conclusion is that the world could be fed in a sustainable manner. Obviously, the other benefits of sustainable agro-ecological farming are huge: repairing the soil, increasing water retention and organic matter content, a reduction in pesticides, water pollution, and animal deaths, and increases in biodiversity—let alone better-tasting and healthier food.

The conclusion is clear: if we got rid of the warped priorities of capitalist accumulation with all its gargantuan waste of resources, the environmental "footprint" of humanity, even with nine billion of us, would be far less than it currently is with six. Accomplishing this would bring down population and reassert the integrity of the earth for the benefit of future generations while advancing rather than attacking the interests of workers and peasants from all countries.

The fact that people have taken to the streets by the tens of thousands around the globe in response to the food crisis of 2008 to demand that their governments provide what should be regarded as a human right—access to food—should be welcomed, not fretted over. Fighting for a reduction in the extreme levels of poverty that exist in the Global South as well as the hunger that exists in the North, means fighting alongside the workers and peasants of the developing world to confront the entrenched corporate power of the multinationals and their enablers in government that exploit and oppress all of us.

Rather than seeing the poor as some kind of demographic threat, as neo-Malthusians such as Brown do today, we should recognize them as our allies in struggle. Indeed, some of the most inspiring struggles to preserve livelihoods, decent jobs, environmental integrity, and indigenous cultures over the last fifteen years have come from peasants and workers in the developing world fighting against water privatization, deforestation, and the strip-mining of local resources and food supplies by Western multinationals and financial institutions. We need to categorically reject the argument that population growth is at the heart of world hunger or that people in the developing world are not producers of wealth as well as consumers—that they are somehow not part of the struggle for a better world. To do otherwise is to accept that the division of rich and poor is an eternal law of nature, whereby there are always destined to be "too many" poor. To quote Engels, Malthus claims that:

> the earth is perennially overpopulated, whence poverty, misery, distress, and immorality must prevail; that it is the lot, the eternal destiny of mankind, to exist in too great numbers, and therefore in diverse classes, of which some are rich, educated, and moral, and others more or less poor, distressed, ignorant, and immoral...The problem is not to make the "surplus population" useful, to transform it into available population, but merely to let it starve to death in the least objectionable way and to prevent its having too many children, this, of course, is simple enough, provided the surplus population perceives its own superfluousness and takes kindly to starvation. There is, however, in spite of the violent exertions of the humane bourgeoisie, no immediate prospect of its succeeding in bringing about such a disposition among the workers. The workers have taken it into their heads that they, with their busy hands, are the necessary, and the rich capitalists, who do nothing, the surplus population."[64]

Each addition to world population does contribute to the production of greenhouse gases to a greater or lesser extent, the amount dependent on where that person is born. It is also true that over the last thirty years, as two hundred to three hundred million Chinese have been lifted out of poverty by economic development, Chinese emissions have risen dramatically. But environmental degradation and emissions increases in China are a direct product of the state-orchestrated capitalist mode of development that China is following. This is precisely what we are refusing to take as given when we call capitalism into question—development doesn't have to follow this model, and more people don't have to be a problem. Apart from the fact that population growth is declining as shown above, if we follow the argument for population control, this puts us in the same camp as the ruling classes of the North and pits us against our natural allies; the workers and peasants of the South.

The richest 7 percent of the global population are responsible for 50 percent of the world's CO_2 emissions, whereas the poorest 50 percent are responsible for a mere 7 percent.[65] The conclusion is clear: it's capitalism that needs restraining, not people. We must aim for real development that takes social, cultural, and ecological improvement as its primary goal.

The article in *Focus* mentioned earlier expresses a sentiment with which I couldn't agree more: "As far as the environment is concerned, the last thing we need is more rich people."[66]

CHAPTER THREE

Why Capitalism Cannot Solve the Problem

"Capitalism as we know it today is incapable of sustaining the environment."

> —James Gustave Speth, dean of the Yale School of Forestry and Environmental Studies, former environmental advisor to Jimmy Carter[1]

The Energy Dilemma

On a planet being slowly poisoned by the economic system under which it is run, transforming energy sources is the single biggest item that needs to change. And it has to be done rapidly. Most scientists agree that CO_2 emissions need to be reduced by up to 80–90 percent globally by 2050 to avoid serious and irreversible climate change.[2] The fact that the entire economy runs on essentially three substances—oil, coal, and natural gas—and that these are the three most responsible for global warming presents capitalism with an essentially insurmountable problem.

Some renewable energy technologies, such as photovoltaic cells, lend themselves to more decentralized and smaller local applications, cutting against the needs of the giant energy corporations for huge power stations and a centralized energy grid, but there is nothing inherent to capitalism that sets it against deriving energy from renewable sources. Indeed, in theory, there is nothing that capitalism will not and cannot make profitable; one only needs to see the ability of the system to make money from previously worthless pollution to recognize the validity of that statement. However, now that capitalism has evolved in a particular way and has developed a world economic system predicated on fossil-fuel-driven growth, it is caught on the horns of its own historical development.

Marx wrote of once-productive social relations becoming a fetter to the further development of society's productive powers.[3] Here Marx was was not arguing for unending expansion of production, for which he is commonly criticized. It is capitalism that expands production for its own sake, driven by the competitive pursuit of profit—the expansion of exchange value. Marx was arguing that outmoded social forms stand in the way of the further development of society's powers to answer people's real needs—the expansion of use value. This kind of development of the productive powers would mean an improved ability to produce useful things and useful states of affairs, which, unlike the process of capitalist development, does not entail that more and more things are produced in each round of production.

Nothing illustrates Marx's point better than the incapacity of capitalist social relations to address the issue of fossil fuels. Worldwide, more than $13 trillion dollars of capital are invested in infrastructure directly related to oil and gas production, refining and use: from the oil rigs, oil tankers, refineries, petrochemical plants, gas stations, pipelines, storage, and docking facilities. In the United States alone, there are 150 oil refineries, 4,000 offshore platforms, 160,000 miles of oil pipelines, facilities to handle more than 15 million barrels per day (bpd) in imports and exports, 10,400 fossil-fuel-consuming power plants, 410 underground gas storage fields, 1.4 million miles of natural gas pipelines, and 180,000 gasoline service stations.[4] This doesn't even count all the billions of dollars of investment and government subsidies in roads and the mining, refining and manufacture of asphalt, rubber, steel, aluminum, cars, trucks, etc. The fact that corporations and the governments that facilitate their operation cannot just write this off demonstrates the validity of Marx's observation about how social relations turn from being a driving force of positive societal growth and increase in living standards into their opposite. Previous investments in fixed capital all have to be utilized to the fullest extent until their depreciation costs are acceptable.

Furthermore, the layout, location, and growth of entire towns, cities, and ports, particularly later developing ones such as those in the United States, are explicitly designed to facilitate the needs of an automobile-centered culture. Motorized road traffic based on the internal combustion engine is given primacy of place while public transportation or human or animal powered transport is relegated to second or third class status.

The U.S. energy bill passed in 2007, the Energy Independence and Security Act (EISA)—deliberations over which we (unlike the energy corporations) were never allowed to participate—demonstrate this point. After heavy lobbying by the oil industry and utilities, provisions offensive to business, such as a $13 billion tax increase and a requirement to provide 15 percent of electricity from renewable sources, were removed by "reluctant" Senate majority leader Harry Reid, a

Democrat, and passed in the Senate 86 to 8.[5] According to James Ford, director of government affairs at the American Petroleum Institute: "We made sure that everybody knew our point of view—the White House, the House, the Senate... We told our story and told it thoroughly."[6] The overwhelming vote in favor of this legislation prompted Brent Blackwelder, president of Friends of the Earth, to accuse Senate Democrats of, to use his words, "capitulating" to Senate Republicans and the White House:

> When the Republican leadership and the polluter lobby have blocked important legislation, Senate Democrats have been all too willing to move in their direction. The result is that the two most positive provisions of the energy bill—a clean energy mandate and a tax package reining in handouts for fossil fuels and promoting clean energy—are being removed, while detrimental provisions, such as a radical five-fold increase in unsustainable biofuel use, remain.[7]

In a bipartisan vote of 314 to 100, the watered-down bill passed the House and was declared "groundbreaking" by House Democratic majority leader Nancy Pelosi, though a more accurate term might be "earth-breaking." The bill allocates $25 billion to a resurgent nuclear industry, $2 billion for a uranium enrichment plant, $10 billion to build plants to turn coal into a liquid vehicle-fuel, and $2 billion to turn coal into natural gas.

Moreover, while there are $10 billion dollars in provisions for alternative energy, much of this is being funneled to the large corporations involved in the development of agro-fuels, such as Monsanto and Archer Daniels Midland. These are fuels such as ethanol, which is made from fermenting corn (in the United States) or sugarcane (Brazil) and can then be used as an additive in gasoline, and biodiesel, made from palm, soybean, or rapeseed oil.

Agro-fuels are being hailed as "carbon neutral" because the CO_2 released when the ethanol or agro-fuel is burned is only the same amount as that taken in when the plant was growing. But despite the push of the major agribusiness corporations for the spread of agro-fuels, more and more scientists are concerned about their energy efficiency, their role in the food crisis, and their contribution to accelerating rates of deforestation[8] that is taking place in some of the world's last remaining tropical rainforests, such as those in Brazil and Indonesia.[9] According to the *Times* of London it would in fact be more environmentally sound to continue driving a gasoline-fueled car than one whose fuel is made from crops:

> The expansion of plantations [for biofuel production] has pushed the orangutan to the brink of extinction in Sumatra, where it takes 840 years for a palm oil plantation to soak up the carbon emitted when rainforest is burnt.
>
> Using fossil fuel in vehicles is better for the environment than so-called green fuels made from crops, according to a government study seen by The Times.
>
> The findings show that the Department for Transport's target for raising the level of biofuel in all fuel sold in Britain will result in millions of acres of forest being logged or burnt down and converted to plantations. The study…concludes that some of the most commonly used biofuel crops fail to meet the minimum sustainability standard set by the European Commission.[10]

While the carbon neutrality of agro-fuels is technically true, in a move that typifies the sleight of hand practiced by capitalist accounting methods, it omits to take into consideration the fertilizer and pesticides used to grow the plants, which are all derived from energy-intensive fossil-fuel-driven sources. Furthermore, the amount of energy derived from burning corn-based ethanol is, at best, only about the same amount as the amount of energy that has to be put in to turn it into ethanol in the first place.[11] Therefore, it cannot be said to be an energy source. Consequently, there has been a turn to "cellulosic" ethanol from grasses, because here there is a net energy gain (as there is for ethanol from sugarcane). Nevertheless, land (and labor) still has to be devoted to growing these crops, in a world where, according to the UN, 16,000 children die from hunger-related diseases every day—one every five seconds. According to a recent report in the journal *Science* that backs up the European Commission's report cited by the *Times* above, when considering the whole life cycle, some agro-fuels are in fact worse than fossil fuels for carbon dioxide emission.[12]

There has been a huge increase in the price of corn and other food crops as more and more arable land is devoted to growing corn to turn into fuel to burn in cars, rather than feed humans.[13] While powerful economic forces encourage developing countries to hack away at what little remains of the rainforests and replace them with monocultures, the "free market" lesson is clear: feed cars in order to starve people. The passage of the energy bill means the situation will only get worse. It calls for further ramping up of ethanol production, mostly from corn, to hit 36 billion gallons by 2022. This is an ecological and social catastrophe in the making as more land will be devoted to corn to make ethanol in the United States and further deforestation for palm oil and sugarcane plantations overseas to export into America to make up any shortfall.[14]

Before the vote on EISA, Democrat Nancy Pelosi told colleagues, "You are present at a moment of change, of real change."[15] This was in reference to the bill's requirement that cars and light trucks meet a fleetwide average of 35 miles a gallon—but not until 2020. Car fleets in Europe and Japan *already* exceed this number and the EU and Japan have goals of 48.9mpg by 2012 and 46.9mpg by 2015 respectively.[16]

The story of attempts so far to discipline the auto industry to produce lower- or non-emissions vehicles is a sad one. With the backing of the first Bush administration, the oil and auto industry strenuously lobbied in California against the 1990 Zero Emissions Vehicle mandate that required 2 percent of cars sold in California to be "zero emissions" by 1998, 5 percent by 2001, and 10 percent by 2003. Under pressure from auto and oil interests, the California Air Resources Board (CARB) removed the 1998 2 percent requirement. The mandate then went through four more changes. Finally, in spring 2008 the board mandated the auto industry to produce only 7,500 electric and hydrogen fuel cell vehicles from 2012–2014—down from 25,000 that were called for in the previous revision made in 2003.

While there had been a fleeting attempt by GM to pioneer production of an electric car to meet CARB requirements, this attempt seems to have been deliberately doomed to failure. In 1996, GM produced more than 600 first-generation and 500 second-generation EV1 electric cars, offering to lease them to customers. Interest in the popular car immediately mushroomed far beyond their supply, yet GM discontinued production in 1999, citing battery problems. Then in 2003 the cars were recalled and most of them crushed, based on the claim that there was not sufficient demand for them. An independent study commissioned by the California Electric Transportation Coalition found that had it been mass produced, the EV1 would have had enough eager customers to absorb 12 to 18 percent of California's auto market. The oil industry was also involved in killing the EV1. According to the 2006 film *Who Killed the Electric Car?* GM sold the patent for the EV1 car battery (which they had purchased from its inventor) to Texaco in 2000 just before Texaco merged with Chevron. Chevron would not make the battery available.[17] In a big slap in the face to the public, GM announced in August 2002 that it was going to meet California's emissions requirements by giving away a bunch of golf-cart-style electric vehicles that could not be driven in traffic.

What Progress under Obama?

Many people in the United States and across the world were inspired by President Obama's commitment during his 2008 presidential campaign to take strong action on the environment. There was a welcome change from the Bush-Cheney oil administration's outright denial of the dangers of climate change and the "drill, baby, drill" war cry of the McCain-Palin campaign.

With the Democrats in control of both houses of Congress and a president formally committed to the creation of a "green economy" and millions of "green-collar" jobs, expectations were high for the bill pushed by Representatives Henry Waxman (D-Calif.) and Edward Markey (D-Mass.), the American Clean Energy and Security Act (ACES, HR 2454) in 2009.

The ACES bill was intended to restore U.S. credibility and leadership on the environment in the run-up to the international conference in Copenhagen at the end of the year. However, as it meandered through congressional subcommittees subject to corporate lobbying, the bill was substantially watered down to make it palatable to the fossil-fuel sector and win the support of wavering Democrats from oil- and coal-producing and agricultural states. Yet it still barely scraped through the House by a 219–212 vote. The bill, or what little remains of it, now looks dead in the water as government priorities shift.

While much was made of the bill's promise to cut 17 percent of CO_2 emissions by 2020, in a little highlighted but extremely important shift the baseline has been changed from 1990 (when the baseline for Kyoto began) to 2005. Therefore, in the best-case scenario—i.e., if the system actually works like it's supposed to—this represents at best a 4 percent reduction of U.S. emissions from 1990. The United States would therefore remain in violation of the 1997 Kyoto Protocol that then-President George W. Bush refused to sign—hardly the leap into a brighter, greener future that is so urgently needed.

Even before the bill was substantially watered down, as successfully demanded by various polluter lobbies, it hardly marked a serious attempt at tackling the escalating deterioration of the ecosphere. But just to make sure, the oil industry increased its lobbying budget 73 percent in 2008 over the previous year and spent $44.5 million in just the first three months of 2009 alone.[18] Since then, oil and gas spending on lobbying in 2009 set a new record: over $154 million, a 16 percent increase from 2008. Electricity utilities spent a further $134.6 million to influence a supposedly democratic process; dwarfing by ten times the amount spent by alternative energy companies or environmental groups.[19]

Nevertheless, the Republicans and the right wing have gone into full-throttle apoplexy about the supposed dire implications that the bill will have for the U.S. economy and

American workers. To listen to them, the ACES bill is an almost existential threat to the very fabric of American society.

Iain Murray wrote in the *National Review* that the bill represents "a 1,201-page economic suicide note." He added, "Those members of the House who vote for it are voting for long-term economic decline and for turning the United States into a second-rate economy."[20]

Representative Frank Lucas (R-Okla.) declared that a cap-and-trade system like the one proposed by Waxman and Markey "promises to cap our incomes, our livelihoods and our standard of living" and will therefore "hurt American agriculture." And Representative "Smokey" Joe Barton, (R-Texas) wants the bill renamed: "They like to call it ACES, but I call it C.R.A.P.—continue ruining America's prosperity."[21] While Murray, Lucas, and Barton are ridiculously overstating the case, there is also truth to the argument that under capitalism, placing environmental regulations on your own corporations while other countries don't will lead to competitive disadvantage. This is why the competitive pressures between nation-states drive them all to do the minimum to stop greenhouse gas emissions. The Republicans are distinguished by having the nerve to admit this and present it as a virtue.

At the heart of the legislation lies the concept of cap and trade, which will be outlined in some detail in the following chapter. President Obama's campaign literature promised that 100 percent of the original carbon credits that companies are allocated under the cap would be auctioned—not given away as under the European carbon-trading system. Despite Obama's campaign pledge to oppose any free permits—the one significant advantage over the European system if one is prepared to accept the extremely dubious logic of carbon trading in the first place—the ACES bill nevertheless allows for 85 percent of them to be given away for free.[21]

Furthermore, the ACES bill provides for $2 billion in offsets—companies can "offset" their carbon emissions by buying carbon credits from another company. The vast majority of these offsets—$1.5 billion—are tagged for international projects, which are the most difficult to verify and open to all kinds of fraud.[22] This essentially amounts to a corporate license to print money.

The U.S. government itself released a report in late 2008 that was highly critical of the UN's Clean Development Mechanism that oversees international offsets and verifies whether they are effective. According to the Government Accounting Office report, "Carbon offsets involve fundamental trade-offs and may not be a reliable long-term approach to climate change mitigation...It is not possible to ensure that every credit represents a real, measurable and long-term reduction in emissions."[23]

In reference to the European Union's disastrous record of reducing carbon emissions by cap and trade, James Kanter, writing in the *New York Times* reported in December 2008: "Indeed, it seems clearer by the day that while carbon trading represents a neat and economically sound solution to cutting emissions on paper, in practice it may be unleashing a new bonanza of corporate lobbying and political brinksmanship."[24]

Ronald Bailey, *Reason* magazine's science correspondent, commented, "The problem with Europe is that each country got to set its own emission allocations, and the temptation to cheat was overwhelming—in fact, all of them cheated."[25] Of course they cheated. Under the competitive anarchy of global capitalism, all nation-states, like all corporations, have a permanent incentive to cheat on agreements that might limit their profits. That's why a vast army of bureaucrats would be needed to oversee and check every capitalist enterprise for cheating on health and safety and environmental laws.

The Emissions Trading Scheme (ETS) scheme has yet to deliver any greenhouse gas reductions, and according to the *Wall Street Journal*, European emissions have actually risen by 1 percent every year since 2005, when the scheme began.[26] Is it really any wonder that the bill was backed by some of the most-polluting fossil-fuel-based corporations on the planet: Shell, Duke Energy, Rio Tinto, DuPont, ConocoPhillips, Dow, and BP? According to the *Wall Street Journal*, Wall Street traders called the bill's carbon markets a "huge playground" where "bucks [will] be made" and are similarly backing the bill.[27]

Though the political winds have shifted most recently, should the bill pass the Senate and be signed into law by President Obama it is predicted to massively expand the market for pollution credits into a $2 to $3 trillion bazaar. This will then come to rival the market for "exotic" financial instruments that brought the world economy to a screeching halt in 2008. In fact, some predict the next financial bubble to be in the carbon trading market.

Alongside cap-and-trade handouts, handouts to the coal industry continue, with the ACES bill allocating funds to the tune of $10 billion for the development of "clean coal" technologies such as Carbon Capture and Sequestration (CCS).

According to a statement released by Friends of the Earth, which along with Greenpeace is opposing passage of the bill, it is in fact *worse* than no bill at all:

> There's a simple reason polluting and irresponsible corpora-
> tions support the Waxman-Markey bill: It showers them with

hundreds of billions of dollars, but doesn't require them to reduce pollution fast enough to avoid devastating climate change impacts. Worse, the bill guts the EPA's preexisting authority to use the Clean Air Act to reduce this pollution. That means the bill is actually counterproductive—enacting it into law would be a step backward.[28]

So the flagship environmental bill backed by Obama requires us to rely on Wall Street to "self-regulate" in a brand-new multibillion-dollar derivatives market. If it passes in anything like its current form, what we will get is a "pollution casino" and windfall profits for those corporations astute enough to learn from their European corporate friends and engage in the age-old capitalist tactic known as cheating.

While some prominent environmentalists are backing the bill as "the best realistically possible," Michael O'Hare, quoted in the *New York Times* Opinionator blog, expresses how disappointing President Obama's leadership on this issue, among others, has been:

It's not easy to exaggerate just how bad this [bill] is. Waxman-Markey has been savaged on the implicit principle that climate stabilization is good, but only if no one important has to actually do anything different to accomplish it. Among the people who get a pass are anyone who burns coal, and anyone who grows corn or makes fuel out of it; I was worried months ago that a president from a coal state and a corn state might be a problem, but then he promised flatly that in his administration, science was not going to be yoked to a political ox.

Boy, is the bloom off this rose: DADT [Don't Ask, Don't Tell], climate and energy, transparency... "Better than Bush in some ways" is a mighty big comedown from the PR of a few months ago.[29]

Since then, expectations for Obama taking concrete and positive action on climate change have spiraled further downwards. The debacle at Copenhagen has been followed by Obama's capitulation to the nuclear, fossil fuel, and agro-fuels lobby, as evidenced by his first State of the Union address in January 2010, where, commenting on energy, he had this to say: "That means building a new generation of safe, clean nuclear power plants in this country. It means making tough decisions about opening new offshore areas for oil and gas development. It means continued investment in advanced biofuels and clean coal technologies."[30]

None of these are solutions to global warming. For all Obama's much-vaunted and justified oratorical skills, the words "safe," "clean," and "nuclear" should never be placed next to each other in the same sentence. "Clean coal" technology doesn't exist and is another example of a phrase containing two words that simply can't logically coexist. Biofuels, as noted above, have been shown to very effective at fueling hunger but certainly are not a transition to a clean energy future.

Effecting "change we can believe in" on environmental questions, as with a raft of other policy areas, will come about not by relying on Democrats; self-evidently even the charismatic, progressive-sounding ones are beholden to the same corporate interests as Republicans. Change will instead depend on mobilizing against the corporate agenda fronted by politicians of both major parties and independently organizing for the priorities of working people: clean air and water, safe, reliable public transport, and an energy policy driven by those needs.

This is not part of President Obama's agenda. In yet another government handout to big business, this time to the nuclear industry, the Obama administration just added an extra $36 billion in federal loan guarantees to the nuclear industry, increasing the total amount guaranteed to them should there be cost overruns, budget problems, or difficulty with financing projects—all symptomatic of nuclear construction—to $54 billion.

Democrats are now so gung-ho about building nuclear plants they are even baiting Republicans on how serious is their commitment to nuclear power. Senator Tom Carper (D-Del.) said it is time for Republicans who support nuclear to back their words up with action: "If the Republicans are interested in helping to ensure a renaissance for nuclear power in this country, I think the path is clear for how we might do that" and went on, "They want to see as many as 100 plants built in the next 40 years. We'll find out if they're really serious about getting started. If they are, they've got a great opportunity to work with us."[31]

If any further proof were needed for how President Obama has given up on pretty much any notion of a progressive new direction for energy policy, Obama provided it himself when he had this to say of Senate minority leader Mitch McConnell (R-Ky.) in a recent meeting on a possible energy bill: "[McConnell] said something very nice...on how he supports our goals on nuclear energy, and clean coal technology and more drilling to increase oil production." "Well, of course he likes that," Obama added. "That's part of the Republican agenda for energy, which I accept."[32]

Capitalism Takes the Most Dirty Road

Coal liquefaction and gasification, something President Obama is championing alongside the "next generation" of agro-fuels,[33] are part of the strategy for the promotion of "clean coal" technologies; that is, using coal without emitting the extra greenhouse gases, which will be achieved by something called "carbon sequestration." In recognition that coal—the reserves of which are predicted to last far longer than oil or gas—is more heavily polluting than either oil or, in particular, natural gas, the plan is to bury the CO_2 emitted by coal power plants in underground reservoirs below the plant itself—pump it into empty coal mines, depleted oil and gas reservoirs, and so forth. While there have been some small-scale experiments with this technology in Norway and other countries, it is far from commercialization. The most authoritative study so far, completed by MIT in 2007, *The Future of Coal*, concluded that the first commercial plant couldn't come on-stream until 2030 at the earliest.[34] Apart from begging the question of just where all this CO_2 would be stored if this mechanism were adopted on a global scale or how the infrastructure would be built, sequestration also puts off change "safely" to the distant future. Yet sequestration also has the potential for catastrophic accidents should huge volumes of buried CO_2 escape. The Lake Nyos tragedy is an example of what can happen even on a relatively small scale. In 1986, this volcanic lake in Nigeria had become saturated at depth with odorless, colorless CO_2. When the pressurized gas finally escaped, it asphyxiated more than 1,700 people in their sleep, killing all animal life within a 15-mile radius.[35]

Clean coal is a myth dreamed up by Big Coal and latched onto by politicians as a way to continue with business as usual as most electricity is currently generated from coal-fired plants.[36] Coal is particularly attractive to U.S. coal operators and policy makers because the United States, along with China, India, and Australia, has some of the largest coal deposits of any country. U.S. coal supplies are predicted to last for at least another two hundred years. This is a major reason why the U.S. government, urged on by the politically powerful coal lobby, is so determined to try to legitimize coal production despite the extreme levels of air pollution, toxic waste, and production of CO_2 that accompanies coal mining, refining, and burning; planners see a geopolitical strategic advantage in pursuing coal power. As Amy Jaffe, an energy expert at the James A. Baker Institute for Public Policy at Rice University explains: "We are going dirtier.... If you need to come up with a fuel source other than drilling for oil under the ground in the Middle East, what is the most obvious thing with today's economy, today's infrastructure and today's technology? Oil shale, liquefied coal and tar sands. It's all dirty but it's fast."[37]

Furthermore, the energy required to "clean up" coal will inevitably mean using more coal as a significant percentage of each ton of coal burned will be required to fuel the process of coal liquefaction and CO_2 extraction and burial. Using more of the dirty fuel to clean up the stuff you're already burning hardly seems the answer required to move away from the dirtiest fossil fuel of them all. But the depth and strength of the coal lobby is immense.

Coal is a significant economic actor in thirty-four states from mining, transportation, or burning. In states such as Illinois, Obama's home state, it generates 95 percent of the electricity. It is also responsible nationally for 75 percent of railroad shipments and 25 percent of barge traffic. Indeed, only two states out of fifty, Vermont and Rhode Island, are untouched by the long economic reach of coal. Moving away from this nineteenth century fuel would therefore be a wrenching and all-encompassing experience. Despite the ravages of layoffs in the coal industry, it still employs 134,000 people in the United States and remains one of the most heavily unionized sectors of the economy.[38] It will be critical to win over coal miners and other workers whose jobs are threatened by a transition away from fossil fuels. Therefore, a central and leading part of environmental activism needs to incorporate the fight for a coherent and well-funded plan for retraining these highly skilled workers and reemploying them in well-paid union work in a new green economy building the new infrastructure we need. Only a steadfast commitment to solidarity with workers for real replacement jobs, not de-skilled, low-paid, non-unionized substitutes in the service or tourist sectors, stands the chance of success.

An excellent example of this type of environmental activism in support of unionized workers in a heavily CO_2-producing industry occurred during March 2010 in Britain. Despite mass campaigns by climate activists in Britain against another runway at Heathrow Airport and against air travel in general, a clear reason for supporting striking British Airways cabin staff was illustrated in a letter published in the *Guardian* newspaper by Khwaja Salim, with the group Workers' Climate Action:

> Climate change activists are mobilising to support the British Airways workers. We do not believe workers should pay for an economic crisis their bosses have created any more than the planet should pay for capitalism's endless chasing after profit. Strikes, workplace occupations and other militant actions are the only way to prevent the costs of the recession being unloaded on to working people. Workers in high-emissions industries have an important role in curbing climate change. They cannot do this if they are pushed down and their union broken. We want to build an alliance between the labour movement and the climate

change movement so we can transform both into an effective force for social change.[39]

This is exactly the kind of commitment that environmental activists need to make to workers everywhere, whether they are unionized or not. To create genuinely mass campaigns for serious action against climate change, workers and environmental activists need to start by building bonds of solidarity in smaller struggles for more immediate needs. These can help shift the balance of forces to the point where politicians and bosses are forced to make significant shifts in investment priorities. With the right kind of pressure from a revitalized, environmentally conscious workers' movement, we can make sure that there will be no shortage of jobs available to manufacture and lay train track, build and deploy wind turbines and solar panels, retrofit commercial, residential, and industrial buildings for energy efficiency, and upgrade the dilapidated sewage system and antiquated electrical grid.

Even oil companies that have striven to create a "green" image, such as BP, are investing in technologies to extract and refine oil from low-quality sources such as oil shale and tar sands. Extracting oil from such low-quality sources requires more energy and so has not been economically viable with low oil prices. In 2007 when prices spiked to more than $100 per barrel, all that changed, prompting a wave of investment to develop and enlarge this additional source of oil. The recent fall of oil prices to around a third of their $147 dollar per barrel peak in the summer of 2007—prompted by the decline in oil consumption brought on by the worldwide recession—has led to a decline in investment in these projects, in some cases by half. Industry experts say that oil must be $70–$80 a barrel for the oil sands industry to be profitable.[40] However, when the crisis abates and oil prices reset at higher rates, which they are predicted to do as a result of decreasing conventional oil supplies, this industry will resume its growth.

The amount of oil shale and tar sands waiting to be developed eclipses all known reserves of oil, including that already extracted and used—in excess of two trillion barrels.[41] If these corporations are allowed to develop oil sands as an alternative source of oil, the planet is certainly cooked. Extraction not only requires a lot more energy and vast quantities of water, it produces significantly more greenhouse gases (not to mention huge volumes of rock and dirt that must be removed) to do so. According to the *Independent*:

> Producing crude oil from the tar sands—a heavy mixture of bitumen, water, sand and clay—found beneath more than 54,000 square miles of prime forest in northern Alberta—an area the size of England and Wales combined—generates up to four times more carbon dioxide, the principal global warming gas, than conventional drilling. The booming oil sands industry will produce 100 million tonnes of CO_2 (equivalent to a fifth of the UK's entire annual emissions) a year by 2012…
>
> The oil rush is also scarring a wilderness landscape: millions of tons of plant life and top soil is scooped away in vast open-pit mines and millions of litres of water are diverted from rivers—up to five barrels of water are needed to produce a single barrel of crude and the process requires huge amounts of natural gas. The industry, which now includes all the major oil multinationals, including the Anglo-Dutch Shell and American combine Exxon-Mobil, boasts that it takes two tonnes of the raw sands to produce a single barrel of oil.[42]

This has not stopped Tony Hayward, BP's new chief executive, from declaring the acquisition of Sunrise oil sand refinery in Canada an "excellent asset." With a proposed investment of $5.5 billion, "BP's move into oil sands," according to Hayward, "is an opportunity to build a strategic, material position and the huge potential of Sunrise is the ideal entry point for BP into Canadian oil sands."[43]

At the same time that BP—whose slogan "Beyond Petroleum" would be more accurate if it were "Burn the Planet"—was cutting this lucrative deal, Shell quietly announced that it had sold off almost all its solar energy business. The reason given: "It was not bringing in any profit for us there so we transferred it to another operator."[44] This prompted Jeremy Leggett, chief executive of Solar Century to lament:

> Shell and Solar Century were among the 150 companies that recently signed up to the hard-hitting Bali Declaration. It is vital that companies act consistently with the rhetoric in such declarations, and as I have told Shell senior management on several occasions, an all-out assault on the Canadian tar sands and extracting oil from coal is completely inconsistent with climate protection...This latest evidence of half-heartedness or worse in Shell's renewables activities leaves me even more disappointed. Unless fossil-fuel energy companies evolve their core activities meaningfully, we are in deep trouble.[45]

BP, having shed its commitment to solar power, is now investing in wind energy in California in anticipation of acquiring market share there if, as expected, President Obama increases subsidies to wind power. However, BP makes more profit in thirteen weeks than it intends to spend on renewables over the next six years.[46] Hence this commitment should be interpreted as BP cornering a niche market, rather than a real commitment to expand wind power.

Oil company priorities are clear: In 2005, according to Shell, only 1 percent of total capital investment went into renewables. This contrasts with 69 percent going toward "scouring the planet for new sources of fossil fuels."[47] Overall, investment in energy research and development, a mere $3 billion in the 2006 federal budget, has declined in real terms by 50 percent since 1979.[48] Over the same time period, military research has increased by 260 percent to more than $75 billion a year.[49]

As traditional sources of oil diminish, the response from corporations and governments is not to launch a full-scale redirection of resources away from oil extraction, but to prolong its use to secure every single last drop through enhanced recovery techniques such as saltwater injection and horizontal drilling as well as the exploration and annexing of hitherto drill-free wilderness areas and extreme environments under the polar ice cap. In addition, they plan the creation of an even more polluting industry for the extraction of oil from previously marginal sources such as oil sands and oil shale. Therefore, whether we ever reach "the end of oil" or "peak oil" will not be determined by a physical limit or environmental destabilization, but by a social one—what profit can be made versus what resistance to this insanity can be organized.

Another case in point whereby capitalist market relations drive production in environmentally unsustainable and more polluting ways is the recent explosion of interest in the extraction of previously-marginal deposits of natural gas locked inside deep rock deposits. For many years the natural gas known to be trapped inside shale deposits that extend from New York and Pennsylvania all the way through to Texas were thought to be non-recoverable due to the technical difficulties and expense of fracturing the rock to allow the gas to be pumped to the surface. However, thanks to technological innovations such as horizontal drilling and hydraulic fracturing along with increases in the price of natural gas, widespread "hydrofracking" is the new oil rush (known as the "Shale Gale") down the entire length of the United States.

A few years ago there were plans for the construction of new liquefied natural gas (LNG) loading and storage facilities at ports around the United States to cope with the need to import it from other countries as U.S. reserves declined. Now all those plans have been shelved as the amount of gas trapped in shale has *doubled* the gas reserves of the United States and will provide enough supply for the next hundred years. In a complete turnaround, there's so much gas that by some industry accounts the United States could become a net *exporter* of natural gas. Shale gas already accounts for 20 percent of U.S. gas supplies, up from 1 percent in 2000. At a recent major oil and gas conference in Houston, ConocoPhillips CEO Jim Mulva referred to shale gas discoveries in his keynote address as "nature's gift to the people of the world."[50]

While it's true that gas has half the carbon emissions of coal, continuing with the extraction and burning of gas for another hundred years is not taking us any nearer climate stability or moving the United States away from fossil fuels.

In fact, because of the energy and water intensive method of extraction, a recent study by Robert Howarth at Cornell University questions whether hydrofracking really is more environmentally benign than coal in terms of CO_2 emissions.[51] In addition, hydrofracking is implicated in the pollution of ground water and drinking supplies. The process requires massive quantities of water, sand, toxic chemicals, and sometimes diesel to be driven underground at high pressure through boreholes to crack open the shale rock and force the gas to the surface. The process is currently exempt from regulation under the Safe Drinking Water Act, and, outside of the companies doing the fracturing, no one knows the exact composition of the chemicals because they are protected by patent law. There is already mounting evidence of company negligence and false statements to the EPA about how strictly they are preventing diesel—which is regulated under the act—from getting into water supplies.[52] Around the country, communities and activists have risen up to prevent the practice and force Congress to act to regulate it. In response to this groundswell of activism around the country, the gas industry, in an all-too-predictable stance, is opposing any federal regulation of the process as lawmakers in Washington come under pressure to pass bills restricting the practice, and the EPA carries out a new impact assessment on hydraulic fracturing.[53] More recently, industry groups are lobbying hard to make sure that any climate bill that does emerge from the U.S. Senate in 2010 strongly supports the procedure:

> The oil and gas industry yesterday leapt up to join BP America Inc. in its push to add to the new Senate climate bill a recommendation against regulating hydraulic fracturing.
>
> "Amidst all of the other worthy priorities your bill will seek to address, we hope that you can find space in your draft legislation to make your commitment to natural gas explicitly clear," wrote Lee Fuller, executive director of Energy In Depth, to the three senators drafting the new bill, John Kerry (D-Mass.), Lindsey Graham (R-S.C.) and Joe Lieberman (I-Conn.).[54]

Geopolitical Tensions and Oil Depletion

Even optimistic (read oil industry) predictions of when
"peak (conventional) oil" will be reached—when 50 percent of
reserves have been used, signaling inexorable price increases
as demand outstrips supply—only extend to 2040.[55] This fact
not only helps to explain the burgeoning investments in "non-
conventional" sources of oil in tar sands and oil shale, it can
also only lead in one direction. It is axiomatic that under unfettered capitalism, as long as profits can be made from oil, the
"lifeblood of the global economy,"[56] they will seek to extract
every last drop. Over the last two years ExxonMobil as well as
Shell have reported unprecedented profits.[57] The crash of oil
prices from their peak, prompted by the current economic crisis, will slow but not stop this process.

The competition for declining oil resources has already
led to increased geopolitical tension in the pristine wilderness
of the Arctic after a resurgent Russia, buoyed by profits from
natural gas and intent on reestablishing itself as a world
power, planted a Russian flag two miles below the surface of
the Arctic Ocean and claimed it as Russian "land." In the Arctic, sea ice and extreme climate have until recently made offshore rigs an impossible feat of engineering. For the first time
however, with global warming and the reduction in sea ice,
offshore rigs are fast becoming feasible. The Arctic is be-
lieved to contain 25 percent of the remaining undiscovered reserves and so represents an irresistible prize well worth
going to war over.[58] The United States, Canada, Norway, and
Russia are all vying for rights and arguing about how to classify the waters and the land underneath.[59]

Furthermore, in a move likely to terminate any possibility

of survival for the polar bear, let alone a host of other species clinging to a precarious existence in one of the most extreme environments on earth, global warming has opened up the possibility of turning into reality the fabled Northwest Passage to shipping. Large container ships from Europe will be able to make the trip to Asia one third quicker—an irresistible competitive advantage.[60]

The conflicts in Iraq and Afghanistan, and the United States' unwavering commitment to occupy both countries and dictate their forms of government, can only be explained by the world's biggest user seeking to control supply of the world's most important commodity. To maintain global economic and military supremacy is simply impossible without control over the single most important resource. Ever since Lord Curzon made his famous observation about how the Allies had won the First World War by "floating to victory on a wave of oil,"[61] this is recognized as a necessary goal and one to which the U.S. ruling class is fully committed, no matter which party is in power.

The conflicts erupting in other oil-producing regions, the jockeying for position by the Great Powers in various oil states in Africa, the U.S. hostility to Venezuela, the growing U.S. animosity with Russia, the antagonism between Russia and the countries of the European Union that import its natural gas, the friction around the Caspian and South China Seas: all are potential flashpoints as competition over resources intensifies and threatens to boil over into the traditional way capitalist states resolve their disagreements over "vital questions of national security"—via open warfare.[62] As Chinese and Indian economies expand and their energy demands increase, this can only lead to increasing levels of inter-imperial rivalry as all countries seek to ramp up military spending and annex their share of the remaining resources available. As Michael Klare's *Resource Wars* makes clear, potential conflicts over oil, water, and other dwindling resources are already threatening stability in a succession of areas around the world as global and regional powers make new alliances and seek to maintain or extend their hold over geostrategically important areas.[63]

Acceptance of the Imperial Status Quo

There is a connection between the discussion of population in chapter two and the inter-imperial rivalry examined above. When people focus on population as the main determinant behind ecological disruption and resource depletion this often leads them into an acceptance and defense of the prevailing imperial order. Once "surplus" populations become the problem, it is difficult to see them as part of the solution; they are merely consumers rather than equally as much producers and initiators of change. It is a short step from there to see stabilization and redress coming from the intervention of the powers that be as the enlightened agents of change. Hence for example, Lester Brown does advocate for a more progressive and welcome set of objectives other than just population control, arguing for a massive effort to cut carbon emissions, eradicate poverty, and restore forests, soils, and aquifers. However, it is difficult to see how these objectives could be reached without a radical transformation of the geopolitical status quo, something Brown refuses to acknowledge.

Notwithstanding this critique of the limits of change set by a world dominated by inter-imperial rivalry, activists cannot stand aside from the short-term struggle but resolutely and determinedly fight for all the goals just mentioned as necessary for the fundamental reorganization of society. Victories in alleviating poverty, slowing down ecological degradation, or for women's rights not only improve people's lives in the here and now, but act as inspiration to continue and deepen the struggle by encouraging more people to join in. All movements against entrenched power need victories, no matter how small they may initially appear to be. Any advance for our side is of necessity a setback for the other.

Brown argues that governmental collapse in developing countries increasingly prone to water and food shortages as a result of overpopulation and climate change will lead to more "failed states" that will then become leading exporters of "refugees, terrorism, disease, illicit drugs and weapons" thereby destabilizing the whole of world civilization. Brown states:

> Unable to buy grain or grow their own, hungry people take to the streets. Indeed, even before the steep climb in grain prices in 2008, the number of failing states was expanding. Many of their problems stem from a failure to slow the growth of their populations. But if the food situation continues to deteriorate, entire nations will break down at an ever increasing rate. We have entered a new era in geopolitics. In the 20th century the main threat to international security was superpower conflict; today it is failing states. It is not the concentration of power but its absence that puts us at risk.[64]

Thus he shifts the blame for environmental crisis from the leading economic and military powers to regions that are the victims of these powers' policies.

One good question might be: what caused these states to fail in the first place? By propping up authoritarian regimes and dictators during the cold war, and then abandoning any responsibility for these regions when the superpower rivalry sub-sided, imperial powers in fact bear direct responsibility for the creation of failed states. Somalia and Afghanistan, for example, fell apart in the early 1990s when both the U.S. and the USSR devastated the two respective regions. Afghanistan's economy collapsed when the two superpowers stopped pumping money into the country's civil war.[65] And the Somali state collapsed when its dictator lost his imperial sponsorships, first from Russia (late 1970s), then from the United States (early 1990s). After the fall of the Soviet Union in 1991 and the end of the cold war, there was a massive withdrawal of aid to the "Third World" from the United States, Russia, and Europe. At the same time, it marked the intensification of the period of neoliberal plunder—whose ideology called for the rule of open, privatized markets, further relaxation of import tariffs, and the weakening of the role of the very states that were on the edge of failure.

Even a cursory glance at U.S. foreign policy shows that it is not so-called failed states that are responsible for exporting terrorism, disease, weapons, refugees, and illicit drugs. The United States is by far the biggest arms supplier in the world, as well as the largest market for illicit drugs. It spends almost more on arms than all other countries *combined* and happily sells them to any state that will serve its interests.[66] Moreover, as already noted, the neoliberal policies pushed by Washington are responsible for destroying subsistence farming in poor countries and creating the food insecurity that so alarms Lester Brown.

Two countries Brown highlights as failed states, Iraq and Afghanistan, are direct victims of U.S. policy—places that have indeed become ridden with poverty, disease, soaring drug production, ethnic tensions, and the resentment that can lead directly to terroristic acts. Are we meant to take seriously the idea that Afghanistan and Iraq became "failed states" because they suddenly became vastly overpopulated? And why not classify dropping 500-pound bombs on villages in Pakistan—a supposed U.S. ally—as "terrorism"?

With the United States responsible for 25 percent of global emissions of climate changing gases, and the West more generally almost exclusively responsible for their buildup over the last hundred years, Western countries are by extension responsible for the growing number of climate refugees. This has led to calls by activists, particularly from developing countries, for "climate reparations," an idea flatly rejected by the top U.S. government environmental spokesperson at the Copenhagen conference in December 2009, Todd Stern: "I actually completely reject the notion of a debt or reparations or anything of the like…We absolutely recognize our historical role in putting emissions in the atmosphere that are there now. But the sense of guilt or culpability or reparations, I categorically reject that."[67]

This statement is equivalent to admitting that you set your neighbor's house on fire by dousing it with gasoline and then stood aside watching it burn, but rejecting the idea that you somehow might bear responsibility for rebuilding it. Without a transfer of funds and technology on the order of $100 billion/year—still a small fraction of U.S. defense spending—to the developing world, it is impossible to see how they can adapt to climate change and implement strategies for alternative development pathways. Given the level of technological development currently available worldwide, there's no reason developing countries have to follow the fossil-fuel-dependent developmental pathway taken by the West. They could leapfrog over that stage and move straightaway to a clean, renewable energy future. But they would need a massive injection of capital to do that. Unfortunately, capital currently flows the other way. According to a recent report by Raymond Baker, director of the U.S.-based research body Global Financial Integrity (GFI), almost $2 trillion has left Africa since 1970, the vast majority of it to Western financial institutions:

> In recent years [in Africa] much attention has been focused on corruption—the proceeds of bribery and theft by government officials—[but] this only makes up about 3 percent of the cross-border flow of illicit money around the world...It is not unreasonable to estimate total illicit outflows from the continent across the 39 years at some $1.8tn...This massive flow of illicit money out of Africa is facilitated by a global shadow financial system comprising tax havens, secrecy jurisdictions, disguised corporations, anonymous trust accounts, fake foundations, trade mis-pricing and money laundering techniques.[68]

This amount of money dwarfs by 10 to 1 the money given as aid by Western governments and explains why poverty reduction strategies have been such a failure. The report continues: "According to recent studies by GFI and other researchers, developing countries lose at least $10 through illegal capital flight for every $1 they receive in external assistance."

Lester Brown writes, "Our global civilization depends on a functioning network of politically healthy nation-states to control the spread of infectious disease, to manage the international monetary system, to control international terrorism and to reach scores of other common goals."[69] In short, his assumptions are those of the dominant world imperialist powers, who claim to represent world "civilization" and the needs of humanity, but whose activities are in fact responsible for destroying it.

The above analysis has examined some of the main reasons why there has been so little progress in tackling climate change to date and the structural constraints that bind the capitalist system to continued dependence on fossil fuels as the core global energy source. These constraints are due to the historical development of the system and the resulting gargantuan investments and vested interests in fossil fuel extraction, refining, transportation, infrastructure, distribution and the profits that flow from this historical development. Further narrowing of options is imposed by international economic and political competition as it plays out between nation-states in inter-imperial geopolitical strategy.

An objective, rational appraisal of the degenerating ecological situation based on the best available scientific data and the promulgation of real solutions extrapolated from that appraisal are beyond the ability of competing nation-states to coordinate and put in practice. For these reasons, the only "solutions" that the system is prepared to countenance are not selected for their efficacy in actually alleviating global climate change. The solutions they do put forward are the subject of the next chapter.

CHAPTER FOUR

False Solutions Favored by the System

> "If you didn't auction the permits, it would represent the largest corporate welfare program that has ever been enacted in the history of the United States. All of the evidence suggests that what would occur is that corporate profits would increase by approximately the value of the permits."
>
> —Peter Orszag, President Obama's budget director, testimony before the House Budget Committee, March 2009[1]

Proposed Mitigating Solutions

Governments and scientists were concerned enough about global warming in 1989—two decades ago—to set up the IPCC. Since that time, very little has been accomplished. To date, the most serious international attempt to do something to reduce greenhouse gas emissions was the 1997 Kyoto Protocol, negotiated under the auspices of the United Nations Framework Convention on Climate Change (UNFCCC), which evolved out of the 1992 Earth Summit in Rio de Janeiro. This agreement, hailed at the time as an historic breakthrough in limiting the growth of greenhouse gases, committed the industrialized countries to reduce their emissions of six different greenhouse gases below the levels emitted in 1990 by between 0 and 8 percent averaged over the years 2008 to 2012. Kyoto did not go into effect officially until February 16, 2005, because until the Russian Federation ratified it on November 4, 2004, it did not have enough signatories; notably, both the United States and Australia refused to sign on. By that time, the U.S. Senate had already voted 95 to 0 not to ratify anything that committed the United States to any kind of emissions targets that might negatively impact its economic development. Bill Clinton never even sent the measure to Congress to seek ratification. Indeed, the person leading the U.S. delegation to the talks and responsible for much of the watering down of the agreement—for example, cutting the 15 percent reductions by 2010 asked for by the EU to an average of 5.2 percent by 2012—was none other than Al Gore.[2]

The deal hammered out in Kyoto was not only unenforceable without the United States—the world's biggest polluter, responsible for 25 percent of global CO_2 emissions—signing on, but from a practical perspective pointless.

To the extent that the signatories have attempted to comply with Kyoto, what are the results? While Britain has achieved some measurable decreases in emissions, these never approached the 12.5 percent below 1990 levels that they set for themselves and were almost all due to switching from burning coal to burning natural gas. All fossil fuels emit carbon dioxide when they burn, but not all fuels are equally polluting. Natural gas has lower carbon content and so emits significantly less CO_2 per unit of energy generated, while coal emits the most. However, in order to meet a developing energy crisis, Gordon Brown, then prime minister of Britain, was set to authorize the building of eight new coal-fired power plants—the first such plants to be built in thirty years. According to James Hansen, a leading and early advocate of the need to halt climate change and director of the NASA Goddard Institute for Space Studies in New York, building these plants would completely invalidate any commitment given by the UK at the recent climate talks in Bali or any hope that it will meet its emissions targets.[3]

At the end of 2009, government plans to build those plants, labeled "death factories" by Hansen,[4] took a major hit as a mass campaign by environmental groups struck down what was to be the flagship new plant at Kingsnorth in Kent, England. This is one of the biggest victories for climate change activists as the three-year campaign to inform the public and shut down the existing plant on the same site through mass invasions was subject to heavy-handed police intimidation tactics, judicial interference, and intransigence from the giant German energy operating company, E.On. Despite all this, and despite the company's prior insistence on the need to build the massive new coal plant, E.On, in a dramatic reversal—citing a reduction in demand for energy— pulled out of the deal to build the plant in October 2009. As noted by activists, the plant was designed to operate for forty years and so an annual dip in demand is hardly a legitimate reason for suspension of the multimillion dollar construction.[5] This victory against entrenched corporate interests by grassroots activism highlights what is possible and sets the stage for a fight against existing coal plants.

Activists from all over the country had successfully mobilized against the coal-fired plant and their campaign clearly resonated with the public. After five Greenpeace activists scaled the smokestack at Kingsnorth in 2006 a jury refused to convict them of criminal damage as they successfully argued the environmental damage from the proposed plant would cause far more public harm than they ever could. Much to the annoyance of E.On, they were acquitted on all charges.[6]

To the extent that Europe has been able to reduce its greenhouse emissions to 1990 levels, it was helped enormously by the catastrophic economic collapse of the Eastern Bloc and the demise of the Soviet Union in the early 1990s. By setting the date at 1990, when the Soviet Union and other East European countries were pouring out emissions from outdated and ramshackle power stations and factories with no environmental constraints whatsoever, Europe managed to take the ecological high ground and look environmentally committed by not doing anything other than sitting back and watching the economies of Eastern Europe implode.[7] While EU governments are generally more committed than the United States is to the regulation of emissions—due principally to a stronger environmental movement, the presence of significant Green parties, and a somewhat different path of economic development based on a lack of oil and gas deposits—no one should think that this is anything other than a calculated position that allows them to place the blame for global warming on the intransigence of the United States.

Meanwhile, the United States, which has never ratified the Kyoto Protocols, increased its greenhouse gas emissions by a cumulative 17 percent throughout the 1990s under the environmental stewardship of Bill Clinton and Al Gore. As a result of these increases, were the United States to make any attempt at fulfilling the pledge it reneged on at Kyoto to 7 percent cuts from 1990 levels—itself totally inadequate in terms of addressing the scale of the problem—this would mean making 20 percent cuts to 2000 levels by 2012.[8]

Given that no one from either party in the election of 2008 put much of a priority on global warming it is perhaps unsurprising that President Obama has taken little action to significantly cut U.S. contributions to greenhouse gas emissions. This is not unrelated to the substantial sums that industry polluters give to both parties, as reported by George Monbiot:

> Since 1990, the energy and natural resources sector—mostly coal, oil, gas, logging and agribusiness—has given $418m to federal politicians in the U.S. Transport companies have given $355m…. [T]he undiscriminating nature of this munificence [is bipartisan]. The big polluters favor the Republicans, but most of them also fund Democrats. During the 2000 presidential campaign, oil and gas companies lavished money on Bush, but they also gave Gore $142,000, while transport companies gave him $347,000.[9]

More recently, since Democrats now control all the levers of government, campaign contributions from energy corporations, historically tilted toward the Republicans, have effortlessly switched sides:

> Electric utilities, energy producers and other major players in the fossil-fuel based sector have significantly increased the percentage of their campaign contributions that go to Democrats, with many donating to the majority party at a greater rate than at any point in at least 15 years.
>
> The shift in industry giving is particularly noticeable among major electric utilities, many of whom are for the first time in recent history giving the majority of their dollars to Democratic politicians.
>
> Through the first six months of 2009, electric companies and utilities gave about 59 percent of their campaign dollars to Democrats…through much of President George W. Bush's tenure, some Democrats and others on the left often

accused the Republican Party of being in the pockets of corporate energy interests—a theme that was repeated again
and again in campaign advertising. Now, it is the Democrats who see large number of industry contributions while
crafting legislation that will have major ramifications for
nearly all corners of the energy sector.[10]

Since Australia's decision to accept Kyoto at the end of
2007, things have only gotten worse as far as climate conferences go. The latest IPCC report was meant to inform governments meeting in Bali at the end of 2007 for another round
of climate talks and to lead to some agreement that would su-
persede Kyoto. While there was much huffing and puffing
about the stubbornness of the United States, and then the
hailing of the eventual eleventh hour agreement as, once
again, "historic," the Bali document doesn't commit anyone to
targets or dates. According to Nelson Muffuh, a Christian Aid
senior climate change policy analyst, "We were expecting a
road map, and we've got one... But it lacks signposts and
there is no agreed destination."[11] Bali is, therefore, a worse
compromise than Kyoto. What it does do is extend the market in carbon trading, which has done nothing but line the
pockets of a large variety of carbon traders, banks, and, incredibly—or predictably—large polluters. Carbon trading will
be dealt with in some detail later in this chapter.

So far, government efforts to curb carbon emissions have
done nothing but allow countries to claim that they are doing
something meaningful when they are not. The purpose of de-
tailing the wretched efforts taken by politicians so far is to
highlight an essential point: namely, that while many global
leaders, and indeed CEOs of major corporations, including oil
and car companies, profess a knowledge of global warming and

its likely effects and a seemingly genuine and heartfelt desire to do something meaningful about it, nothing is actually being done—as emissions continue to climb. In November 2006, scientists working on the Global Carbon Project announced that emissions were rising *four times faster* than a decade ago. To quote Mark Lynas: "In other words, all of our efforts—of carbon trading, switching off lights, the Kyoto Protocol and so on—have had a discernible effect so far: *less than zero*."[12]

Why Copenhagen Failed

Since the Bali conference, the international climate change conference jamboree has moved on to Copenhagen. The incompatibility of capitalism with long-term ecological sustainability has a variety of sources, one of which, inter-imperial rivalry between competing nation-states, was on abundant display in Copenhagen. Without the intervention of massive social protest, this rivalry guarantees that international treaties on issues such as climate change will be pathetic and toothless charades. No country can accept a treaty that "unfairly" disadvantages it in the mad scramble to promote their national set of capitalists. Even the absolutely minimal requirements of the Kyoto Protocol were unacceptable to the capitalist ruling classes of the United States and Australia despite the fact that they came nowhere near a comprehensive or even partial solution to CO_2 emissions.

Furthermore, if major powers refuse to comply with an international treaty on any grounds whatsoever, even if it's generally recognized to be a "good thing," there is little to no recourse in international law for penalizing them. The United States is a serial breaker of international law, as is its protégé in the Middle East, Israel, and yet there are no UN sanctions against either country. They can act with impunity and there is barely a word of protest from other governments or international censure, except from those on the streets of the world's cities. Canada is going to exceed its Kyoto commitments by at least 30 percent; yet the drums of war or international sanctions do not beat upon the doors of the Canadian parliament.[13]

Despite the gravity of the climate crisis, the world climate conference in Copenhagen, which was billed as the "last best chance" to replace the ineffectual Kyoto Protocol generated voluminous quantities of hot air but little else. Writing in the September/October 2009 issue of the magazine *Foreign Affairs*, mouthpiece for the more forward-thinking sections of the U.S. ruling class, Michael Levi, Senior Fellow for Energy and the Environment at the Council on Foreign Relations, gives a succinct picture of what to expect due to these competing imperial interests: "The odds of signing a comprehensive treaty in December are vanishingly small. And even reaching such a deal the following year would be an extraordinary challenge, given the domestic political constraints in Washington and in other capitals that make such an agreement difficult to negotiate and ratify."

Were a deal to be struck, something they essentially didn't even manage, Levi adds that a global agreement on paper is "only half the problem"; precisely because, depending of course on who's doing the cheating, there is no international enforcement. "Even a blockbuster deal in which every country signed up to binding emissions caps would come nowhere near close to guaranteeing success, since the world has few useful options for enforcing commitments to slash emissions short of punitive trade sanctions or similarly unpalatable penalties."[14]

If corporations are compelled by competition to pursue short-term profits at the cost of long-term ecocide, then governments will be compelled to support those efforts. Each country has to protect and, where possible, extend the influence and competitive advantage of its own national corporations. Every political, economic, military, and diplomatic lever must be pulled to further those interests.

This dynamic naturally pits nation against nation as they squabble over the details and thrash out compromises based on the balance of world power, rather than a coherent and objective assessment of what's needed.

The Copenhagen conference was no different. The UN meeting and similar international conferences represent the neutral gathering points for each round of diplomatic arm-twisting. National emissaries maneuver to consolidate old positions of power, or secure new ground in the never-ending economic and political battle for supremacy—all shrouded in the polite language appropriate to diplomatic discourse in civilized society, though negotiations became notably fractious at Copenhagen.

All this makes a meaningful agreement almost impossible, as every country seeks to angle for its own advantage—and insert escape clauses and exclusions that are large enough to drive a fleet of Hummers through. Meanwhile, there is a clear schism between the competing interests of the developed and developing world, especially as the United States, European Union, and Japan tried to place the blame for the lack of progress on rising powers China and India.

However, as Vandana Shiva makes clear in her book *Soil Not Oil*, the primary schism isn't between rich countries and poor countries: "It is between corporate industry in the

North, and farmers, indigenous people and vulnerable communities. Corporations in the North and South have now formed partnerships, and the corporations in the South must first pollute and then reduce pollution to get credits."[15]

While Shiva omits the most significant and majority actor, the workers, in both North and South who need to be mobilized if we are to reorient society, her point is nevertheless accurate; corporations the world over share the same interests and while they compete against each other, they share the same fundamental agenda.

Again, this was on display in Copenhagen where suddenly there was a coming together of major polluters from both hemispheres as they found common ground to co-author the three-page Copenhagen Accord. The five countries who drafted the accord represent the major polluters from four continents: the United States, China, India, South Africa, and Brazil.[16] This re-alignment is significant as it shatters the hoped-for unity among developing countries to form a united block. Furthermore, it highlights the point about whose interests the respective governments have at heart and their need to prevent or delay any comprehensive climate treaty. The United States, China, India, and South Africa are all disproportionately heavy polluters due in large part to their reliance on coal. As such they face competitive disadvantages under any wide-ranging and inclusive international carbon regulatory regime. Brazil has some recently discovered oil and gas deposits of its own though it is primarily a major emitter due to the relentless deforestation of the Amazon. China, India, and Brazil all have some of the highest growth rates in CO_2 emissions as they seek to develop their economies as mirror images of capital accumulation associated with developed

Northern countries. South Africa was just awarded a World Bank loan of $3.75 billion to build the world's seventh biggest coal-fired power station. Therefore, despite their other disagreements, these five countries cooked up the last-minute deal not to push the conference forward toward a real agreement, but to do precisely the opposite by subverting the possibility of other countries coming up with one.

But what makes an agreement on climate change different—and more difficult to achieve—than a treaty on trade is that it would limit corporations' freedom to ransack and plunder the planet with impunity. All countries would have to enact an international treaty equally. Otherwise, the countries that unilaterally put in place environmental legislation would be "unfairly disadvantaged"—and lose out in the competitive race to make the most money in the shortest possible time.

Hence there's an extra complication with conferences that seek to address global warming. Political leaders know they need to show up and make polite noises to divert attention and public pressure from more unpalatable options. Some of them even realize they need to do something real to avoid climate disaster. But none of these leaders are really committed to the process, whatever fine words flow from their mouths.

There is an important contradiction here. Part of the function of the state is to counterbalance the competing short-term interests of individual corporations and look to the longer-term needs of the whole national commercial enterprise. The state is responsible for enabling capital to operate in the most profit-friendly environment possible, and hence, for example, will seek to ensure that adequate infrastructure exists for transportation to get workers to their jobs and to move goods to markets.

This relationship between the state and capital is in itself an impediment to any agreement on climate change. But the obstacles are still greater after the ideological assault on social spending and "big government" over the last thirty years that characterizes neoliberal economic orthodoxy. Since addressing the roots of climate change means a frontal assault on the citadels of capitalist power and restrictions placed on markets and profits that are deemed unacceptable by capitalists, the state is paralyzed by the environmental crisis and political leaders' acceptance of neoliberal ideology.

Furthermore, it's in the economic interests of the major corporations to ensure that the South develops a car culture and fossil-fuel-intensive economy. Northern markets for cars, for example, are at saturation point. By contrast, Southern markets offer a bonanza of expanding markets—especially now that an Indian company has designed small cars such as the Nano that Tata sells for $2,500–$3,000.[17]

Along with an expanding auto market comes the need for road expansion and increased manufacture of steel, aluminum, concrete, and rubber. All this is to the detriment of local cultures, ecologies, and quality of life as public transportation is neglected—and, of course, the global environment.

Thus, the best that could have been hoped for in Copenhagen was a partial, piecemeal plan that's implemented only when it's far too late to avoid climate catastrophe. This was why James Hansen had called for the collapse of the talks as the best possible outcome—something that government representatives managed quite admirably.[18]

It's impossible for even supposedly environmentally conscious governments to develop and implement a real international plan. To do so would require acknowledgement of the deep systemic problems that go to the very root of the entire social system—and a reorientation of social priorities toward workers, peasants, and farmers, and the earth upon which we depend.

That's why it's not viable to win ecological or climate justice without social justice. The inequality and exploitation that lies at the heart of capitalism ravages humans and the planet in the interests of a tiny minority hell-bent on reshaping the planet in the service of profit. Climate justice activists therefore need to be social justice activists in equal measure.

Fixes within the System: Carbon Trading, Lifestyle Changes, Technological Fixes, and Recycling

The international proposals to tackle climate change that get the most discussion all revolve around allowing the market to alter patterns of production and consumption. These market-based solutions, such as carbon trading or carbon taxes, fit neatly with the needs of those who run the world economy—the corporations and their enablers in government. But politicians aren't the only ones seduced by the free market mantra, which decries state intervention and extols the self-healing powers of the market; the idea that the market is the best arbiter of change is accepted by many people— both within and without the green movement—who are genuinely concerned with reducing the impact of humans on the environment.

With this argument for market-based solutions comes a call for individuals to change their lifestyles because "we" consume too much. Many environmentalists seek modification of consumer choices through taxation and the production of "carbon neutral" products while exhorting people to voluntarily change their consumption patterns: fly less, recycle, buy compact fluorescent bulbs and fair-trade goods, invest in "ethical" companies, turn down thermostats in winter, use fans in summer rather than air conditioning, make your next car a hybrid, and so on.

Some of these recommendations are certainly laudable and those that are we should pursue. The real question, however, is whether market-based solutions or changes to personal consumption will measurably and effectively reduce emissions and energy consumption—and the answer is a definitive no, as is shown by the following review of the proposed solutions and their effects.

Cap-and-Trade Schemes

Under the "cap-and-trade" system or Emissions Trading Scheme (ETS)—the first phase of which has been in place in the EU since January 2005—a maximum or cap is placed on the amount of carbon that companies in participating countries are allowed to produce annually. If individual companies exceed their quota, they can buy carbon credits from other companies, including those outside the EU, in order to carry on with their own business. The idea is to create a market in carbon trading that will serve as an incentive to companies to reduce their carbon emissions or be forced to pay other companies and so incur additional production costs.

Capitalists have only two uses for the "environment"; it is either a source of raw materials or a sink. Resources—such as oil, coal, metals, etc.—are extracted from the environment and waste products are dumped back in. Capitalists define as waste any byproduct they can't reuse or sell and therefore must dump. Since each capitalist firm, in its competition for market share, attempts to drive down costs and maximize profits, there is a built-in tendency to exclude from expense anything that falls outside the immediate process of production, which leads to capitalists' insistence on dumping for free.

Green economists have long argued that the environmental cost of waste should be included in the overall expense for any given product and noted early on the market's inability to properly take account of "externalities" like production-generated pollution.[19] Carbon trading represents an attempt by economists and governments committed to economic expansion to respond to these criticisms by "internalizing" environmental costs, or bringing them into the market. According to their logic, assigning a price to some measurable form of pollution (carbon dioxide in this case) creates market incentives for companies to move capital investment into less-polluting (in this case, less carbon-intensive) technologies—in other words, carbon trading turns what was previously regarded as a useless and potentially hazardous by-product into a valuable commodity to be bought and sold like any other.

There are a number of problems with this approach. One of the most obvious is the impossibility of putting a price on clean air, drinkable water, and a stable climate. Another is that there is currently no way to prevent companies who are made to pay to pollute ("the polluter pays" principle) from simply passing the extra costs on to the consumer at the same time that they are merely passing the problem from one capitalist or industry to another. Another major problem is that some very large and significant economic actors—airlines and cement and aluminum manufacturers, for example—are exempted from participating in the scheme.

But the most significant problem of all is that carbon trading hasn't worked. The "cap" set by the EU was well above any requirement by companies to make serious changes to production and certainly well above any level that would do anything about climate change. At one point, this led to a fall in the price of carbon emissions (traded per ton) to less than a dollar—hence producing no incentive to anyone to make any kind of switch. When the price rose, companies simply put off applying for carbon credits and used their stored bank (unlike most people's vacation days, carbon credits carry over year to year) to continue to pollute. Or, according to one report, they simply resorted to outright cheating.[20]

A *Financial Times* investigation outlined succinctly the problems with Europe's carbon trading program. It found:

- Widespread instances of people and organizations buying worthless credits that do not yield any reductions in carbon emissions
- Industrial companies profiting from doing very little—or from gaining carbon credits on the basis of efficiency gains from which they have already benefited substantially
- Brokers providing services of questionable or no value
- A shortage of verification, making it difficult for buyers to assess the true value of carbon credits
- Companies and individuals being overcharged for the private purchase of European Union carbon

permits that have plummeted in value because
they do not result in emissions cuts[21]

An example of how the carbon offsetting swindles work in
practice was revealed in a recent edition of *Harper's* magazine
under the title, "Conning the Climate: Inside the Carton-Trad-
ing Shell Game."[7] The article details how Plantar, a major
Brazilian "forest resources" company is set to earn more than
eleven million carbon credits with which it will make an estimated profit of at least $100 million by selling the credits to
European manufacturers and banks over the lifetime of the
following project.

Plantar has set up a eucalyptus plantation where the trees
are harvested then burnt and turned into charcoal for use in a
nearby factory making pig-iron for cars and other appliances.
Each stage of this process has been certified by UN-approved
organizations charged with verifying that Plantar deserves
carbon credits for reducing carbon emissions. One might le-
gitimately ask how a monoculture of eucalyptus trees growing
in a former rainforest that are turned into charcoal for a pig-
iron factory and turning a profit from carbon trading (in addition to selling the pig-iron) could be justified as a carbon
reduction scheme. The explanation lies in how the land had
been cleared for cattle grazing, so planting a monoculture ab-
sorbs more carbon than grassland; this therefore earns carbon credits. The kilns used for making the charcoal are
designed to reduce methane emissions by controlling the very
high burning temperatures—more carbon credits for using
this special "environmentally friendly" technique. Then, because the pig-iron factory burns the charcoal rather than coal
to make the iron, that process also receives carbon credits.[22]

As a result of scams like this and those outlined by the *Financial Times* and others, there has been no net reduction in EU carbon emissions, and the ETS scheme is thoroughly discredited:

> Europe's big polluters pumped more climate-changing gases into the atmosphere in 2006 than during the previous year, according to figures that show the EU's carbon trading system failing to deliver curbs. Critics said the data underlined the gap between the rhetoric of European leaders, who have promised to cut CO_2 emissions by one-fifth by 2020, and the reality of delivering reductions.[23]

Even the architects of ETS realize it has been an exercise in futility, but promise a new and improved "Phase 2." However, power corporations, those responsible for producing most emissions in the first place, are expected to *benefit* from the latest incarnation of the scheme, to the tune of $6 billion dollars.[24] Indeed, according to Faisal Islam, Phase 2 allows many permits to be handed out for free, and power corporations have made an extra $100 billion in "windfall profits." This is because they have passed on to consumers all increases in cost through emissions charges, thereby recouping all losses to profitability. Having been given free polluting permits that they can then sell, some of the biggest polluters end up being rewarded twice: "'A ton of carbon saved above Beijing is the same as a ton saved above Birmingham' is the free market mantra, but free permits have, in essence, been a rather expensive bribe to get power companies to participate in the scheme. It's an entire field of juicy carrots, with little threat of a stick."[25]

The failure of the carbon-trading scheme could be put down to accident or incompetence—maybe the politicians and think tanks that dreamt up this plan just didn't think it through in enough detail, and the next version will be more effective. But this really lets them and capitalism off the hook. The ETS charade is the predictable outcome of an economic system that relies on fossil fuels for energy and has the profit motive as its prime directive. This explains why U.S.-based corporations, having studied the results of the European experiment, have suddenly become quite enthusiastic about cap-and-trade schemes, lobbying hard to ensure that any plan considered allows at least some portion of the permits to be given away rather than auctioned.

Unless politicians are prepared to challenge this dynamic with meaningful regulations and laws—and there is no evidence that they are as Obama has now promised 85 percent be given away for free in any bill that might include cap and trade, a figure directly incorporated into the Waxman-Markey bill— any new cap-and-trade scheme will be as useless in procuring its stated aims as the previous one. Indeed, despite the failure of the first carbon-trading system, the EU's updated version is its only major regulatory policy initiative directed at emissions reduction. Admittedly, there are some improvements, such as a larger share of auctions and the inclusion of previously exempt industries. However, the airline industry has already vowed to fight "all the way" against their inclusion.[26]

Meanwhile, corporations have found new and creative ways of dumping costs onto consumers. In the near-term future, people should expect to hear more about, and pay, so-called "Green Taxes," yet another subsidy to the corporations; we pay for them to upgrade their technology and make it less polluting while they continue to make huge profits. It is the corporations and the rich who should be paying the increased taxes so that they subsidize public services and the move toward a cleaner energy economy.

Ideologically, there is something very significant going on. Carbon trading supports the concept that it's okay to keep polluting by creating, of all things, a market in pollution. Trading pollution and earning pollution credits for carbon offsetting in order to reduce CO_2 emissions has been well satirized by the website cheatneutral.com:

> When you cheat on your partner you add to the heartbreak, pain and jealousy in the atmosphere. Cheatneutral offsets your cheating by funding someone else to be faithful and NOT cheat. This neutralizes the pain and unhappy emotion and leaves you with a clear conscience…When you use Cheatneutral, we'll email you a Cheatneutral Offset Certificate, so you can prove to your loved one that your playing away has been successfully offset. Then you and your partner are both happy, a broken heart is mended, and you can feel good about yourself again, all thanks to Cheatneutral.[27]

Ultimately, these market schemes fail because they are based on an untenable contradiction: the idea that the cause of global warming—the unplanned and unfettered capitalist market—can also be its solution.

Reducing Personal Consumption

If market-driven mechanisms are far and away the least effective method for fighting climate change, blaming ordinary people for consuming too much runs a close second. We are constantly told that there are just *too many people* and that if we are going to save the planet, each of us needs to reduce consumption and live a more frugal life.

Unfortunately, the vast majority of people on earth, including those in the developed countries, can hardly be said to live profligate lives of plenty, gaily sloshing their way through as many products, services, and homes as they can fit into their well-heeled, seventy-plus years of carefree living—although here in the United States we are constantly encouraged to strive for this "ideal." Since capitalism's survival depends upon the endless expansion of markets for capital and consumer goods, we are inundated with the ideology of consumerism; democracy is equated with the freedom to buy, and every possible opportunity is taken to ensure that this message gets rammed home. When how you dress or which car or color cell phone you have represents the extent of your freedom in a society supposedly defined by freedom, it is no surprise that many people conform to this notion. But for most Americans, these "lifestyle choices" are very limited; we get to decide which brands of clothing to buy, whether we want our electronics to break right away or be rendered useless by "upgrades," and what car we can afford that will reliably get us to work. We don't get to choose how things are produced or whether the cities we live in provide reliable public transportation; in fact, the poor quality of the public transportation system in the United States forces tens of millions to use cars even if they don't want to.

But if we step outside the bounds of capitalist logic just for a moment, the reality is there are plenty of things that the system forces us to do that could be eliminated, allowing us to devote more resources to *actually* having a high standard of living. There is no technological barrier that prevents older model computers, photocopiers, or cell phones—all of which fall into the massively expanding category of often highly toxic "e-waste"—from being upgraded rather than thrown away and replaced with new models. The concept of repairing or upgrading older devices and keeping them serviceable is energetically discouraged. The fact that all items are deliberately designed not to last, something known as "planned obsolescence," and that updates are quite deliberately almost never backwards compatible, ensures that every one to five years it becomes necessary to purchase a new piece of electronic equipment whether you want to or not.

More broadly, one should ask: what constitutes a good quality of life? A rational answer would surely include: adequate and nourishing food, access to high-quality housing, efficient and accessible public transport, clean air and water, lots of green space, aesthetically pleasing architecture and town planning, creatively rewarding and dignified work, and most importantly, the *free time* to enjoy all this and engage in a full range of sporting, leisure, and cultural activities.

Reflecting on the above partial list of life-enhancing objectives, one is forced to the conclusion that capitalism is incapable of providing any of them—except to the small sliver of society represented by the ultra-rich. In the developed world, the prime "leisure" activity foisted on us by capitalism is the fetishism of "shopping," to which all roads lead. When we've had the life-force drained out of us from work and when not out shopping, practically the only "leisure" activity we're fit for is to be passively slumped in front of the television. While enjoying some mindless escapism we are again confronted with a torrent of relentless advertising for products that you never realized you couldn't live without until seeing the commercial. For the vast majority of people, work is a soulless drudgery of repetitiveness whose larger purpose, other than a wage, is difficult to ascertain; where each day is the same as the last and the only joy comes when it ends. Free time for many people is consumed with simply trying to hold things together because hours of work and commute time devour almost the entire week.

How could the far higher standard of living outlined above be achieved in an environmentally friendly way? How about the elimination of planned obsolescence? Or building houses that use thermal heating and cooling, shifting resources to public transport, building free public swimming pools, and green spaces in place of parking lots? We could try the rapid conversion of energy production to renewable sources, better agricultural planning with a move away from vast fields of monocultures, and taking all forests into public hands to ensure the elimination of clear-cutting and the success of reforestation projects. A major component of all educational courses from the earliest age should be spent in the "great outdoors" learning firsthand about how we need to co-exist with nature. This is not about learning "environmental science" as much as being given a practical and hands-on experience of how we as a species rely on and obtain all our resources from nature in a socially mediated fashion.

These are just some of the things that could be done that are entirely practical. They require, however, not individual but social solutions as well as a great deal of planning—the kind of planning that could only be based on a completely different economic logic of development.

The Throwaway Society: the Rise of Garbage

The idea that we live in a "throwaway" society is designed to shift the blame for garbage and waste onto ordinary people—as if we are the ones who woke up one day and decided that having disposable *everything* is really right on, that single-serving products are the way to go, and that we just have to satisfy this innate, burning desire of ours to toss out anything we come into contact with as swiftly as humanly possible. It is part of the same ideological onslaught intended to make ordinary people, rather than the system of industrial capitalism, responsible for environmental degradation. However, waste and destruction are essential adjuncts to the success of capitalism. We did not create a world where it's cheaper to throw away a broken appliance than buy a new one; only the vested interests of an irrational economic system could do that.

Contrary to popular belief, recycling or separation of garbage is not the outgrowth of a recent concern for the environment; in the nineteenth and early twentieth centuries, all garbage was separated out for reuse. However, as the gulf between town and country has grown, and the types and nature of garbage have changed, the ideological assault on reuse has increased. With the discovery of plastics and the explosion of the plastics industry over the last sixty years, there has been a push by corporations and their trade organizations to gradually and systematically eradicate reuse and actively promote disposable everything, as this maximizes profits and ensures future markets. Here is Richardson Wright, editor of *House and Garden,* writing in 1930 and quoted in Heather Rogers's excellent book, *Gone Tomorrow: The Hidden Life of Garbage*:

> Saving and thrift would be the worst sort of citizenship today.... To maintain prosperity we must keep the machines working, for when machines are functioning men can labor and earn wages. The good citizen does not repair

the old; he buys anew. The shoes that crack are to be thrown away. Don't patch them. When the car gets crotchety, haul it to the town dump…to maintain prosperity we must keep those machines going. Always we must be prepared to consume their enormous production.[28]

Over the past several years we have been told that the only way to avoid recession is to keep buying and consuming. There is a profound problem of language. The only sense in which a corporation understands the word "waste" is when there is a loss of labor time or an unnecessary expenditure that cuts into profits. In the 1950s, a Fairchild executive stated that, "It is wasteful to make any component more durable than its weakest link, and ideally a product should fall apart all at once."[29] This concept of waste produces the need to engineer consumers for all the new products—in addition to engineering the products themselves—and this need is met ideologically through huge advertising and marketing budgets. Industry took to this concept with gusto. As early as 1960, the *Wall Street Journal* reported car manufacturers were building cars "so that they'll get to the junk pile faster…today almost as soon as new cars hit the street they need replacement parts for all the gadgets they are loaded with."[30] And this is before the advent of the "all new" models that auto companies unveil every year. A marketing consultant spelled out in 1955 capitalism's need for constant market expansion through consumption: "Our enormously productive economy demands that we make consumption our way of life, that we convert buying and use of goods into rituals, that we seek our spiritual satisfactions, our ego satisfactions, in consumption… We need things consumed, burned up, worn out, replaced, and discarded at an ever increasing pace."[31]

Marx noted that there is a built-in contradiction in capitalism in this regard: "The workers are important as buyers of commodities," he noted. "But as sellers of their commodity—labor-power—capitalist society has the tendency to restrict them to their minimum price."[32] Capitalists want their own workers to accept the lowest possible wages in order to boost their profits, whereas they want workers employed by other capitalists to be able to spend more.

As capitalism has increased people's alienation and feeling of powerlessness, omnipresent and relentless corporate propaganda represent "shopping" as a compelling leisure activity through which humans are expected to achieve a sense of life-satisfaction and fulfillment. To take the example of margarine, it is symptomatic of how marketing is designed to work on the atomized, disempowered, and alienated humans sitting in front of their televisions:

> In the marketing of margarine, the product's contribution to the wellbeing of the consumer is wholly divorced from any of its physical properties. The actual usefulness has become irrelevant, so that the consumer does not buy something to spread on bread but a concatenation of feelings associated with idealised family relationships. The complex, clever symbolism of the advertisement is designed to convince the viewer that a tub of vegetable fat that is identical to half a dozen other brands of vegetable fat can give us something very special, something we really need…In a world of social disintegration, modern consumers have a powerful need for family warmth, and humans…make unconscious associations. Unmet emotional needs and unconscious association are the twin psychological pillars of the marketing society.[33]

The fault for so much waste lies not with the people who mindlessly throw things away but the cast-iron requirement of the system to produce as much waste as possible as it simultaneously produces consumers. The switch to the ubiquitous plastic drinking bottle was made not because it was more efficient in terms of resource use or because of consumer demand or resistance to returning empties, but because it's far more profitable to keep producing plastic containers than reusing glass ones. Glass containers have to be collected, cleaned, and refilled. This means devoting space in stores to storage, paying pick-up costs, and having separate bottling plants nearer to cities.

Packaging is another case in point. Thirty percent of municipal waste is packaging and 40 percent of that packaging is plastic. Plastics take from two hundred to one thousand years to degrade. The Pacific Ocean is now six times more abundant in plastic than it is in zooplankton.[34] One of the astoundingly brilliant qualities of plastic is that it lasts practically forever—why is *anything* that is designed only for a single use made from plastic? It should be *illegal* to manufacture anything so recklessly long-lived with all kinds of associated industrial waste and toxic by-products for a single use. This is *antirational*, and yet it is clearly completely rational from the perspective of a system whose sole overriding motivation is profit maximization.

Packaging is important to capitalism. It is part of convincing us that we have choices in the products we buy, as if each different brand were not in many cases identical aside from the packaging and the brand loyalty that packaging seeks to secure. Yet there has never been a popular movement demanding more packaging—quite the opposite. Corporations resist reductions in packaging—even when it might save them money (packaging costs can often be greater than the cost of the item itself)—because packaging persuades consumers to buy their product rather than someone else's. In any case, the cost of packaging can just be passed on to those that buy the product. Effectively, we pay three times for this senseless waste that is so profitable for corporations. First we pay for the packaging itself because the cost is included in the price of the item. Then we pay to dispose of the packaging through garbage collection costs. Finally, we pay through the degradation to the environment caused by the energy required for extraction of the raw material for plastics (oil), the water and energy used to refine the oil into plastics, and the conditions of plastic disposal, usually in a landfill, usually after a single use.

The Rise of Recycling

Again, contrary to what we are told, recycling is the least effective remedy for what is called "consumer" waste but should more properly be called production waste. When the logic of disposability and waste began to be challenged in the late 1960s, it was done most effectively by mass movements of the people calling not for market reforms but government regulation. These protests were carried out in the teeth of corporate resistance to "interference in the market." It was President Nixon, with a proven track record of causing colossal environmental destruction in Southeast Asia (through the indiscriminate use of chemicals such as Agent Orange as a defoliant and dropping a greater tonnate of TNT on Vietnam than during the whole of the Second World War by all combatant nations[35]), who enacted by far the most effective environmental legislation in U.S. history to date.

In 1970, prior to the first Earth Day, when twenty million Americans poured into the streets to protest environmental degradation by corporations, Nixon was forced to include in his State of the Union address a section devoted to pacifying the burgeoning ecology movement. Masses of people had begun to question and fight against some fundamental assumptions in America: the legal right to exclude African Americans from the democratic process in the Jim Crow South and racism in general, the pursuance of imperial wars overseas, the oppression of women and gays. This ideological ferment naturally led people to generalize further and question corporate America's right to pollute. Here is Nixon the environmentalist in his 1970 State of the Union address: "The 1970s absolutely must be the years when America pays its debt to the past by reclaiming the purity of its air, its waters and our living environment. It is literally now or never."[36]

The highly successful movements that actively organized for and won massive societal changes on questions of racism, the war in Vietnam, and government spying also demanded institutional change be extended to place limitations on the untrammeled freedom of corporations to pollute. Building on the gains of the other social movements, the collectively organized power of ordinary Americans to force restrictions on corporations' right to pollute proved irresistible. During Nixon's presidency, the Clean Air Act and the Resource Recovery Act were made law, and the Environmental Protection Agency was created with a mandate to "prevent or eliminate damage to the environment." In 1972 came the Clean Water Act, and in 1976 the Resource Conservation and Recovery Act.

Corporations looked on with horror as their freedom to make money was restricted. Their reaction and counterattack was swift. Similar to corporate greenwashing today, corporations in the 1970s co-opted sections of the movement and came up with their own strategy for resisting further governmental regulation: recycling. The creation of the "litterbug" and the concept of "litter" as the root of all evil was a quite deliberate part of the strategy by industry to move the debate from further regulation by government to self-regulation by individuals. The corporate-funded yet benign sounding Keep America Beautiful (KAB) organization pushed for single-use products and limits to any environmental restrictions on manufacturing. In a phrase familiar from the gun lobby in relation to firearms, the American Can Corporation insisted that "packages don't litter, people do."[37]

Corporate polluters, by turning the spotlight on individuals, weakened the drive toward state regulation. The argument took hold that all we need to do is educate individuals to put their trash in the proper receptacle, not attack the need for so much trash in the first place. The solution, therefore, is to be found not in a reduction in waste through conservation or reuse but by the strong encouragement of recycling and personal responsibility. Today, being exposed as a serial non-recycler is likely to get you the same sort of dirty look as lighting up a cigarette next to a pregnant woman. Yet, for every ton of household discards—and remember, many of these discards are conditioned by the structure of the capitalist market—there are 70 tons of industrial debris created from mining, agriculture, manufacturing, and petrochemicals.[38] In other words, less than 2 percent of all waste is residential. Of course, recycling is better than doing nothing, and I am not arguing that we should just toss things away willy-nilly or ignore garbage cans. However, we should not ignore how this focus on recycling serves a strong ideological purpose validating waste. In addition, it does absolutely nothing to reduce the core of the problem—needless production for the sake of profit; indeed, it sanctifies it.

Furthermore, in the United States, most of what anyone sorts and places to be recycled ends up in landfill. As of 2000, 50 percent of all paper, 75 percent of all glass containers, and half of all aluminum beverage cans go into landfill; only 5 percent of plastics are recycled.[39] The reason is simple and has nothing to do with people who for the most part are eager to recycle when given the opportunity. The profit margins for one of the three large waste management companies such as Waste Management Inc. are ten times greater for landfill than they are for recycling. Fifteen container ships of highly toxic electronic waste from Europe arrive in just one African port, Lagos, *every single day*, even though it contravenes European law. Over half a million broken computers arrive in Lagos every month.[40] Greenpeace estimates that over 80 percent of electronics goods in the United States that have made it into the recycling pile are in fact recycled by child laborers picking through piles of toxic, leaking equipment in developing countries.[41]

While it is sometimes admitted that capitalism may have some flaws as a system, it is also unfailingly asserted that capitalism represents the height of efficiency. There is only one sense in which this is true. Capitalism has a single goal: accumulation for the sake of accumulation. Anything that reduces costs and boosts profits is good. This is what gives capitalism its extreme dynamism—corporations in constant competition as they vie with one another, constantly revolutionizing the means of production in the service of profit. Efficiency under capitalism does not mean anything other than this. As outlined above, the amount of waste under capitalism is gigantic. There is the obvious waste of military expenditure—the U.S.

military is the world's single biggest consumer of energy. While this is still "only" 1 percent of U.S. energy consumption, it is equivalent to the total energy used by Nigeria—a country with a population of 140 million.[42] Advertising budgets, in excess of $1 trillion worldwide, are designed to convince us that two identical products are in fact different and that one of them will change our lives forever. Marketing budgets make sure we keep buying from that certain company and establish "brand loyalty." Then there's the obscene luxury spending of the stratospherically rich. And all of these are on top of the enormous waste in the production process itself through overproduction, the making of useless things like packaging, and in-built obsolescence.

Only massive changes in the way products are designed and made, what they are made from, and the uses to which they are put can reduce capitalism's tendency toward wasteful energy and raw material usage. Making real changes in the production of waste—just like making meaningful lifestyle choices available to ordinary people—will require government regulation and planning that is not driven by the profit motive; it will not be achieved through individual efforts to use less, or reduce one's carbon footprint, or think more deeply about mother earth. The government needs to be pushed into making these changes in the same way it was pushed in the 1970s—through millions of people collectively and actively fighting for change.

What about Nuclear Power?

Nuclear power is expensive and dangerous. Nuclear power plants only emerge as cost competitive with fossil-fueled power stations or alternative energy sources when government subsidies and the huge decommissioning costs are not included as part of the cost of building and running them. This is one of the main reasons no private company will build a nuclear power station without cast-iron guarantees from the government that they will be covered for any accidents and decommissioning costs, and will receive generous subsidies during the construction and operational phases of the plant.

The inefficiency of production of electricity from nuclear power, even from a capitalist point of view, is recognized by corporations and governments. A recent report by Citibank, "New Nuclear—the Economics Say No" concludes that "the risks faced by developers [from new nuclear plants]...are so large and variable that individually they could each bring even the largest utility company to its knees financially."[43] The Citibank paper lists five major risks developers and operators of new nuclear power plants must take on: planning, construction, power price, operation, and decommissioning risks. The three most serious risks according to Citibank are those associated with construction, power price, and operational costs, i.e., essentially the whole project. The paper labels these risks "the corporate killers."[44] This is why the Obama administration, as mentioned earlier, has plans to increase loan guarantees to the nuclear industry by an additional $36 billion to take the total to more than $50 billion.

But government handouts to rejuvenate the nuclear industry don't stop there. A 2009 proposal by the U.S. nuclear industry outlines what they'd like: $100 billion boost for the entire loan guarantee program, an extension of the production tax credits for new nuclear reactors through 2025; the removal of the 6,000-megawatt limitation for those credits; a 30 percent investment tax credit or a grant in lieu of the production tax credit; tax credits for new or expanded manufacturing and worker training; and the reduction or elimination of tariffs on nuclear components under certain conditions. With Democrats now about as pro-nuclear as Republicans it is very likely that these measures will be approved as they feature in the climate bill of Senator John Kerry, which is currently under negotiation. To quote Kerry, "I know a lot of Republicans were impressed by the president's listing of priorities in terms of energy, particularly nuclear and the drilling and those other components. They thought it was good. They thought it was positive."[45]

An article in *Scientific American* cited a recent report by economist Mark Cooper at the Vermont Law School outlines the cost of adding one hundred new nuclear reactors to the U.S. power grid. The cost to the taxpayer, over and above the costs associated with the costs if renewable sources and energy conservation measures had been used instead, comes out to an astronomical $1.9–$4.1 trillion over the lifetimes of the reactors. As nuclear projects traditionally suffer from some of the most extreme cost overruns and delays of any industry, the higher figure is the more likely one. As noted by Cooper, "It is telling that in the few short years since the so-called 'Nuclear Renaissance' began there has been a four-fold increase in projected costs…The original low-ball estimates were promotional, not practical; they were based on hope and hype intended to promote the industry."[46]

Cooper's analysis factors in studies from Wall Street and independent energy analysts that estimates the efficiency of renewable energy at 6 cents per kilowatt hour versus 12 to 20 cents per kilowatt hour for nuclear. So the financial inefficiencies, to say nothing of the safety concerns, can only be made up from government subsidies (i.e., we bail out the nuclear industry indirectly) or increases in electricity bills (we bail them out directly).

A report by MIT reaches similar conclusions; that nuclear power is not cost effective and continues to have serious safety and waste management issues.[47]

While nuclear power enjoys a renaissance as an allegedly "environmentally friendly" alternative to fossil fuels, there has yet to be any serious long-term proposal by any country about what to do with the radioactive nuclear waste that is piling up next to nuclear reactors all over the world (36,000 tons in the United States alone). The most highly radioactive waste has to be kept in storage for ten thousand years—this means designing and building storage containers that will remain intact longer than human civilization has been on the planet. Many nuclear power stations built three decades ago are coming to the end of their operational lives and decommissioning costs to entomb reactors in concrete are gigantic. Unfortunately, even some environmental campaigners such as James Hansen have been seduced by the siren song of nuclear power and the proposed new Generation IV nuclear plants. Although none have been built and the technology is unlikely to be viable for at least another decade, these plants are touted as safe and able to overcome the radioactive waste issue. But these are not part of the plans in the United States, only Generation III plants are scheduled to be built. As for Generation IV technology itself, Amory Lovins, a leading expert in sustainable energy with the Rocky Mountain Institute in Colorado has extensively critiqued the supposed benefits in a 2009 report and concluded that they are not the answer economically or environmentally.[48]

Many people cite France as the poster child for a nuclear success story. However, the newest nuclear plant being built in France is 20 percent over budget and requires complete subsidy by the French government after eighteen months of construction.[49] The French nuclear company AREVA is responsible for the ongoing, very expensive fiasco at the Finnish nuclear plant Olkiluoto 3. They have been building it since 2004. It was slated to come on line by May 2009 but due to safety issues and construction delays this is now being put back until 2012. Cost overruns have spiraled from an initial estimated cost of three billion euros ($4.1 billion dollars) to a current total of 5.3 billion euros ($7.2 billion dollars) with the potential for more increases down the line.[50]

As for nuclear power being environmentally friendly, when the Chernobyl nuclear power plant in the Ukraine exploded in 1986, it released between 50 and 250 million curies of radiation over half of Europe, with radiation reaching Japan to the east and the United States' eastern coast to the west. This is equivalent to almost one hundred medium-sized atomic bombs.[51]

The fuel for nuclear power plants, uranium ore, is not common, and its extraction and refinement to useable form is highly energy intensive—giving the lie to it being "carbon neutral." According to one report,

> the use of nuclear power causes, at the end of the road and under the most favorable conditions, approximately one third as much carbon dioxide emission as gas-fired electricity production. The rich uranium ores required to achieve this reduction are, however, so limited that if the entire present world electricity demand were to be provided by nuclear power, these ores would be exhausted in nine years. Use of the remaining poorer ores in nuclear reactors would produce more CO_2 emission than burning fossil fuels directly.[52]

The mining and refining of uranium is a highly pollution- and energy-intensive business in its own right. The fissile material needed in nuclear reactors, the isotope of uranium, U-235, is only 0.7 percent of uranium ore. This means more than 99 percent of the rock that has been mined to obtain the uranium ore is left behind as highly toxic "tailings" containing over a dozen radioactive elements. One processing plant in India, at Jaduguda, processes more than 1,000 tons of ore *per day* to generate a mere 200 tons of uranium ore *per year* from an original 350,000 tons of mined rock. To make it useful in power plants, this then has to be "enriched" up to a concentration of 3–5 percent. The tailings cannot be left lying around as they will dry and spread radioactive particles via the wind into the surrounding watercourses, fields, and plants.

Similar to the "containment" of coal ash, they are pumped into giant dams containing millions of tons of radioactive waste. According to one report, Indians living within 1 kilometer of a tailing dam "showed that 47 percent of women had developed menstrual problems, 18 percent had suffered miscarriages or had given birth to stillborn babies, and 30 percent had other fertility problems." Many of the children who do survive are born with "deformities, skeletal distortions, partly deformed skulls and organs."[53]

While many people have heard of the 1979 near-meltdown at Three Mile Island in Pennsylvania and the explosion in 1986 of the nuclear power station at Chernobyl, hundreds of other accidents, leaks, and near-misses have occurred with less media attention. For example:

A recent simple power failure at a Swedish nuclear plant... [resulted in] Sweden [having to] shut down four of its 10 nuclear plants after faults were discovered. Emergency power systems at the Forsmark plant failed for 20 minutes during a power cut. If power was not restored there could have been a major incident within hours. A former director of the plant later said that "it was pure luck there wasn't a meltdown." The closure of the plants removed at a stroke roughly 20 percent of Sweden's electricity supply.[54]

Nuclear power plants are best seen as very expensive, wildly inefficient, and extremely dangerous ways to boil water while doubling up as atomic bomb factories. It is nuclear power's strategic role—in potentially reducing a nation's dependence on foreign energy sources and in providing the basis for nuclear weapons programs—that attracts countries like the United States to it, not its alleged environmental benefits. The cost of nuclear defense and spending on nuclear weapons in the United States between 1945 and 1996 was $5.5 trillion (in 1996 dollars). That amount represents more than the combined federal spending on: education, agriculture, training, employment, social services, natural resources, space, technology, community and regional development, law enforcement, and energy production and regulation over the same time period.[55]

It is true that if nuclear power really did go through a renaissance, most likely more uranium deposits would be found. There is also uranium in seawater, but its extraction has yet to be proven commercially viable. There is also the possibility of moving to breeder reactors, which reuse the fuel and generate, according to industry estimates, up to sixty times more energy for the same amount of nuclear fuel. However, they also generate plutonium, the key ingredient in nuclear bombs, in even more significant quantities than regular fission reactors. They are also unproven as commercially viable, as are ideas about moving to thorium as a fuel.

As we need solutions to climate change very quickly, for a host of reasons nuclear power is a non-starter. Leaving aside planning permission and regulatory hurdles, it takes at least five years to construct a nuclear power plant and often considerably longer, as evidenced by the Finnish example. Wind farms take only eighteen months, while combined-cycle natural gas plants take four years to bring on line. Just to offset the closing of old nuclear plants over the next fifty years and increase the percentage of global nuclear energy would require building at least twenty-one to twenty-five large (1 gigawatt capacity) new nuclear plants every year for fifty years. All kind of bottlenecks exist for this kind of rapid construction, which only took place for a relatively short period of time in the 1980s, not least a lack of highly skilled and trained nuclear construction workers, engineers and plant operators.

Even the International Atomic Energy Agency (IAEA), part of whose mission is to "foster the efficient and safe use of nuclear power," published an article that recognized that nuclear cannot be an answer to global climate change because of its long lead times—and went on to propose things that can:

> Nuclear power is not a near-term solution to the challenge of climate change. The need to immediately and dramatically reduce carbon emissions calls for approaches that can be implemented more quickly than building nuclear reactors. It also calls for actions that span all energy applications, not just electricity. Improved efficiency in residential and commercial buildings, industry, and transport is the first choice among all options in virtually all analyses of the problem.[56]

Money allocated to nuclear is money that could have been spent on technologies that are cheaper, safer, don't lead to the production and spread of nuclear weaponry, are much quicker to bring on line and are much more environmentally benign, such as solar, wind, wave, and geothermal. Not only does nuclear power compete for funding, but because nuclear plants need to be operated at full capacity all the time, they compete directly with alternative energies that similarly cannot be optimally designed to be switched on and off. In addition, to make the huge construction costs of nuclear plants even remotely cost effective, they have to be run for as long as possible—forty to fifty years. Therefore, if the world shifted to nuclear power, we would not be starting on an energy transition to genuine renewable energy until well into the latter half of the twenty-first century, when there would be tens of thousands more tons of nuclear waste to deal with.

CHAPTER FIVE

Real Solutions Right Now: What We Need to Fight For

"At least we know now: scientific evidence and rationality are not going to be enough to persuade our leaders... Nobody is going to sort this out—unless we, the populations of the warming-gas countries, make them... The time for changing your light-bulbs and hoping for the best is over. It is time to take collective action...The cost of trashing the climate needs to be raised."

—Johann Hari[1]

The Problem Is Social, Not Technical

A recent special issue of *Scientific American* entitled "Beyond Carbon," put forward "clean coal," nuclear power, biofuels, and hydrogen cells as the best way to reduce our burning of fossil fuels.[2] But it should be clear by now that these proposed solutions (including carbon-trading schemes) are all a smoke screen for the continuation of business as usual—whatever the cost to the biosphere.

Capitalism is certainly a dynamic economic system, but the last thing it can be described as is rational. The market system of production, particularly under its deregulated incarnation, is a sprawling, anarchic, and out-of-control monster that has run amok with the planet. One of the central and inescapable contradictions inherent to capitalism is that even as production in an individual plant or company is highly planned and organized, there is no plan within the broader market—hence the disorganization and overproduction intrinsic to the system. Capital will flow to whatever area will make the largest profit. This is not a choice but a compulsion. That is why oil will not be abandoned. As another example, agro-fuels, despite their increasingly obvious and well-documented negative impact on food supply, are being touted purely to maintain a car-based (and hence highly profitable) economic structure. Apart from anything else, growing crops in developing countries that are in need of food, only to transport them to developed countries to set fire to them in cars, should be regarded under any rational and ethical social system as a grotesque crime.

So what can be done? Quite clearly, engaging in individual acts of conservation, recycling, resource restraint, and other actions to reduce your personal "carbon footprint" are not going to be enough. These millions of individual acts do show that people are far from apathetic about environmental issues, and we should celebrate this spirit of ecological concern. But to concentrate solely on these actions, or worse, berate people who are unable to do so, is misdirected effort when the kinds of action that are really necessary are qualitatively different—and collective. It is self-evident that no individual can build a wind turbine on their own, dismantle a coal-fired power station, or set up a light rail system in their city. But these are precisely the kind of systemic and infrastructural changes that are needed to make any kind of difference. Writing in *Red Pepper*, Kevin Smith, researcher with Carbon Trade Watch, had this to say about the effectiveness and underlying ideological traps that accompany the promotion of changes to personal consumption and carbon offset schemes:

> No matter how many low-energy light bulbs you install, or how much recycling you do, there is still the need for more systemic changes to take place in society. No amount of individualistic action is going to bring about this change in itself.
>
> Such changes will not happen without community organizing and collective political action. Yet there are no offset schemes that encourage individuals to engage in collective action to bring about wider structural change. [Carbon o]ffset schemes place the onus for climate action on individuals acting in isolation from others. This inhibits their political effectiveness.
>
> The act of commodification at the heart of offset schemes assigns a financial value to the impetus that someone may feel to take climate action, and neatly transforms this potential to bring about change into another market transaction. There is then no urgent need for people to question the underlying assumptions about the nature of the social and economic structures that brought about climate change in the first place.[3]

Wider structural change must mean curtailing the power of the corporations by forcing governments to regulate their operation. Real environmental reforms can and have been won under capitalism, but only under one condition—when we collectively demand, organize, and fight for them. The self-regulating capitalist enterprise is a contradiction in terms. Only through governmental regulation such as occurred in the 1970s—changes to laws and the redirection of government subsidies through collective and determined action—can we hope to have an impact on emissions within the timeframe available to us. George Monbiot, the British journalist and environmental activist, in his recent book, *Heat*, argues that governments will not act until the political cost becomes too high not to:

> Governments will pursue this course of inaction [regarding tackling climate change]—irrespective of the human impacts—while it remains politically less costly than the alternative. The task of climate change campaigners is to make it as [politically] expensive as possible...Of course [the Internet] is marvelously useful, allows us to exchange information, find the facts we need, alert each other to the coming dangers and all the rest of it. But it also creates a false impression of action. It allows us to believe that we can change the world without leaving our chairs.... But by itself, as I know to my cost, writing, reading, debate and dissent change nothing. They are only of value if they inspire action. Action means moving your legs.[4]

A Government Action Plan on the Environment

What should the demands of a new and revitalized environmental justice movement call on President Obama and a Democratic Congress to do? Obama keeps saying he wants to prioritize energy and climate change, yet he is also heavily backed by entrenched business interests who want to limit those changes and so far have been highly successful in doing so. It is now transparently clear: only if he comes under sufficient pressure from below will he feel compelled to fight for real reforms. Some recent developments have swung things in our favor.

Amid all the disappointment and disillusionment, there are significant reasons for hope. First and foremost, the prevailing idea of the last thirty years—that the market is the single best arbiter of change—has been shattered. The economic turmoil beginning in 2008 has ended capitalist triumphalism and its bastard child neoliberalism's hegemonic claim to legitimacy. Second, despite the repeated disappointments, there is still a great deal of hope in Obama and an expectation for change that can be channeled into a movement to pressure him to go significantly beyond his rhetorical promises. Third, many people who were firmly of the belief that Obama would be different have not just sunk into disillusionment and apathy. Rather, driven by the urgency of the need for action many, especially students and young people, are coming to the conclusion that such action will only come about through their own independent self-activity. Finally, it has become clear to millions of people that money is available when ruling elites want it to be. Vast quantities of cash suddenly came on tap to bail out of the banking system. According to Joseph Stiglitz, the United States will eventually end up paying $3 trillion for the wars in Afghanistan and Iraq.[5]

But we won't get nearly enough of this money diverted to socially useful causes, such as de-carbonizing energy, unless we fight for it. Ultimately, the extent to which we get positive change will depend on the balance of class forces—how much pressure our side can bring to bear on these issues versus the corporations and vested interests. The arguments for market mechanisms for shared sacrifice to save the environment are part of a class-based response by the ruling elite to allow profit-making to continue,while we pay for them to do so. We need to respond with our own class-based solutions—ones that reject market mechanisms and the idea that we must—or even can—make sacrifices. The solutions below are not about sacrifices, but about enhancing our standard of living while delivering real cuts to emissions. It is the corporations that must make sacrifices, not us. The technological capabilities and resources exist to make the dramatic changes needed to reverse climate change; it is the ruling economic interests in society that prevent them from being implemented on the necessary scale.

The energy coming from the sun each day is more than 15,000 times greater than humans consume—four orders of magnitude larger—meaning that we only need to harness a fraction of 1 percent in order to satisfy our energy needs.[6] According to the authors of a January 2008 *Scientific American* article, the United States could obtain 69 percent of all its electricity requirements and 35 percent of its total energy demands by 2050 from a single source—the sun—with the input of $420 billion of investment between 2011 and 2050. In 2050 U.S. carbon dioxide emissions would then be 62 percent below 2005 levels. Such a price tag—$420 billion over forty years—is considerably less than the Pentagon budget for a single year; it's also less than the U.S. Farm Price Support Program over the same period.[7]

ENERGY SOURCE	POTENTIAL CONTRIBUTION
Concentrating Solar Power	Seven states in the U.S. Southwest could provide more than 7,000 GW of solar generating capacity—nearly seven times U.S. electric capacity from all sources
Solar Water Heaters	Could easily provide half the world's hot water
Rooftop Solar Cells	Could provide 10 percent of grid electricity in the United States by 2030
Wind Power	Could easily provide 20 percent of world's electricity;

offshore wind farms could meet all of the European Union's electricity needs

Geothermal Heat	Could provide 100 GW of generating capacity in the United States alone
Wave and Ocean Thermal Energy	Contribution could be on same order of magnitude as current world energy use

Depending on the study, estimates for exactly how much renewable energy is realistically available for human use do vary. However, all point to the conclusion that with present technology and the correct mix of sources, more than enough exists to power the world. Source: Worldwatch Institute Report 178, 2008[8]

A more recent report in the same journal makes a compelling case for 100 percent of the world's energy coming from renewable sources by an even earlier date of 2030. They project the need to build 3.8 million large wind turbines and 90,000 solar panels. Even spread over a twenty year period 3.8 million wind turbines sounds like a lot—except, as the article points out, the world manufactures almost 70 million cars *every year*. The article also illustrates how a mix of renewable sources of energy (wind, solar, hydro, and geothermal) in California could provide reliable energy twenty-four hours a day, seven days a week as, contrary to common assumption, wind and solar power plants have considerably less downtime for maintenance than coal or nuclear plants, thereby undermining one of the main supposed benefits of conventional power sources.[9] Coal plants have an average maintenance down time of forty-six days, compared to only seven for wind turbines and photovoltaic cells.

One of the technological hurdles making impractical the situating of electricity generators far from population centers is that all electricity is transported as AC (alternating current), making energy losses over long distances prohibitive. Furthermore, there was no equivalent method for transporting and using it as DC (direct current) and carrying extremely large quantities of power. However, that problem has been overcome, making the placement of vast arrays of free solar-energy-collecting photovoltaic cells and solar concentrators in the desert Southwest eminently feasible. High-voltage DC (HVDC) cables already over 1000km long are in place in China, the United States, South Africa, Brazil, and Congo capable of transmitting 2 gigawatts of power. HVDC transmission networks would have to be built to transport electrical energy all over the country. A similar scheme for Europe and Africa, using electricity generated in the Sahara, is entirely feasible. A separate calculation has estimated that 600km x 600km covered with solar panels could supply enough power for 500 million people (the combined populations of the United States, Canada, Mexico, Central America, and the Caribbean) with the equivalent U.S. consumption of 250kWh/day, twice the European average. The same size square located in the North African desert would be enough for one billion people at average western European consumption levels (125kWh/day).[10]

According to the authors of the *Scientific American* article first mentioned, the area required would be just 19 percent of suitable (i.e., barren, with no competing uses) land in the Southwest and would negate the need for three hundred coal plants and three hundred natural gas plants. If this system were set up in conjunction with a massive expansion of wind, tidal, and wave power, the United States could generate all its energy from renewable sources. The potential for power generation using the wind is similarly enormous, particularly from offshore wind farms. But even onshore, by one estimate, 80 percent of current electrical demand in the United States could be met by the wind energy of North Dakota and South Dakota alone.[5] Another recent study of eight thousand wind records from all continents calculated a wind power potential of 72 terawatts. This is forty times the amount of electricity consumed by every country on the planet in 2000.[11]

Of course, one obvious drawback to using the sun and wind as a basis for power generation is that it's not always sunny or windy, and this has been one of the major advantages of conventional power stations. In recognition of this, other than ensuring a mix of renewable supplies and geographical distribution (it's guaranteed to be windy or sunny somewhere), and back-up generation capacity, large storage facilities can be built to ensure a continuous supply of base-load electricity. This can now be done as successful demonstrations of storing energy as compressed air in underground caverns have shown, as well as storing energy as hot salt in insulated containers. According to the Electric Power Research Institute, suitable geologic formations for underground storage exist in 75 percent of the country—far more environmentally benign than using them to store high pressure CO_2. The natural gas industry currently stores eight trillion cubic feet of natural gas underground in 400 underground reservoirs—so we know there's capacity and the technology is already well proven.[12] There is also the possibility of pumped storage. Here water is pumped back up hill during times of low demand and low cost and stored behind a dam. This kind of storage mechanism can provide power in seconds to augment any shortfall from renewable sources and recovers 70 percent of the energy used to pump the water uphill.

Alongside these storage facilities to supplement fluctuating renewable sources, there is the largely untapped potential of geothermal energy. According to a recent article in a publication of the British Royal Society and based on an MIT study, the potential for geothermal energy in the United States—with currently available technology and energy that is easily extractable with minimal environmental impacts or emissions—represents *2,000 times the current primary energy use of the United States.*[13]

Of course none of the above should be taken as an argument that there is any technological panacea. First and foremost, these changes will require a massive redistribution of power away from corporations to workers, farmers, and local communities connected together for mutual benefit. But the emphasis here is to show that, in contrast to general perceptions, a transition to non-carbon-based fuels within two to three decades is wholly realistic.

However, it should be recognized that there is no such thing as a free lunch. Alternative energy technologies such as wind, solar, and geothermal are much more environmentally benign than digging up and burning fossil fuels or uranium. But there are restrictions based on possible limitations of supply for some rare earth metals required for wind turbine gearing mechanisms for example and other elements needed for solar panels. There are also significant differences and environmental costs to using photovoltaic cells versus solar furnaces (concentrated solar power). In addition, the impact of geothermal plants on tectonic activity and the long-term implications for wildlife and water use from alternative energy power stations need to be fully and transparently assessed.

My argument should not be seen as a blueprint, merely the starting point for discussion. My point is that real solutions for clean energy are all technologically feasible and practically possible within a fairly short time frame. Rather than the one-size-fits-all model of giant centralized utilities using their economic and political clout to determine what kind of power stations get built and where, we need a judicious mix of renewable energy solutions. Some of these solutions will be local or community based, some of them will be part of large regional grids. The exact energy mix, will logically and of necessity, look different in different geographical and climatic locations. Input will come from those affected by the decisions in consultation with scientific and technical experts as to what would make the most sensible choices based on need, energy efficiency, minimization of pollution, and use of resources.

The point is that only a full democratic debate of alternatives, including the need to radically curtail our energy consumption via energy-efficiency measures, can allow this process to bear fruit. If all that frames the discussion are the short-term profit dynamics of capitalism where the focus is on cap and trade, nuclear and offshore drilling, the relevant debate cannot even begin.

The Challenge of Chemical Pollution

A renewed emphasis on alternative energy and the infrastructure to support it would have the added beneficial effect of making us not only carbon-free by 2050 but creating millions of new, high-skilled jobs. In addition, by reducing the number of coal plants, air quality would see major improvement as the single biggest emitter of carcinogenic dioxins and mercury into the atmosphere are coal-fired power plants. Coal plants are also a major emitter of small (less than 10 microns) particulates. This type of particle is part of a "deadly cocktail of ash, soot, diesel exhaust, chemicals, metals and aerosols that [in major U.S. cities] can spike dangerously for hours to weeks on end. The body's natural defenses, coughing and sneezing, fail to keep these microscopic particles from burrowing deep within the lungs, triggering serious problems such as breathing, asthma and heart attacks, strokes, lung cancer and even early death."[14]

Ozone, along with these small particulates, is a major component of the brown haze over all cities around the world—collectively known as "smog"—which is given off by car exhausts. While ozone is good for stopping UV (ultraviolet) rays in the upper atmosphere, when breathed in at ground level it irritates the respiratory tract and "causes health problems such as asthma attacks, coughing, wheezing, chest pain and even premature death."[15] According to the American Lung Association's 2008 *State of the Air* report, one in ten Americans live in areas with unhealthful levels of all three types of air pollution—ozone and short-term and year-round particulate pollution. Two in five people live in counties that have either ozone or particulate pollution and nearly a third live in areas with unhealthful ozone levels.[16]

No matter how much organic food you eat or whether you live in a city or far out in the countryside, nothing can insulate you from having to breathe the air or use the products manufactured by capitalism. Persistent toxic chemicals and Persistent Organic Pollutants, many of them strongly carcinogenic or related to birth defects, can be found everywhere. Each of us has at least 200 of them in our bodies right now. A Canadian study that tested for 88 harmful chemicals found that on average each person had 44 in their bodies. Blood and urine samples from a Toronto mother were found to contain 38 known reproductive and respiratory toxins, 19 chemicals that disrupt hormones, and 27 carcinogens. And before everyone leaves for the wilderness, they also tested a First Nation volunteer who lives in a remote region of Hudson Bay—that person tested positive for 51 of the 88.[17] If Inuit mothers were to try to sell their breast milk in the United States, it would be classified as hazardous waste due to the levels of PCBs it contains. PCBs are fat soluble and so become concentrated in mother's milk, as they do in the blubber of Arctic species common in a traditional Inuit diet. Through a process of biomagnification, PCB concentrations can increase up to twenty times for a diet that is high in end-of-the-food-chain sea predators. Carried on the winds to all corners of the earth, these toxic, long-lived chemicals are lodged in living beings despite their existence in a seemingly pristine environment far from their industrial sources.

Another set of fat-soluble industrial compounds, polybrominated diphenyl ethers, PBDEs, are a class of chemicals that paradoxically became common when new fire safety standards were implemented in the United States in the 1970s. The flame retardants are used in foam furniture, electronics, fabrics, carpets, plastics, and a host of other common items found in the home, and studies illustrate widespread contamination of house dust by PBDEs, which bio-accumulate in fat cells. Ninety-seven percent of U.S. residents have detectable levels of PBDEs in their blood with the levels in Americans twenty times higher than in Europeans.[18] The Centers for Disease Control's latest biomonitoring study of 2,500 people detected 212 toxic chemicals in their bodies. A biomonitoring study by the Learning and Developmental Disabilities Initiative identified sixty-one "neurotoxic and endocrine disrupting chemicals" in the twelve people tested.[19] Much of the risk depends not on the levels of exposure as it does on the time of exposure, for example, whether exposure is prolonged or occurs at a critical developmental growth stage in children. With the manufacture of tens of thousands of chemicals and their dispersal around the globe, a giant and largely unregulated experiment is being carried out on every living creature. This is a fact recognized by the U.S. government agency supposedly responsible for protecting people from harmful substances, the Environmental Protection Agency. According to the conclusions of a report by the agency's inspector general: "EPA's assurance that new chemicals or organisms introduced into commerce do not pose unreasonable risks to workers, consumers, or the environment is not supported by data or actual testing."[20]

Of the more than 21,000 chemicals required to be registered under the 1976 Toxic Substances Control Act, only 15 percent have been submitted with health and safety data. The EPA has no legal ability to enforce testing unless there's unequivocal evidence of harm (the kind you'd find if you did the testing). Ninety-five percent of new chemicals are protected by confidentiality clauses, and even when a chemical is known to cause harm, asbestos for example, federal courts have overturned every EPA effort to limit manufacture. As a result, of the more than 80,000 chemicals in the United States, only five have been restricted or banned.

This is not because all the other 79,995 are therefore safe. Bisphenol A, more commonly known as BPA, is a case in point. The CDC has reported that 93 percent of Americans have detectable levels of BPA in their urine. BPA, one of a range of chemicals known as endocrine disruptors, is a chemical used in plastics manufacture for all kinds of uses such as polycarbonate plastic for baby bottles and other hard plastic containers, eyeglass lenses, polyester clothing, and epoxy resins. Though there was evidence of BPA's ability to mimic the hormone estrogen back in the 1930s, scientists' concerns about BPA became more serious in the 1990s when it was discovered that mice developed chromosomally abnormal eggs when kept in cages that were leaching their coating of BPA. Since then the chemical has been linked to asthma, behavioral changes, cardiovascular disease, diabetes, and some cancers. Yet, the EPA has still not taken strong action to regulate or ban BPA, along with 60,000 other chemicals—because it can't; the 1976 act excluded from evaluation all those chemicals that were already in use by the time of passage of the law.[21] The best the Food and Drug Administration has been able to do is warn parents not to pour hot liquids into plastic baby bottles and to discard bottles that are scratched.

Measures to Reduce Energy Use

The heating of water and the heating and cooling of residential and commercial space account for almost 40 percent of electrical power generation requirements and are therefore a substantial contributor to CO_2 emissions. Buildings need to be either retrofitted for insulation or torn down and rebuilt with energy efficiency in mind. Currently, buildings are often constructed to the lowest standards of energy efficiency, and beyond some construction safety codes, any further meddling by the government is regarded as unwarranted intrusion into the market. This means that major percentages of the energy used to heat or cool a home are lost through badly insulated walls, poorly fitted windows and doors and leaky roofs and floors. Millions of homes, for example, are built without cavity wall insulation, even though injecting mineral microfibers between the bricks pays for itself in two to five years.[22] As the turnover for building stock is very slow, around 1 to 2 percent a year, it is extremely important to focus on retro-fitting old buildings to bring them up to the standards of what is possible today.

In the late 1980s, the "Passivhaus" was designed, and in Germany several thousand have been built since the 1990s. The house, which looks like any other house from the outside, is super-insulated and so well designed that it does not need an active heating or cooling system at all. This type of house uses three-quarters less energy than a typical building of comparable size and only costs around 10 percent more than an equivalent home. The government should require that new buildings be constructed to this standard and enforce energy efficiency regulations on construction companies. Using regulation to force companies to comply, rather than market incentives such as subsidies to corporations or tax deductions to consumers, ensures that far more rapid progress is made. This is because rather than relying on the minority of middle-class people with some disposable income or "responsible" corporations to make changes, everyone has to comply. In Germany, where a mix of tighter government building regulations, public information campaigns, energy-saving incentives, loans, and subsidies have been in place for some years, the energy savings of old buildings range from 60 to 80 percent.[23] An "eco-renovation" of an apartment block in Austria built in the 1950s reduced its electrical consumption by 90 percent. As a result of the German building refit plan, the government estimates that 200,000 new jobs have been created. Due to the more technical nature of building long-lived, energy-conserving buildings, the technical demands are much more exacting. Thus, as an additional benefit, these jobs are highly skilled and rewarding.

In terms of transportation, rail and bus systems need to be nationalized so that a coherent national plan can be developed to enhance the quality of travel and reduce energy use. Currently private companies only run extensive services along commuter routes that are highly trafficked, predictable, and hence highly profitable. Subsidies currently given to the private airline companies should be cut off and redirected to the building of high-speed train lines to massively reduce or eradicate the need for superfluous business and short-haul flights. If people need more holiday time because they're taking the train, how about increasing paid vacation time by four days a year? Or bringing it in line with Europe, where people have four to six weeks of paid vacation?

Public tram lines and light rail need to be built in all major cities. Subway and bus lines need to be increased and made free, with buses running on electricity generated by renewable sources. This would allow for the banning of cars from congested areas of city centers and for enlarged green spaces by reducing the need for parking lots and on-street car parking. City centers need to be made bike- and people-friendly by closing off streets to private cars and massively extending and augmenting bike routes. When the amount of space cars take up even when empty, and the number of road deaths, injuries, and respiratory illnesses from cars is taken into account, banning them from dense urban centers would immediately improve the quality of life. Imagine what it would be like to live in a city that was people-centered rather than car-centered: clean, safe, quiet; a place of tranquility, space, breathable air, urban farms, and human community.

Regulations for fuel efficiency need to be tightened to move beyond current European efficiency standards. With the strategic building of new rail lines from manufacturers and air and sea ports to distribution points near cities, freight—the vast bulk of which is moved around the country by trucks in the United States and other developed countries—can be moved back to trains, which are much more efficient and less polluting.

Who's going to build all these new trains and tracks, buses, and wind turbines? Instead of an Obama administration handing further billions over to GM, Ford, and Chrysler to continue to make earth-despoiling products that nobody needs, the government should take ownership and control: rehire and retrain the already skilled workforce and switch the factories to make the things we need. If they can partially nationalize the banks, we can fully nationalize (with control as well as ownership) the auto companies and stop their begging before Congress for more blank checks as they private-jet it back to Detroit.

However, any rational energy plan needs to be part of a national transportation, housing, product manufacturing, and energy-efficiency plan. As European capitalism has survived and prospered with tougher governmental regulatory controls and greater restrictions on corporations, it is clear that we can win important and life-enhancing reforms without threatening the overall structure of capitalism. However, it is equally clear that we will only achieve these if we push our elected representatives to represent our interests and not those of the corporations.

The Need for Independent Politics

The above would seem like a good program for a genuinely reform-minded social democratic government that has cast off the sickness of neoliberal economics and raging militarism. A program such as this could even get couched as "a Green New Deal for the Twenty-First Century—good for the planet, good for people, good for profits." These proposals could *theoretically* be carried out under capitalist social relations through governmental regulation, particularly by a proactive and forward-thinking Obama administration. But while there has certainly been a most welcome change of tone and a more serious approach to energy and climate change, after one year in office, rhetoric aside, Obama has largely backed the dictates of Big Business.

If it wasn't apparent before, it is now crystal clear that the Democrats and Obama cannot be relied upon to take action on climate change seriously. Only mass collective organizations, social pressure, and action can possibly bring to fruition the kind of plans outlined above as they fly in the face of the short-term interests of the corporations that have the political parties on their speed dials. Put another way, reforms that are theoretically possible under capitalism won't be made because they "make sense," but because the politicians are forced to implement them. Otherwise we will get fobbed off with false solutions and only make progress that is too slow and piecemeal to make real inroads to dramatically slowing climate change.

We need a far bigger vision for change than any of the mainstream parties are prepared to sanction. To cut costs, mass production is what's needed, not just more research. Between 2002 and 2008 federal subsidies to the fossil fuel industry in direct spending and tax breaks amounted to $72 billion. A further $16.8 billion went to corn ethanol production for biofuels. Over the same period, only $12.2 billion went to federal subsidies for renewable energy. These priorities need reversing.[24]

It took Congress—pushed by Obama—less than a week to decide to hand over $700 billion to the banks with no democratic oversight or control. Every year, they vote to hand the Pentagon sums now approaching a staggering $1 trillion and further tens of billions to the oil, coal, nuclear, and gas industries. The $664 billion allocated to the U.S. defense budget for 2010 dwarfs the second largest military budget; China has a military budget less than one tenth of the United States, at $78 billion.[25] To put that in perspective, spending $700 billion plus per year on military hardware is equivalent to taking more than $2,000 from every one of the three hundred million men, women, and children in America. These are the kind of amounts we need to be talking about spending to implement a comprehensive, effective and timely national plan on energy and emissions. Rather than cuts to state and federal budgets, cuts need to be made to the Pentagon and more money raised by a "windfall tax" on the superprofits being made by the oil giants as well as increases to the top rate of tax for the stratospherically rich. Is there any doubt that, if put to a popular vote, prior to which information was made freely available to the public, such a program of infrastructure

spending, job retraining, and employment, along with taxes
on the rich, would be wildly popular?

A stupendous river of cash flows from corporations and
the rich to tax havens purely as a way of avoiding the few
taxes they are actually supposed to pay. Since financial markets were deregulated in the 1980s more than $600 billion
dollars has been siphoned from sub-Saharan Africa and
parked in offshore accounts. This represents more than three
times the international debt of those countries. Estimates of
how much money is sequestered in off-shore accounts by
wealthy individuals and corporations around the world range
from $11.5 trillion dollars and up. This represents an annual
tax loss of $250 billion dollars. Commercial tax evasion
amounts to a staggering $700–$1,000 billion dollars annually.[26]
Barely has the public disgust at bankers settled down, let
alone layoffs and foreclosures declined, then we find they're
at it again. Aided by government bailouts of taxpayer money,
the top twenty-five hedge fund managers, who play no socially
useful role in society, "earned" $25.3 billion in 2009. For
hedge-fund managers, 2009, barely one year after almost total
financial meltdown, was a year when pay "roared back."[27]

Apart from being for nuclear power, "clean coal" technology, ethanol from corn, and a cap-and-trade scheme, Obama
is for offshore drilling and boosting domestic production of
oil even though, by his own admission, it is totally inadequate
to wean the United States off "foreign oil." The unfolding catastrophic explosion of BP's Deepwater Horizon oil rig in the
Gulf of Mexico starkly illustrates how ever-deeper offshore
drilling alongside lax government oversight inevitably leads
to environmental disaster—in this case, quite likely to surpass the destruction of habitat, wildlife, and human industry

that ensued from the *Exxon Valdez* spill of 1989. According to his campaign literature, he is for opening up more land to drilling across the United States, including the National Petroleum Reserve in Alaska and prioritizing the building of a second Alaska pipeline for natural gas extraction. Unbelievably, he is also for developing low-grade oil shale reserves, one of the most polluting industries imaginable, in Montana and North Dakota. These are not the kind of changes we need or that people voted to see. He has now moved firmly in to the "drill, baby, drill" camp by opening up almost the entire coastline of the United States to offshore drilling.

As planetary environmental degradation increases and individual climate-related disasters such as Hurricane Katrina multiply, even without an environmental justice movement it is probable governments and corporations will be pushed into implementing some genuine, albeit limited, reforms. It is also quite possible that they will be pushed into some of these reforms by actions taken by workers, farmers, peasants, and their communities being devastated by environmental changes, regardless of whether they call themselves environmentalists or not.

Some of the more far-sighted corporations without significant investments in fossil fuels will see the way the wind is blowing and that money can be made from investing in alternative energies, as is already the case. This will create tension and splits among ruling elites and between conflicting corporate interests, which will open up space for social and labor movements to demand swifter and more coordinated action.

Bringing about the kind of changes we need, however, systematically and in the near term, will require building a mass movement that combines the best aspects of the social movements of the 1960s with the workers' radicalism of the 1930s. Such a movement needs to argue and fight for these changes and take head-on the argument that the market is the best arbiter of what should and shouldn't be produced. In addition, such a movement will require squarely placing the blame where it lies: unregulated free-market capitalism. Any ecological movement that develops needs to forcefully argue that this is not about sacrifice but improving lives and creating jobs. If it does not seek to establish connections and link up with the people who make all the products in the world and who in many instances are already organized into mass collective organizations—the global working class—it is hard to see how it could be even minimally successful. Recently a number of unions have signed onto exactly this kind of program to tackle climate change through investments in alternative technologies and retraining of workers. The environmental justice movement must be prepared to support workers fighting for safer, healthier conditions, job security and benefits. For too long, environmental groups and trade unions have been mutually exclusive, to the detriment of both. This leaves an ideological space open for capitalists to pit them against each other as if the two groups have mutually antagonistic goals.

The successful fight to stop the privatization of the water supply in Bolivia is one example of how workers can lead the way in the battle against multinational domination and how we can learn from the vibrant and successful struggles in the South. Oscar Olivera, president of the Cochabamba Federation of Factory Workers sees the victory as a way of encouraging people in the North to join the struggle:

> I believe people in the U.S. need the experience of some real political victories…In April 2000, in Cochabamba, we

won an important victory against the transnationals and against the World Bank—a victory in which we overturned the privatization of drinking water...Victory is possible. These victories, and the opportunities for the development of social movements, will spread to North America. Given the wars in Iraq and Afghanistan, the brutality practiced against the Palestinians, the constant assault of U.S. capitalism on the living standards of ordinary working people in the U.S.—no day is better than today to start to rebuild the social movement in the U.S.[28]

Given the recurring economic crises that have wracked capitalism since the early 1970s, any movement for environmental change will require a more steadfast, determined, and clear-sighted set of politics and organization than ever before. Concessions that eat into short-term profitability and that disadvantage those corporations and countries that enact them will provoke steadfast resistance from the vested corporate interests that stand to lose out. To take on the oil industry, with a global turnover of $2.4 trillion,[29] would require a truly massive international movement. Ultimately, even if some of these reforms were to be granted—and we should fight for them as we push for more—they will ultimately be insufficient to address the scale of the crisis.

The real difficulty with fulfilling this reform-minded scenario, even with a militant and broad-based mass environmental movement to demand it, is that the environmental crisis is global, close at hand, and vast in scope. Over the medium to longer term, it requires the complete retooling of society in every sphere of activity: energy production, distribution, and storage; transportation; housing design and town planning; agricultural and industrial production. As can be seen from the abject failure at Kyoto and Copenhagen, and the imperial conflicts around the globe, it is impossible for competing capitalist states to plan and coordinate on this level. Such planning could only realistically come about through a completely different way of organizing production—one based not on making a profit but meeting human need.

CHAPTER SIX

Marxism and the Environment

"The analysis of Nature into its individual parts, the grouping of the different natural processes and objects in definite classes, the study of the internal anatomy of organized bodies in their manifold forms—these were the fundamental conditions of the gigantic strides in our knowledge of Nature that have been made during the last 400 years. But this method of work has also left us as legacy the habit of observing natural objects and processes in isolation, apart from their connection with the vast whole; of observing them in repose, not in motion; as constraints, not as essentially variables; in their death, not in their life."

—Frederick Engels, *Socialism: Utopian and Scientific*[1]

There is a widespread assumption among environmentalists that Marxism, as a "productivist" ideology, has little to say, and little concern, for the fate of the environment. Contrary to a common perception—much of it understandably based on the diabolical environmental depredations carried out in the name of socialism by the former Soviet Union, Eastern Bloc, and China—Marx and Engels had a much more holistic view of humankind's place in the environment.

The idea that Marx and Engels were obsessed only with the conditions of workers comes from all quarters, right and left. They are often portrayed as writers who, it is conceded, may have been ahead of their times with their insightful economic analysis of capitalism but were typical of nineteenth century men enamored of the wonderful powers of technology to solve all of society's ills. Their only contention, it is argued, was that technology should be owned and controlled by the workers, not the capitalists. Thenceforth, it could be unleashed upon the planet for the furthering of the interests of the entire human race without a thought to natural limits.

According to this view attributed to Marx, through control of the means of production and mastery of nature mankind would be set free. Most often Marx's ideas are described as "productivist" or Promethean after the Greek god Prometheus, who stole the technology of fire from Zeus and gave it to mortals. The Promethean view is shown to be true by selected excerpts from the writings of Marx and Engels and the evidence of "actually existing socialism" as it used to be in the Soviet Union and its satellites, and as it still exists in China and other "socialist" countries not known for their ecological stewardship, such as North Korea and Vietnam. Marxist scholars John Bellamy Foster and Paul Burkett have done much to refute this version of Marxism and the presumptive original sin of Marx and Engels with which all past and future socialist projects are taken to be tainted.[2]

This chapter is important because we need not just a critique of the past but also a vision for the future, one that is rooted in historical experience and theoretical cogency that we can build on and develop. Just as socialism needs to be rescued from the distortions of some of its supposed practitioners, so the writings of Marx and Engels should be recognized for their usefulness in examining the natural world and human relationships to it. This is not to take every word of Marx and Engels as the gospel truth more than a hundred years after they wrote them. Rather it is to argue that the methodology of Marxism holds key insights into our relationship to nature that are extremely useful for understanding our place in the biosphere and interaction with it.

The language of socialism and the mantle of Marx and Engels were adopted by Stalin in the USSR, Mao in China, and other "socialist" societies not to further the course of socialism but to derail it. While going into detail on the nature of these regimes is beyond the scope of this book, it should be clear that if socialism means anything, it is the free association of the people who do the work raising themselves into power to collectively and democratically decide the future course of society.[3] The workers and peasants who make the revolution should bear its fruits. That is, they democratically decide the direction of the economy and society in the interests of the vast majority; a society where production of goods is based on human need, not profit.

After the Stalinist counterrevolution in the Soviet Union of the 1920s, nowhere has this been true of any society claiming to be socialist. Each society is run from the top down in the interests of a bureaucratic ruling elite who run the state as a one-party fiefdom. The interests of the ruling Soviet elite became associated with the interests of a state in economic and military competition with the West.

In other words, the same factors that propel capitalist production—the need to compete and drive out the competition—reigned within these regimes. Flowing directly from this came the need of each of these one-party states to constantly raise productivity and dispense with any environmental, democratic, or labor concerns in the manic drive toward economic and technological parity with the Western powers. It was the severe lack of power of the working class in the "socialist" countries, not its untrammeled freedom, which created the conditions for the extreme ecological vandalism seen there. As Stalin commented, what took the West one hundred years to accomplish, the Soviet Union would do in ten.[4] This chapter will therefore explore the real legacy of Marx and Engels and subsequent Marxist thinkers as it relates to enhancing our understanding of the human social relationship to the natural world.

While life will evolve and biodiversity will eventually be reestablished on a planet that is 6^0 C warmer than today, it will do so on a timescale vastly greater than human planning and life spans could possibly contemplate. As mentioned earlier, it took fifty million years for biodiversity to recover from the Permian-Triassic mass extinction. In the interim period, 50 to 90 percent of species currently extant will die out as they will be unable to adapt fast enough to such rapid changes and the resulting breakdown in ecosystems within which these species are embedded. It is not just the overall amount of climatic change that will be so devastating to ecosystems, but just as importantly, the rate at which that change occurs. Alongside such drastic reductions in biodiversity, human misery will multiply. Mass migration, droughts, floods, wars, and famine will be endemic rather than periodic features of a greatly constrained human society.

Frederick Engels outlined over one hundred years ago the contradictions between an exploitative, short-term relationship of humanity to nature and the long-term problems that would inevitably engender:

> Let us not, however, flatter ourselves overmuch on account of our human victories over nature. For each victory nature takes its revenge on us. Each victory, it is true, in the first place brings about the results we expected, but in the second and third places it has quite different, unforeseen effects which only too often cancel out the first. The people who, in Mesopotamia, Greece, Asia Minor and elsewhere, destroyed forests to obtain cultivable land, never dreamed that by removing along with the forests the collecting centers and reservoirs of moisture they were laying the basis for the present forlorn state of those countries. When the Italians of the Alps used up the pine forests on the southern slopes, so carefully cherished on the northern slopes, they had no inkling that by doing so they were thereby depriving their mountain springs of water for the greater part of the year, making possible for them to pour still more furious torrents on the plains during the rainy season... Thus at every step we are reminded that we by no means rule over nature like a conqueror over a foreign people, like someone standing outside of nature—but that we, with flesh, blood and brain, belong to nature, exist in its midst, and that all our mastery of it consists in the fact that we have the advantage of all other creatures of being able to learn its laws and apply them correctly.[5]

This failure to take into account the long-term, unintended consequences of human actions reaches its height of contradiction under capitalism where both the scale of the destructive impact of these unintended consequences, as well as the scientific and material means to overcome them, develop in tandem. Writes Engels:

> Classical political economy, the social science of the bour-

geoisie, in the main examines only social effects of human actions in the fields of production and exchange that are actually intended. This fully corresponds to the social organization of which it is the theoretical expression. As individual capitalists are engaged in production and exchange for the sake of the immediate profit, only the nearest, most immediate results must first be taken into account. As long as the individual manufacturer or merchant sells a manufactured or purchased commodity with the usual coveted profit, he is satisfied and does not concern himself with what afterwards becomes of the commodity and its purchasers. The same thing applies to the natural effects of the same actions. What cared the Spanish planters in Cuba, who burned down forests on the slopes of the mountains and obtained from the ashes sufficient fertilizer for one generation of very highly profitable coffee trees—what cared they that the heavy tropical rainfall afterwards washed away the unprotected upper stratum of the soil, leaving behind only bare rock! In relation to nature, as to society, the present mode of production is predominantly concerned only about the immediate, the most tangible result.[6]

Today, all the solutions to climate change are already technologically feasible, and we have the means to implement them on a global scale, as well as the knowledge of what will happen if we don't. We are being held back not because solutions don't exist or money is not available, but because current social relations will not allow for them. As Leon Trotsky wrote in 1926:

> I remember the time when men wrote that the development of aircraft would put an end to war, because it would draw the whole population into military operations, would bring to ruin the economic and cultural life of entire countries, etc. In fact, however, the invention of the flying ma-

chine heavier than air opened a new and crueler chapter in the history of militarism. There is no doubt now, too, we are approaching the beginning of a still more frightful and bloody chapter. Technology and science have their own logic—the logic of the cognition of nature and the mastering of it in the interests of man. But technology in itself cannot be called either militaristic or pacifistic. In a society in which the ruling class is militaristic, technology is in the service of militarism.[7]

Today, we clearly have governments overtly committed to militarism to extend the economic reach of their own national group of capitalists. As all mainstream predictions by the United Nations and the International Energy Agency point toward growing worldwide use of fossil fuel energy, waiting for real and meaningful solutions to emerge from governments guarantees humanity a desperate future and many species a short one. The raison d'être of capitalism is profit based on continual economic expansion. Capitalism has, in effect and in practice, alienated humanity from nature by privatizing the land and making all things into commodities—even pollution itself. On this alienation from nature, Marx explains, "As for the farmer, the industrial capitalist and the agricultural worker, they are no more bound to the land they exploit than are the employer and the worker in the factories to the cotton and wool they manufacture; they feel an attachment only for the price of their production, the monetary product."[8]

Capitalism is an economic system profoundly and irrevocably at odds with a sustainable planet, as it requires ever-greater material and energy throughput to keep expanding. According to a 2000 study carried out by five major European and U.S. research centers:

Industrial economies are becoming more efficient in their use of materials, but waste generation continues to increase...Even as decoupling between economic growth and resource throughput occurred on a per capita and per unit of GDP basis, overall resource use and waste flows to the environment continued to grow. We found no evidence of an absolute reduction in resource throughput. One half to three quarters of annual resource inputs to industrial economies are returned to the environment as wastes within a year.[9]

Let's dwell on that last sentence for a second: One-half to three-quarters of industrial inputs returned to the environment as wastes within a year!

Capitalism simultaneously and of necessity exploits the land and the people and sacrifices the interests of both on the altar of profit. Philosophically, the approach that capitalism takes to the environment, and the attitude it forces us to adopt, is one of separation and alienation. As a species we are forcibly cut off from the land, separated from nature, and alienated from coevolving with it. It's an attitude amply summed up by Marx in volume 1 of *Capital*:

Capitalist production...disturbs the metabolic interaction between man and the earth, i.e. prevents the return to the soil of its constituent elements consumed by man in the form of food and clothing; it therefore violates the conditions necessary to lasting fertility of the soil.... The social combination and organization of the labor processes is turned into an organized mode of crushing out the workman's individual vitality, freedom and independence... Moreover, all progress in capitalist agriculture is a progress in the art, not only of robbing the worker, but of robbing the soil; all progress in increasing the fertility of the soil for a given time is a progress towards ruining the more long-lasting sources of that fertility. The more a country starts its development on the foundation of modern industry, like the United States, for example, the more rapid is this process of destruction. Capitalist production, therefore, develops technology... only by sapping the original sources of all wealth—the soil and the worker.[10]

Marx and Engels viewed humans not as something separate from the environment, as capitalist ideological orthodoxy does, but dialectically interconnected. Writes Marx on the relationship between nature and humanity:

Nature is man's inorganic body, that is to say, nature in so far as it is not the human body. Man lives from nature, i.e. nature is his body, and he must maintain a continuing dialogue with it if he is not to die. To say man's physical and mental life is linked to nature simply means that nature is linked to itself, for man is a part of nature.[11]

The organism interacts with its environment while simultaneously the environment acts back on the organism. In the process, both are changed. The environment is no longer a passive object to be shaped at will by whatever life-form comes along, but plays a role in making the organism what it is. In this view, it is impossible to speak of any living thing, humans and their activity included, as anything but deeply enmeshed with each other, in a constant process of mutual interaction and transformation. Environmental niches don't just pre-exist so that some happy organism that just happens to wander by at the right time can slot itself in. The very idea of an environment has no meaning unless we are talking about an organism's relationship to it. For Marx and Engels, writing in *The German Ideology*, human activity had the potential to alienate all creatures from their environments:

The "essence" of the fish is its "being," water... The

"essence" of the freshwater fish is the water of a river. But the latter ceases to be the essence of the fish and so is no longer a suitable medium for existence as soon as the river is made to serve industry, as soon as it is polluted by dyes and other waste products and navigated by steamboats, or as soon as its water is diverted into canals where simple drainage can deprive fish of its medium of existence.[12]

Climate, and the earth's ecosystem more generally, is dynamic and complex; it is best viewed as a process of many interacting factors. Every change feeds back and creates new effects on all actors. This leads to the concepts of tipping points and holism—both central within Marxism. Violent shocks to the system over relatively brief timescales have dominated previous climate swings, as have the revolutionary social changes that ushered capitalism onto the world historic stage. Rapid changes to natural and social systems can be seen to operate in analogous ways. Stresses that accumulate in climate systems and human societies often do so without much outward sign until rapid and extreme changes seem to burst forth almost out of nowhere. Under the surface however, what seem like small, inconsequential "molecular" changes were taking place that eventually led to the radical and abrupt shifts to entirely new systems. In regard to climate change, this is the thesis of Fred Pearce's book *With Speed and Violence: Why Scientists Fear Tipping Points in Climate Change.*

In this sense, rapid climate change and revolutionary social change are analogous because they both exemplify the sudden transformation of quantity into quality. The great concern among scientists is that we are fast approaching just such a tipping point with regard to global climate. In the social realm, the great concern among many other people is that we are not approaching just such a corresponding social upheaval fast enough to prevent us from going beyond a systemic breakdown in a stable global climate.

To end the contradiction between humanity and nature requires "something more than mere knowledge. It requires a complete revolution in our hitherto existing mode of production, and simultaneously a revolution in our whole contemporary social order."[13] To truly end the exploitation of nature in the service of profit requires that the profit motive be excised from society in a revolutionary reconstitution by the majority on whose labor the system depends. The right to privately own the land and the means of production, which lies at the very root of capitalist economics and forces the population at large to work for a living at the behest of private capital, must be abolished. Only by holding land, along with the instruments of production, in common and producing to meet social need will the simultaneous exploitation of nature and humanity end. Only then can we interact with nature according to a conscious plan, utilizing the scientific knowledge and technique that we already possess to organize production and distribution on a completely new footing that thus establishes a more harmonious relationship between humanity and nature. The methodology developed and used by Marx and Engels offers insightful clues as to how to do that.

Socialist Ecological Thought Since Marx

Marxism is a science, not a religion. As such it is a continually evolving body of thought, adapting and learning from new situations and knowledge. It is no surprise therefore to learn that several Marxists and socialists have made significant contributions to ecological thought.

The term "biosphere," encompassing the entirety of an open system that supports all life and its interaction with the atmosphere and the energy coming from the sun, was coined in the 1920s by a leading scientist of the Bolshevik Soviet government, Vladimir Vernadsky. Vernadsky was one of the very first—in a prophetic speech in 1922—to warn of the dangers of the misuse of atomic power. In 1926 Vernadsky published *The Biosphere*. This was before Soviet science became intensely productivist, anti-ecological and, in some important and notorious episodes, anti-scientific.

Well before James Lovelock's rather mystical notions of Gaia and the earth as a self-regulating living organism, Vernadsky, in echoes of Marx, wrote in his book of the essential link and interconnection between all biotic and abiotic matter in shaping the earth:

> Life is, thus, potently and continuously the disturbing chemical inertia on the surface of our planet. It creates colors and forms of nature, the associations of animals and plants, and the creative labor of civilized humanity, and also becomes a part of the diverse chemical processes of the earth's crust. There is not substantial chemical equilibrium on the crust in which the influence of life is not evident, and in which chemistry does not display life's work. Life is, therefore, not an external or accidental phenomenon of the earth's crust...All living matter can be regarded as a single entity in the mechanism of the biosphere.[14]

Here the biosphere, encompassing all living and nonliving matter, is the system, human society is an interacting sub-system of that, and the economy a subsystem of human society, even if the key one through which society evolves. For conventional economists it is the exact reverse: the economy is the system; human society, and, to the extent that the biosphere is even considered, are both subsystems. This reversal gives rise to the idea, essential under capitalism, that the economy can expand without limits, that capitalism is a *boundless* system. That this runs counter to the physical and biological laws of the universe goes without acknowledgment. The capitalist economy runs as a perpetual motion machine, the practical possibility of which was discredited in the nineteenth century with the enunciation of the First and Second Laws of Thermodynamics. Nevertheless, in order to continue, it requires a belief system that suspends knowledge of those very laws even as it utilizes them in other spheres of scientific endeavor. Hence the entirely necessary but nonsensical notion under capitalism: the economy is essentially independent of nature.

Committed to the unity of theory and practice, the Bolsheviks did not limit themselves to theoretical reconceptions of a dynamic and interactive organic and inorganic world but actively supported little-known but nevertheless groundbreaking ecological practice. The Soviet Union, particularly through the leadership of Lenin while he was alive, and Lunacharsky while he was head of the People's Commissariat for Education, Narkompros, (before his forced resignation by Stalin in 1929) were strong backers of an ecologically minded policy toward agricultural sustainability, biodiversity, and ecological research. This was in the face of the most desperate economic circumstances bequeathed to the young Soviet state due to the deprivations of the First World War and the unrestrained savagery with which the counterrevolutionary White armies and Allied Western governments prosecuted the ensuing three year civil war.

For a short period of time, studies in Soviet ecology blossomed as in no other country. That brief period was brought to an abrupt end when Stalin and the ascendant bureaucracy demonized "science for the sake of science" as a "bourgeois deviation." Stalin insisted not only that true "proletarian science" must first and foremost justify itself in the interests of the economy, but also that scientific theory had as much to gain from "practice" as it did from the unearthing of scientific relationships. In other words, what was happening on the ground, with Trofim Lysenko's infamous crop-yield experiments and theory of "vernalization," for example, should be accepted by scientists because it was in the interests of Soviet agriculture, rather than critically examined for scientific soundness.[15] Even science was not immune to the ideological manipulations and distortions required by Stalin as political considerations came to trump scientific conclusions.

Prior to the Stalinist counterrevolution, the Soviet Union in fact pioneered ecological theory and practice. The government was the first in the world to listen to its scientific and ecological researchers and implement a policy of setting aside large tracts of land, *zapovedniki* (nature reserves), that were completely inviolable to any form of human intervention other than scientific research. There was to be no logging, animal hunting, or crop growing—even tourism was banned.

These areas, linked together in a nationwide network were to serve as *etalony*—baseline standards similar to the surrounding region that could be used to track how virgin nature existed in order to better understand how industrialized society was changing natural habitats in nonprotected areas. Russian ecologists similarly pioneered the idea that despoiled land could be rejuvenated through rational use and through the development of a regional plan on the basis of the study of etalony. It was Russian scientists who were among the first to consider the idea of plant distribution as communities (phytosociology) and initiated the concept of ecological energetics (trophic dynamics).

Two days after the October Revolution, the crucial decree "On Land" was passed, abolishing the ability of anyone to privately own "alienated" land. Because all land, forests, waterways, and natural resources were now publically owned, a rational plan for their sustainable use and renewal could be put in to action. Despite this, the journal *Lesa respubliki* (Forests of the Republic) reported that forests were being degraded by illegal logging and hunting and something needed to be done. In May 1918, in a meeting chaired by Lenin, the government responded by passing the decree "On Forests," which created a Central Administration of Forests of the Republic to design a plan for reforestation and sustained yield. Forests were to be divided into an exploitable sector and a protected one. The purpose of the protected part was specifically to engage with issues of the control of erosion, the protection of watersheds, and the "preservation of monuments of nature." Another law, the Forest Code, was adopted into law in 1923 which further enhanced the protected status of forests.[16]

By January 1919, from a Soviet perspective, the civil war had reached its nadir. The continued existence of the worker's and peasants' government was in serious doubt. Bolshevik-controlled areas had been severely curtailed and the Red Army pushed back almost to the gates of Petrograd. The government was hanging by a thread as White armies crossed the Urals and seemed headed for the desperately beating heart of Soviet power. U.S., British, French, and Japanese troops occupied and controlled key Russian ports, and much of the fertile Ukraine and the south were under the control of the Germans. Despite the almost hopelessly dire situation, Lenin took time out to personally meet with the well-known agronomist, N. N. Podiapolsky, to hear about proposals for the first zapovednik. As Podiapolsky recounts:

> Having asked me some questions about the military and political situation in the Astrakhan region, Vladimir Ilyich expressed his approval of all of our initiatives and in particular the one concerning the project for the zapovednik. He stated that the cause of conservation was important not only for the Asktrakhan region, but for the whole republic as well, and that he considered it an urgent priority.

Lenin proposed that Podialpolsky immediately draft national legislation on conservation for consideration. After submitting the legislation, Podiapolsky received the examined draft back from Lenin the very same day!

Once land was retaken by the Red Army, this decree, "On the Protection of Monuments of Nature, Gardens, and Parks" could eventually be signed in to law by Lenin in September of 1921. In May 1919 Lenin approved passage of the decree "On Hunting Seasons and the Right to Possess Hunting Weapons," which prohibited hunting of endangered moose and wild goats and initiated closed seasons for hunting other animals in order to ensure sustainable yield.

In 1924, the All-Russian Society for Conservation (VOOP) was created through the Conservation Department of the Commissariat of Education to help build a mass social base for conservation and to incorporate conservation and the study of nature into school curricula. VOOP published its own journal, *Okhrana prirody* (Conservation), which carried vigorous debates inside its pages on critical academic issues in ecology, the history of ecological research in Russia, news from national parks in other countries, including translations of Theodore Roosevelt's thoughts on Yellowstone, articles for and about children, special profiles on various endangered species, and articles for biological pest control and against monocultures. The journal even discussed the positive role shamans had historically played in ensuring sustainable yields of game in Siberian culture. Ecology as a separate field of academic study began to appear in Russian university curricula by 1924.

All this stood as law; academic debate and research flourished and popular organizations sought to further the rational use and study of nature with governmental support, even as the most far-reaching goals were constrained by the need to feed the people and earn foreign currency through fur and timber sales. These advances were circumvented, curtailed, and ultimately reversed by the requirements of Stalin's First Five-Year Plan, when unrestrained productivism was the order of the day and animals and plants were reclassified. Species, in a mirror image of the short-termism inherent to capitalism, were now to be classified either as "useful" to the most immediate needs of "socialist construction" or "harmful"—and therefore penciled in for extermination.

The early years of Soviet rule could not be more different from the usual picture of total disregard for the environment, leading to horrific pollution and environmental crimes. The entirety of Soviet ecological misrule is presented as a continuum from the modernizing despot Lenin all the way through to Chernobyl in a smooth unbroken line. In fact, the Soviet Union under Lenin and through the 1920s was characterized by a stunning series of pioneering ecological policies, education, research, and theorizing. Compare the enlightened policies sketched above with Maxim Gorky's paean to the concept of the total "transformation of nature" inaugurated once Stalin had consolidated his rule through repeated purges in the 1930s:

> Stalin holds a pencil. Before him lies a map of the region. Deserted shores. Remote villages. Virgin soil, covered with boulders. Primeval forests. Too much forest as a matter of fact; it covers the best soil. And swamps. The swamps are always crawling about, making life dull and slovenly. Tillage must be increased. The swamps must be drained...The Karelian Republic wants to enter the stage of classless society as a republic of factories and mills. And the Karelian Republic will enter classless society by changing its own nature.[17]

The ascension of Stalin, as in all other areas of postrevolutionary life, represents a clearly delineated rupture with the pioneering ecological policies and environmental research of the 1920s. Under Stalin, who had little use for any scientific theory if it didn't ideologically justify party rule or enhance economic competitiveness with the West, meant that anyone charged with carrying out "science for science's sake" automatically became a potential "wrecker"—the charge that precipitated trial, the gulag, execution, or frequently all three. The ecology movement, along with independent scientists, had to be broken and entire governmental departments purged, reordered, renamed, or simply abolished. To examine just the Ukraine, formerly a center of ecological research, every single voluntary scientific or professional society concerned with conservation or nature protection was terminated in the 1930s. Many were accused of cooperating with "counterrevolutionary nationalist groups," due to their continued opposition to economic issues taking primacy over those of conservation. This amounted to a certain death sentence; more than a third of the Ukrainian Committee for the Preservation of Monuments of Nature were executed.

A British socialist, A. G. Tansley, who went on to become the first president of the British Ecological Society and in the 1930s coined the term "ecosystem," a concept central to our modern understanding of ecosystems ecology, now an academic research field of its own. Tansley wanted to explain how his materialist conception of natural communities had become fused with all physical and chemical factors such as soil and climate and so came up with the term "ecosystem" to speak effectively of this dynamic equilibrium and essential unity. As he explained:

> It is the systems so formed which, from the point of view of the ecologist, are the basic units of nature on the face of the earth. Our natural human prejudices force us to consider the organisms as the most important parts of these systems, but certainly inorganic "factors" are also parts—there could be no systems without them, and there is constant interchange of the most various kinds within each system, not only between the organisms but between the organic and the inorganic. These ecosystems, as we may call them, are the most various kinds and sizes. They form one category of the multitudinous physical systems of the universe, which range from the universe as a whole down to the atom.[18]

And, in an image of how Marxist dialectics can help us understand the constant motion and interconnectivity of life processes, Tansley goes on to explain how "the systems we isolate mentally are not only included as parts of larger ones, but they also overlap, interlock, and interact with one another."[19]

The reason I bring up these examples is to illustrate that a central preoccupation of socialists, beginning with Marx and Engels, but including scientists and leading Bolsheviks from the 1920s among others, has been our relationship to the environment. Socialists have made serious and fundamental contributions to ecological or "green" thought and practice. In addition, socialists were thinking along these lines and were able to make these contributions precisely *because* they were socialists. Marxism provides by far the best framework for understanding the concept of sustainability.

This is in contrast with much of green thought that for far too long has neglected the issue of class and the nature of the economic system. Many people truly concerned with environmental degradation and global warming view sustainability through the lens of individual responsibility—working within the system to reduce one's personal carbon footprint, biking to work, not eating meat, making sure to recycle or not drinking bottled water. There is a focus on individual lifestyle changes in order to show in practice what an alternative, more sustainable life would look like and prefigure a sustainable world, one person at a time.

I am all for making those personal choices if you can, but it shouldn't be confused with a political strategy that will actually bring about the change everyone wants to see. If we subscribe to lifestyle politics we then see ourselves exactly as corporate and political elites want us to see ourselves—as consumers. This is not where our power lies. It allows capitalism to go on as before, with more and more environmental damage and pollution, while we are lulled into believing we're actually doing something—recycling is the classic case. If we view ourselves primarily as consumers, they will figure out a way to sell us crap. As they have successfully done with all of the new "green" merchandise, organic and "carbon-neutral" products, hybrid vehicles, and so on, which are doing nothing to challenge the competition-driven growth imperative hard-wired into a system based on profit as its prime objective.

Marx was concerned with taking a long-term view of the earth over a century before the UN discovered a problem. In the third volume of *Capital* he essentially defines sustainability thus:

> From the standpoint of a higher socio-economic formation, the private property of particular individuals in the earth will appear just as absurd as the private property of one man in other men. Even an entire society, a nation, or all simultaneously existing societies taken together, are not owners of the earth, they are simply its possessors, its beneficiaries, and have to bequeath it in an improved state to succeeding generations, as boni patres familias [good heads of household].[20]

Nature and society cannot be seen as diametrically opposed but should co-develop with one another as natural history and human history become different aspects of the same thing. For Marx it was necessary to heal the "metabolic rift," to use his term, created between humanity and nature by capitalism.

Given this mode of ecological thought, which, as I have argued, was deeply embedded within Marxism from the very beginning, what would it actually take to live sustainably on planet earth with today's level of technology and almost seven billion people?

CHAPTER SEVEN

From Capitalist Crisis to Socialist Sustainability

> *"This Commission believes that people can build a future that is more prosperous, more just, and more secure. Our report,* Our Common Future, *is not a prediction of ever increasing environmental decay, poverty, and hardship in an ever more polluted world among ever decreasing resources. We see instead the possibility for a new era of economic growth, one that must be based on policies that sustain and expand the environmental resource base."*
>
> —excerpt from *Our Common Future*: Report of the World Commission on Environment and Development, 1987[1]

> *"'Sustainable" means to create and maintain conditions, under which humans and nature can exist in productive harmony, that permit fulfilling the social, economic, and other requirements of present and future generations of Americans."*
>
> —definition of "sustainable," Executive Order 13423, Strengthening Federal Environmental, Energy, and Transportation Management, George W. Bush, January 2, 2007[2]

> *"Being socially responsible as a corporation means that we care about the environment around us—and that*

> *our actions reflect a commitment to invest in a sustain-*
> *able future."*
> —Taking Care of Our Environment, Cargill, Inc.[3]

Arguably, there is no word more in vogue today than "sustain-able." It has become de rigueur for political and economic fig-ures of every stripe and persuasion to pepper their public pronouncements with the word. No speech on the goals of busi-ness and government is complete without paying homage to the concept of "sustainability." Indeed, the word has so wrig-gled free of any real meaning that an entire book has been writ-ten on the hijacking of "sustainability."[4] Everyone wants to be "sustainable" and create a sustainable environment, a sustain-able economy, sustainable agriculture, or live sustainably. Most idiotically, even the U.S. military has its own ambitious "green" and "sustainable energy" blueprints. According to Secretary of the Navy Ray Mabus these include switching half naval and ma-rine energy consumption to renewable and alternate sources by 2020, making half their installations "net zero" energy users by the same year and, by 2016, sailing what Mabus calls "the Great Green Fleet"—nuclear- and hybrid-powered ships and aircraft that run on biofuel.[5]

But what does "sustainable" really mean? Can capitalism be "sustainable"? What is the Marxist attitude to sustainability and would a socialist society be "sustainable"? If so, in broad outline, what would a sustainable socialist society look like?

This chapter and the next will attempt to answer these questions. Capitalist social relations systematically compel certain types of behavior that dictate the way in which "the environment" is viewed and treated. It will be argued that this compulsion results in the capitalist system being fundamentally incapable of developing in a sustainable manner. If this is in fact the case, then there can be no such thing as "green" capitalism or "environmentally friendly" capitalism. In the short term, grassroots socio-ecological movements must build independent struggles for reforms that will slow down the daily degradation of the environment caused by the current economic and social structure. This will both buy time and build confidence for the more profound social change that will ultimately be necessary. As is becoming clearer with each passing scientific report, the only long-term, viable solution to living in harmony with the earth is to overthrow capitalism and replace it with a different socioeconomic system of production and distribution, one that puts people and the planet before profit.

But what should that system be? The attitude of Marxism, primarily evidenced through the writings of Marx and Engels themselves will be scrutinized in order to argue that a socialist society would have the possibility of sustainability denied to a society organized along capitalist lines. No one can predict the future, and there are no guarantees; however, socialism, a democratically controlled workers' global society that produces for use and not for exchange, would have a substantial chance of success toward attaining sustainability. The next chapter will give a brief outline of what a sustainable human interaction with the earth would look like over the short and longer term.

Sustainable Development and Capitalism

In 1983, the United Nations, in recognition of the worsening state of the global environment, established the World Commission on Environment and Development to address the question of "the accelerating deterioration of the human environment and natural resources and the consequences of that deterioration for economic and social development" and acknowledged that it was in the best interests of all countries to move toward something called "sustainable development."

In 1987, the commission published their report, entitled *Our Common Future,* and defined sustainable development as "development that meets the needs of the present without compromising the ability of future generations to meet their own needs." which, as we saw with Marx's quote at the end of the last chapter, is very similar to how he articulated the concept of sustainability.

The UN definition contains within it two key concepts:

- the concept of '**needs**,' in particular the essential needs of the world's poor, to which overriding priority should be given; and second,
- the idea of **limitations** imposed by the state of technology and social organization on the environment's ability to meet present and future needs.[6]

Over twenty years separate the publication of this report and the present where we are: fast approaching an array of environmental tipping points while the number of malnourished and chronically poor in the world remain at entirely unacceptable levels. It therefore seems only fair to ask why so little progress has occurred; indeed, on many fronts, colossal regression.

According to the UN's definition of sustainable development, sustainability requires a view of the earth and humans in three critical areas—economics, society, and the environment.[7] These should be viewed as a single system of interactions over space and time, which gives us an indication as to why it's been such a spectacular failure. It is utterly impossible for the system of social relations characterized as capitalism to view the earth *and* humanity as a single system, particularly if this system is meant to be viewed regionally, globally, and over time. On the other hand, this kind of holism and interactive, process-driven approach is precisely the view taken by Marxism, a stance that gives socialism a uniquely and fundamentally ecological outlook.

Three of capitalism's basic features make it anti-ecological: an imperative for constant expansion of the economy as a whole; the drive for profit in each economic unit; and a built-in focus on the short term.

Marx captured capitalism's general drive for expansion with his classic definition of the root purpose of the system—the "self-expansion" of capital, symbolized as $M–C–M'$. The process begins with money, M, which is turned into a commodity C, to be sold on the market for M', where M' is more money than the original M. The cycle then repeats on an enlarged basis with a larger starting pot of capital, M'. Thus capitalism entirely abstracts the exchange value of a commodity from its use value. Put another way, the only thing that matters is whether a commodity can be sold for more money than was used to manufacture it, not whether it's actually useful. Furthermore, Marx's schema captures the relentlessly expansive drive for exchange value (money-price), otherwise known as the drive for profit. To quote Burkett from *Marx and Nature*: "[W]hile a viable co-evolution of society and nature requires quantitative limits on human production, the value form of wealth by definition imbues production with an expansive character. As a result, capitalist societies are on an unsustainable "treadmill of production" featuring ever greater quantities of material and energy throughput."[8]

We see today, if the economy is not expanding by at least 2 percent per year—or worse, if it is contracting—millions of people are thrown out of work and cast into poverty and homelessness. Government tax revenue falls and budgets must all be slashed, with the notable exception of defense and government subsidies and tax breaks and loopholes to corporations. It doesn't matter if the goods that workers have made are required—food, for example—it only matters if those goods can be sold at a profit.

The capitalist devotion to profit, the second and inescapable internal contradiction that drives the first, is the ultimate god of the "free market" system. Daily and hourly sacrifices of the two ingredients necessary to make profit—workers' labor power and nature's resources—must be continually made upon the altar of capitalism. Accumulation, to use Marx's words, is for the sake of accumulation. In the infamous words of Bethlehem Steel CEO Donald Trautlein, "We are not in the business of making steel. We are in the business of making money."[9] This is indeed a true statement of the compulsion that impels capitalism forward; apparently CEO Trautlein was familiar with Marx's writings on this subject.

Capitalism regards nature as a free source of raw materials—a "gift" to use mainstream economics language. Commenting on the views of mainstream economists in 1997 Stanford biologist and climate scientist Stephen Schneider summed up their attitude: *Most conventional economists… thought that even this gargantuan climate change—equivalent to the scale of the change from the ice age to an interglacial epoch in a hundred years, rather than thousands of years—*

would have only a few percent impact on the world economy. In essence, they accept the paradigm that society is almost independent of nature."[10] Now, more than ten years later, given how much *worse* we know the situation to be, and yet still with no serious remedial action being taken, it is difficult to see how this outlook has changed.

The essentially fantastical and irrational notion of independence from nature reached its apogee during the 1990s, when the idea of the "weightless economy" emerged; of how the economy had "decoupled," or "dematerialized" from energy and material inputs by the spread of technology. Technological innovations, even with a growing economy, would automatically give human society a lighter, almost imperceptible, ecological footprint on the earth. Decoupling, as defined by the OECD, "refers to breaking the link between 'environmental bads' and 'economic goods'" and occurs when "the growth rate of an environmental pressure is less than that of its economic driving force (e.g., GDP) over a given period."[11] Yet there is much evidence pointing toward a direct correlation between GDP growth and environmental damage under capitalism and so makes the OECD concept of "decoupling" phantasmagorical. A fixation on GDP growth represents another point where capitalism's success is measured in exchange value, in contrast to, and at the expense of, use value.

Mainstream economists, as bulwarks of the prevailing order, have never been ones for letting reality get in the way of their prognostications. "Decoupling," the idea that we are essentially independent of nature, is the logic behind the idea of "adaptation" to climate change. That there will always be a technological silver bullet engineered by the ingenuity of free market capitalism. There is an ever-growing chorus explaining how we can "cope with" truly gigantic changes to world climate where life will go on more or less as before with only a few percent decline in economic growth. Many high-profile economic commentators, such as internationally renowned Yale economist William Nordhaus and media darling Bjorn Lomborg, author of *The Skeptical Environmentalist*, are adamant that it would be the height of folly to impose strict restrictions on the economy to ameliorate climate change. They insist that making serious inroads and radical changes to the economic direction of society in order to avert what most physical scientists regard as catastrophic climate change would end up costing more than more modest alterations.[12]

Nature, being something separate from and external to us, is a free lunch for capitalism. When in its unregulated, laissez-faire form, it's also a free dumping ground for the increasingly toxic and ever-growing volume of waste products. Humans are ground up and made into extensions of the machine, while the earth is similarly despoiled and degraded in order to maximize profits. The inbuilt and relentless drive to make profit at all costs leads to the cast-iron requirement for larger and larger throughputs of raw materials and energy.

Because this is the imperative of capitalist accumulation it dictates its behavior toward nature, and explains why purely technological solutions—the ones favored by the system—will never work. In aggregate, efficiency gains or improvements in technology under capitalism simply lead to increases in scale, more accumulation and economic growth, which typically outweigh any of the original efficiency gains. Making more fuel-efficient cars for example is a worthy goal and, to the extent we even want cars made, we should force automakers to make them—but the efficiency gains in engine technology over the last three decades have just led to larger vehicles, more vehicles, and increased driving. This effect was analyzed a long time ago. It is something known as Jevons paradox after William Stanley Jevons, the British economist who analyzed and wrote about efficiency gains in the coal industry in 1864.[13]

Any company that makes efficiency gains does so in order to cut production costs, undercut rivals, and thereby increase market share; an activity that leads to increased investment in production as the over riding objective is competition-driven accumulation. Jevons argued that growing scarcity of coal, leading to higher costs, wouldn't lead to a move away from coal. Rather, it would speed up the building of more extraction and refining capacity to take advantage of the increased profits: "It is a confusion of ideas to suppose that the economical use of fuel is equivalent to diminished consumption," he wrote. "The very contrary is the truth."[14] The correlation with oil prices and the oil corporation's investments in enhanced recovery techniques, increased exploration, and an emergent oil and gas shale and tar sands sector is the modern-day example of this phenomenon.

To be clear, this is not an argument against efficiency gains; we do need more efficient technology: the average car engine wastes more than around three quarters of the fuel that's poured into it for example, and a typical coal-burning power station wastes almost two thirds. In addition, in a world where more than 50 percent of all the energy generated is wasted, substantial increases to the amount of research and development money going to socially useful purposes such as energy conservation are absolutely essential. Socio-ecological activists need to fight for a governmental regulatory program focused on efficiency gains in electronic products and heating and cooling of residential, commercial, and industrial buildings, all of which would extensively reduce energy consumption. Furthermore, unlike the time lag involved in constructing new power plants and phasing out old ones, nationally implemented energy conservation targets would have a rapid effect on energy production and consumption. However, because the underlying objective matters, in and of themselves, technology and efficiency gains are not a long-term solution to the environmental crisis. Resource or waste reduction by an individual company, value that would otherwise have appeared in the commodity, takes place within a system of overall net increases in both. It is therefore self-defeating from a long-term sustainability perspective.

As István Mészáros states,

> To say that "science and technology *can* solve all our problems in the long run" is worse than believing in witchcraft; for it tendentiously ignores the devastating social embeddedness of present-day science and technology. In this respect, too, the issue is not *whether* or *not* we use science and technology for solving our problems—for obviously we must—but whether or not we *succeed* in radically *changing* their *direction* which is at present narrowly determined and circumscribed by the self-perpetuating needs of profit maximization.[15]

The requirement for profit-taking gives rise to the third contradiction that makes capitalism unsustainable—its inherent short-termism. The bloody heart of capitalism, competition and the drive for profits, makes economic growth and a short-term outlook imperative and integral components of the system. In an example with clear resonance today, this short-term outlook and lack of foresight derived from the need to make an immediate profit, was analyzed by Marx with respect to the longevity of the worker:

> Capital that has such good reasons for denying the sufferings of the legions of workers that surround it, is in practice moved as much and as little by the sight of the coming degradation and final depopulation of the human race, as by the probable fall of the earth in to the sun. In every stockjobbing swindle everyone knows that some time or other the crash must come, but every one hopes that it may fall on the head of his neighbor, after he himself has caught the shower of gold and placed it in safety. *Après moi le déluge!* is the watchword of every capitalist and every capitalist nation. Hence Capital is reckless of the health or length of life of the labourer, unless under compulsion from society.[16]

But Marx did not limit his concern with the short-termism of capitalism just to the worker, but equally with respect to the longevity of the earth's fertility, which capitalist agricultural practices are incapable of taking into account. Again, the argument made here by Marx was in clear evidence during the recent world food crisis:

> The dependence of the cultivation of particular agricultural products upon fluctuations of market-prices, and the continual changes in this cultivation with these price fluctuations—the whole spirit of capitalist production, which is directed toward the immediate gain of money—are in contradiction to agriculture, which has to minister to the entire range of permanent necessities of life required by the chain of successive generations.[17]

Through their writings and analysis, Marx and Engels demonstrated that capitalism is incompatible with itself internally, due to the diametrically opposed interests of workers and capitalists, and with nature externally because of its view of nature as something separate from us—a free gift. While capitalists do have to pay something to workers to keep us alive and breeding to replenish our stock, as far as they're concerned, nothing has to be paid to the earth.

Marxism, Alienation, and Nature

From a philosophical standpoint, the Marxist concept of alienation is central to understanding why capitalism is unsustainable from a human *and* natural perspective. Marxism views human economy as interwoven with the living ecological relations of society and inseparable from those relations. Yet capitalism splits humans from their evolutionarily developed need to labor to produce what we need to survive and furthermore separates us from the natural world upon which we depend. Thus we are alienated in a double sense—from the products of our labor as we have no control over them and from the earth itself.

It is no coincidence that the first act of privatization at the dawn of capitalism, ushering in the era of generalized commodity production four hundred or so years ago, was the forcible separation of humans from the land. Peasants had to be physically and violently separated from their livelihoods in order to be driven en masse into the "dark satanic mills" of Blake's hellish vision of industrializing England. Capitalism is essentially a parasitic relationship—bosses live off the lifeblood of workers and the raw material of nature. In the process, both humanity and nature are debased, degraded, and denatured. To quote the great abolitionist Frederick Douglass, "They divided each in order to conquer both." While Douglass was referring to capitalist separation of poor whites from enslaved blacks, the same argument reverberates with respect to the earth and humanity.

Because workers have lost control over the products that we make, and the more products we make—i.e., the higher our level of productivity—the greater our loss of control, the more alienated we become from ourselves and nature. An especially popular theme in science-fiction movies is the rise or takeover of the machines coming to control and dominate humans (*Terminator, Matrix,* etc.). Why does this idea and these films have such resonance with us across industrialized cultures? Why can this be seen as a very real fear? Because under capitalism workers are controlled by the machines in a very real way; our day-to-day existence is regulated by the speed of the machines around us. They come to subconsciously seem to us, as Marx argued, an *alien power*, towering over us. The more advanced the machinery, or so-called labor-saving devices, the harder we have to work and the more dominated by them we become.

Just one example will suffice though I am confident anyone living under capitalism can relate hundreds of others. It encompasses both production and consumption. A *Wall Street Journal* article reported in 2000:

> "HimayItakeyourorderplease?" says the drive-through-greeter at Wendy's Old Fashioned Hamburgers. This greeting takes only 1 second—a triumphant two seconds faster than is suggested in Wendy's guidelines—and the speed of it was clocked by a high-tech timer installed this January. In just three months, the timer—which measures nearly every aspect of drive-through performance—helped knock eight seconds off the average take-out delivery time at this restaurant. But manager Ryan Tomney wants more. "Every second," he says, "is business lost."[18]

And when they talk about production being driven by the "desires of consumers," did we all suddenly develop an inbuilt desire to gobble down filth for nutrition as fast as humanly possible—eating while running for the subway or off our laps in the car? I've been on a lot of demonstrations in my time, but I've never experienced one where the chanting was "Feed us crap—only do it faster!" Only a for-profit system, with all its attendant cultural and health degradations, could invent "fast food," or "road rage" for that matter. There was no fast food in Marx's time but I think we can all relate to and recognize the following poetic passage from Marx, on the contradictions engendered by capitalism as even more symptomatic of our time than it was of his:

> In our days, everything seems pregnant with its contrary. Machinery, gifted with the wonderful power of shortening and fructifying human labour, we behold starving and overworking it. The new-fangled sources of wealth, by some strange weird spell, are turned into sources of want. The victories of art seem bought by the loss of character. At the same pace that man masters nature, man seems to become enslaved to other men or to his own infamy…This antagonism between modern industry and science on the one hand, modern misery and dissolution on the other hand; this antagonism between the productive powers and the social relations of our epoch is a fact, palpable, overwhelming, and not to be controverted.[19]

Why spend so much space discussing our relationship to machines and technology when discussing sustainability? Whether machines control workers, as under capitalism, or workers control machines, as under socialism, is a critically important point as it relates to sustainability because the tools and machinery we use are extensions of our physical and mental abilities to manipulate, control, and investigate nature. These tools are the product of thousands of years of human development and are what allow us to understand nature on deeper and deeper levels, right down to the molecular and subatomic. Machinery is, or should be viewed as, the physical materialization of the work carried out by our brains and hands. Viewed from this perspective, it is nature's way of discovering and connecting itself to itself because we are a part of nature.

Technology is not value free or without its own purpose. Its role is determined by the socioeconomic conditions within which it was manufactured. This is why, apart from the Jevons paradox mentioned earlier, technological solutions on their own are not real solutions. However, if machinery and technology were reconstructed on the basis of efficient use of resources, longevity, labor-saving potential, and minimization of waste products, then all of humanity could be freed—freed to fulfill the full range of human interests and pursuits. These would include an exploration and understanding of our fundamental connection to the earth as material beings—rather than enslaved to the rhythm and relentless pace of the faxes, photocopiers, automated machine tools, answering machines, emails, agricultural machinery, computers, drive-ins, and so on.

On this basis, as machines increase in efficiency, take over human functions, and save human labor for more creative forms of work, they would transform humanity's former relation of life-and-death struggle *against* nature into a new relation; one of free time, of leisure, and the opportunity for the fulfillment of distinctively human needs. For the first time in human history, we could begin to relate to external non-human nature in noncompetitive ways and not simply as a utilitarian need—what can we get from nature, how can we use it, what is it good for, how can we subdue and dominate it?

While Marxism has been erroneously associated with notions of the domination of nature due to the later Stalinist distortions of the USSR and associated state-capitalist countries of the Eastern Bloc, this idea has in fact been central to capitalism from the birth of the scientific revolution that occurred simultaneously with the rise of the new economic order. Capitalists need to understand how the world works in order to profit from it, therefore a turn away from religious obscurantism in the late sixteenth and early seventeenth centuries and toward an empirically based mechanical materialism was necessary. Francis Bacon, one of the most cogent and celebrated of the original evangelists of the new scientifically based economic order was clear how nature should be viewed. "I am come in very truth," Bacon declared, "leading to you nature with all her children to bind her to your service and make her your slave."

It is no coincidence that nature, in line with a worldview that took the subordination of women for granted, is viewed as a female to be conquered and subdued. The sexual imagery of male dominance, through torturing the secrets out of a reticent and secretive Mother Nature, is quite explicit in the writings of Bacon, who advised that "Nature must be taken by the forelock," to use his words, "for the further disclosing of the secrets of nature…a man [ought not] make scruple of entering and penetrating into these holes and corners, when the inquisition of truth is his whole object."[20] While today the language of scientific endeavor is not as explicitly violent and misogynistic, the concept of "revealing the secrets of nature" remains the prevailing narrative.

More broadly, as distinct from previous modes of production, Marx relates how capitalism, by its unremitting expansion, its constant uprooting of previously settled relations and the perpetual generation of new needs, only sees in nature its utility toward making profit:

> For the first time, nature becomes purely an object for humankind, purely a matter of utility; ceases to be recognized as a power for itself; and the theoretical discovery of its autonomous laws appears merely as a ruse so as to subjugate it under human needs, whether as an object of consumption or as means of production. In accord with this tendency, capital drives beyond national barriers and prejudices as much as beyond nature worship, as well as all traditional, confined, complacent, encrusted satisfactions of present needs, and reproductions of old ways of life. It is destructive towards all of this, and constantly revolutionizes it, tearing down all the barriers which hem in the development of forces of production, the expansion of needs, the all-sided development of production, and the exploitation and exchange of natural and mental forces.[21]

In sharp contrast, Marx and Engels viewed nature as "a power for itself" and a part of us as we are a part of it, giving an interdependent conception of how the natural world should be viewed and hence treated. On the essential physical and psychological intertwining of nature and humanity, Marx writes:

> The life of the species, both in man and animals, consists physically in the fact that man (like the animal) lives on inorganic nature...Just as plants, animals, stones, air, light, etc. constitute theoretically a part of human consciousness, partly as objects of natural science, partly as objects of art— his spiritual inorganic nature, spiritual nourishment which he must first prepare to make palatable and digestible—so

also in the realm of practice they constitute a part of human life and human activity. Physically man lives only on these products of nature, whether they appear in the form of food, heating, clothes, a dwelling etc. The universality of man appears in practice precisely in the universality which makes all nature his inorganic body—both in as much as nature is (1) his direct means of life, and (2) the material, the object, and the instrument of his life activity...That man's physical and spiritual life is linked to nature means simply that nature is linked to itself, for man is a part of nature.[22]

In this view, "the environment" is no longer a passive, independent object to be plundered, or in the words of Engels, to be made "an object of huckstering,"[23] but plays a role in making us what we are. Given this philosophical perspective, it is impossible to speak of any living thing, humans and their activity included, as anything but profoundly entangled within each other, in a constant process of mutual interaction, transformation, and co-evolution.

Under this paradigm, humans would be able to begin to fulfill our spiritual needs, cultivating non-utilitarian knowledge of the universe that we are inextricably immersed in for beauty, recreation, and for the observation and discovery of plants, animals, and the inorganic world in all its diverse forms. To paraphrase the distinguished ecological and leftist thinker Barry Commoner, nature is a self-enclosed system of energy exchanges: Everything is connected to everything else, nothing totally disappears, and nothing is a "free lunch."[24]

Capitalist Time Versus Human and Natural Time

The competition-driven, ever-changing, and rapidly evolving requirements of capital accumulation dictate that, as noted in *The Communist Manifesto,* "all that is solid melts into air." There is a glaring contradiction between the accelerated throughput required by capital accumulation and the time required by nature to produce and absorb raw materials, energy and waste. The conflict between capitalist turnover and the replenishment and restoration of natural resources is further evidence of capitalism's inherent non-sustainability.

Industrialized agriculture epitomizes how the laws of capital accumulation transcend the cyclical and time-delineated physical and biochemical laws of climate, land regeneration, and plant and animal growth. Capitalist agriculture cannot wait to abide by the geophysical or biochemical limits set by the temporal rhythms of biochemical cycles and organic processes. There is a constant pressure pushing to speed up everything in the interests of enhanced productivity, the holy grail of every capitalist entity. The result is soil degradation, groundwater contamination, chemical pollution, a burgeoning artificial pesticide, herbicide and fertilizer industry, genetically modified organisms (GMOs), Concentrated Animal Feeding Operations (CAFOs), and the like. The fact that capitalism, by creating this alternative, artificially accelerated time, which leads to the unsustainable decay of natural cycles of reproduction and which ultimately undermines its own existence, is merely evidence of the pathological nature of the capitalist mode of production.

The endless hunt for new ways to make money and the associated pursuit of ever-higher levels of productivity simultaneously leads directly to the degradation of us as humans. The relentless intensification of mass production unleashed by the vast productive forces of twenty-first-century capitalism has led to a general sense of a worsening of the quality of societal development; that society is "heading in the wrong direction" even as more and more consumer goods bombard our senses, clamoring to be bought. This phenomenon is a variant and allied component of the alienation fostered by the quickening of time under capitalism.

Despite the system inventing an entire business sector of pointlessness and waste, namely the advertising industry, primed to convince us all that buying things is the one true path to eternal happiness, people are not unaware of how psychologically impoverished consumer culture is making them. In 1995, the report *Yearning for Balance* was released. It examined how Americans viewed consumption and "the American lifestyle" and reported that, "They believe materialism, greed, and selfishness increasingly dominate American life, crowding out a more meaningful set of values of family, responsibility, and community."[25]

The yawning imbalance between the capitalism-impelled mania to express happiness through external material wealth and possessions and the internal fulfillment of genuine human needs leads to profound psychological conflicts of conscience. The way that capitalism encourages a focus on individual possession of commodities frustrates genuine human needs that are also material but don't fit into the commodity form such as having fulfilling relationships with other people, and leisure time that isn't shaped, packaged, and sold for profit. These things in turn, coupled with the strains of living at such an accelerated pace and out-of-control mode of existence, generate increasing levels of depression and other psychological disorders—which manufactures the need for another highly profitable capitalist enterprise: the massive expansion of the depression drug industry. We are taught that the problem is not with a wildly unsustainable society; rather it resides deep inside our individual brains with some maladjusted chemistry. Alongside artificial scarcity, inequality, and inbuilt obsolescence, modern capitalism must engage in the "manufacture of discontent" in order to generate a consumer culture that convinces us that we continually need more things:

> Prodigious intellectual and creative effort is poured into marketing, driven by the imperative of consumer capitalism. All aspects of human psychology—our fears, our sources of shame, our sexuality, our spiritual yearnings— are a treasure house to be plundered in the search for a commercial edge. Thousands of the most creative individuals in modern society...devote their lives to helping corporations manipulate people into buying more of their brand of margarine or running shoes at the expense of another corporation selling a virtually identical product. This is not just a waste of talent. The work of [marketers] is at best meaningless and at worst a subtle form of cultural brainwashing whose purpose is to sustain a system that leaves people miserable. This fact is widely understood but elicits no condemnation. It is regarded as normal.[26]

A journey by any mode of transportation is simply a time obstacle to be navigated as quickly as possible. A leisurely lunch becomes a luxury, rather than a common social occurrence to be enjoyed among colleagues or friends. Eating is a means to continue working rather than a congenial human ritual to be pleasurably experienced. Even as GDP has risen in the United States, making the country "richer" by capitalist standards, the vast majority of people's quality of life, as measured by time spent working, the speed and interest of that work, availability of free time, vacations, and so on has declined, while psychological problems and chronic mental health issues have escalated. The Faustian bargain we are forced into: that more work leads to more money which leads to greater "purchasing power" for consumer goods and so enhanced happiness, is increasingly shown to be an empty shell game. Capitalist self-justification has fought tooth and nail to convince us that human well-being can be effectively and accurately measured solely by income; the greater one's income, the greater one's personal happiness. It has stripped meaningful relationships down until "no other nexus between man and man other than naked self-interest, than callous 'cash payment'" exists.[27] As Marx remarked on this process of human degradation produced by capitalism's insatiable appetite for growth:

> In its blind unrestrainable passion, its werewolf hunger for surplus-labour, capital oversteps not only the moral, but even the merely physical maximum bounds of the working-day. It usurps the time for growth, development, and healthy maintenance of the body. It steals the time required for the consumption of fresh air and sunlight. It higgles over a meal-time, incorporating it where possible with the process of production itself, so that food is supplied to the labourer as to a mere means of production, as coal is supplied to the boiler, grease and oil to the machinery. It reduces the sound sleep needed for the restoration, reparation, refreshment of the bodily powers to just so many hours of torpor as the revival of an organism, absolutely exhausted, renders essential. It is not the normal maintenance of the labour-power which is to determine the limits of the working-day; it is the greatest possible daily expenditure of labour-power, no matter how diseased, compulsory and painful it may be, which is to determine the limits of the labourers' period of repose. Capital cares nothing for the length of labour-power. All that concerns it is simply and solely the maximum of labour-power that can be rendered fluent in a working-day. It attains this end by shortening the extent of the labourer's life,

as a greedy farmer snatches increased produce from the soil by robbing it of its fertility.[28]

A rational regulation of the workday is an ideological contradiction to the principles of "free market" capitalist competition and the oft-expressed need for labor-market "flexibility." Without external limits placed by society on how long workers can work, capital would work them to death; a fact well testified to by history. Wherever the power of capital is actively limited in this sphere, in restrictions to the hours worked in a day or the requirement to pay overtime, it is done by state regulation. The connection to the rational regulation of non-human nature is therefore clear: only state regulation, under pressure from labor and social movements, can compel capital to treat nature with any level of foresight and sustainability. Capital requires humans and nature only as conditions of monetary accumulation, nothing more. Therefore, only explicit social regulation can prevent the overexploitation of both the worker and the earth. This shows how there is a paradox about productivity and leisure time that runs parallel to Jevons paradox about efficiency and resource use. In both cases the efficiencies that capitalism achieves in production get channeled into more production. Only in a society that isn't driven by the profit motive could efficiency gains consistently be used to leisure time and conserve resources.

Capitalism has viscerally corrupted the normal passage of time. Long-held customs and cultural norms must be swept aside in order to accommodate the gushing flood of new consumer goods, "updated" and "all new" models that must be sold to keep the system ticking over. This spawns the requirement to generate new individual and societal "needs" that somehow we never manage to fulfill, a feeling that gets expressed in the oft-heard phrase "how did we ever survive before..."

If an object is to become a commodity, its exchange value—the price it generates on the market—must result in a profitable sale. This fact—not how useful the object is—is what ultimately determines whether it will be produced and in what quantity. Because exchange value dominates use value, and because capitalism is ruthlessly expansive, all manner of useless and wasteful things are produced in an ever-expanding sphere of utter pointlessness alongside things that we do actually need but can't afford to buy. Colossal amounts of overproduction in all spheres, useful or not, occur under capitalism because of a lack of planning and workers being unable to afford the goods produced. A direct consequence of the system that enforces ever-increasing productivity on workers "frees" them up to make even more things. This enlarged social product, if it is not to bring the system to a grinding halt, must be sold and sold profitably. Hence the requirement, alongside the development of new production techniques, for the continual artificial stimulation of new "needs"; as Marx argued:

> For capital and labor which have been set free, a new, qualitatively different branch of production must be created, which satisfies and brings forth a new need...Hence exploration of all nature in order to discover new, useful qualities in things; universal exchange of the products of all alien climates and lands; new (artificial) preparation of natural objects, by which they are given new use values. The exploration of the earth in all directions, to discover new things of use, as well as new useful quantities of the old...The development of a constantly expanding and more comprehensive system of different kinds of labor, different kinds of production, to which a constantly expanding and constantly enriched system of needs corresponds.[29]

CHAPTER EIGHT

What Would a Sustainable Society Look Like?

"Men make their own history, but they do not make it as they please; they do not make it under self-selected circumstances, but under circumstances existing already, given and transmitted from the past. The tradition of all dead generations weighs like a nightmare on the brains of the living."

—Karl Marx

He was first and foremost a materialist. Above is one of Marx's most famous aphorisms. In his time, one of the biggest ecological problems was the depletion of the soil from the intensification of agricultural practices. Before the manufacture of artificial fertilizer, Britain had already pillaged the Napoleonic battlefields of Europe for the gruesome undertaking of digging up human bones to fertilize the fields of England. Naval expeditions were sent to scour the earth for more sources of soil nutrients from bird guano. Marx talked of how capitalism robbed both the worker—in this case, even the dead worker—and the soil, which were equally in his words "the original sources of all wealth."[1]

But Marx and Engels were mostly preoccupied with the

analysis of capitalism in order to overthrow it and replace it with workers' democracy. They did not simultaneously have to worry about impending planetary ecocide as we do. This is one reason why we cannot backdate global environmental concerns onto their shoulders. Despite this, as shown in the previous chapter, Marx and Engels illustrated a genuine concern for ecological degradation based on their analysis of the short-term profit motive at the heart of capitalist industry and agriculture. But it's not just their critique of capitalism and its relationship to the environment that is pertinent. Their ecological insights form a useful basis for understanding our interrelation with the environment in a positive sense.

Based on where we are now, however, even if the revolution were to occur tomorrow, capitalist ecological crimes are vast. We may well be too late to prevent or reverse all of them. According to a UN-commissioned report due out in full in late 2010, the combined environmental despoliation resulting from CO_2 and other greenhouse gas emissions, water and air pollution by the three thousand largest public companies accounts for one third of their profits. From these unaccounted-for costs, the 3,000 corporations make over $2.2 trillion per year.[2]

Because of these technological and historically determined limits on what we can do, and because I don't want to engage in grand utopian schemes for what exactly will be done after private property in the earth is abolished, I will sketch only in outline what I regard to be some of the most important aspects of what a sustainable society might look like. More fundamentally, changes need to be made as part of a fully democratic process carried out by the people who will be affected by the decisions taken, not by some preplanned design into which they had no input.

The proposals that follow are all eminently feasible with social relations based on cooperation whose objective is human and natural sustainability through the co-development of nature and human society. None of them will be implemented under capitalism except in an ad hoc, piecemeal manner—most likely too little, too late to avoid setting off a chain of environmental tipping points that will quickly cascade out of our control and result in calamitous climate change along with a host of other negative impacts.

Every single facet of industrial life—energy production most urgently, but also transportation, housing, trade, agriculture, manufacture of commodities, and waste production and treatment—all require gigantic systemic change and complete structural reorganization. It will be nothing short of totally remodeling the world on a social, political, technological, cultural, and infrastructural level. As pointed out earlier, we cannot make these changes as individuals. The reconstruction of agriculture along sustainable lines, along with the expansion of alternative energy-harnessing technologies is a social project. These are the kinds of changes that need to occur to actually make a difference on the required socioecological level.

Some of the proposed changes could be carried out in a relatively short period of time. For example, over the next twenty to thirty years there is no technological barrier preventing us from moving to an almost totally carbon-free world energy supply, particularly with regard to electricity production. Some changes to agricultural practices, transportation, urban planning, and distribution of human settlements would take more detailed planning, design, thought and a longer time period before fully implementing, but large and significant incremental shifts could happen immediately after a social revolution and take us toward long-term sustainability.

In terms of energy production, we need to quickly switch our sources of energy away from fossil fuels and immediately concentrate on ways to bring down levels of CO_2 already in the atmosphere by a massive internationally coordinated reforestation program. As soon as the words "internationally coordinated" appear in print, it should be obvious an immediate problem jumps off the page. Achieving real international cooperation on profit-related issues under this social system is just not possible; capitalist nation-states would sooner go to war over a disputed oilfield than come up with a joint international plan for planting trees. When reforestation does make it onto the agenda, it is often not as real forests but tree plantations. Reforestation cannot mean simply planting high growth rate monocultures with limited biodiversity just to chop them down to turn into agro-fuels.

Sustainable energy generation will require a mix of solar, wind, wave and geothermal, sources. As stated earlier, the energy coming from the sun each day is more than 15,000 times greater than humans consume—four orders of magnitude larger—meaning that we only need to harness a fraction of 1 percent in order to satisfy our energy needs. The EU has calculated that covering just .3 percent of the desert area of the Sahara with solar panels could supply the entire electricity needs of Europe.[3] Furthermore, waste heat could potentially be used to desalinate saltwater and the shade underneath the mirrors or PV cells used to potentially grow crops. Storing energy as compressed air in underground caverns, hot salt in insulated containers, pumped storage, or geothermal power, a continuous supply of base-load electricity would be possible without resorting to nuclear power.

Fluctuations in solar and wind can be accounted for by geographical distribution of wind farms and solar arrays. A new network of high-voltage DC power lines would be required to minimize transportation losses and make transcontinental and regionwide distribution networks possible. There are concerns about how much water would be needed to keep solar arrays clean, especially when located in dry regions, and this needs to be examined. However, fossil fuel and nuclear plants all require huge quantities of water for the generation of steam and cooling, so closing these down would significantly reduce overall water use, among many other benefits. An additional benefit of photovoltaic and wind systems is that they generate electricity directly, unlike conventional power plants that emit large quantities of waste heat that contribute to global warming.

For transportation, the switch to low-carbon alternatives, particularly electric trains, light rail, and trams would need to be carried out in conjunction with changes to urban planning and human distribution on the planet to reverse a situation where we are more and more permanently bifurcated between town and country, urban and rural communities.

Private cars are incredibly wasteful and use three-quarters of the gasoline poured into them simply heating the car and the surrounding environment. Car traffic, often with a single occupant per vehicle, is a large component of the heat island effect in cities, not to mention air and noise pollution and accidents. Radically reducing world car production from its current seventy million/year figure would lead to huge reductions in the need for steel, concrete, and asphalt, all industries with major greenhouse gas emissions and water requirements. At optimum conditions (i.e., when full) high-speed trains are twenty-seven times more energy efficient than a car, a diesel-powered bus or a trolleybus are around thirteen times more efficient, and underground trains at peak times are eighteen times better than cars.[4]

Certainly, if there is no profit incentive, then we can eliminate pointless air travel for business trips, which are a large percentage of all short-haul flights. Indeed the majority of intra-continental flights can be made much more efficiently by electric train, using electricity generated from renewable sources. We can make beautiful and super-efficient trains, and for shorter journeys have clean, efficient, reliable buses, light rail, underground and tram systems. For very short journeys there will be bikes and electric cars. All these measures around energy and transportation would radically improve air quality so that we can actually breathe clean air and make large cuts in the incidence of all kinds of respiratory ailments, which are becoming ever more prevalent as we transmogrify the atmosphere into a toxic soup of life-threatening chemicals.

Town and city planning would have to be examined to minimize commute times to get to workplaces on subways, trams, and light rail. Indeed, there would need much examination of how to better connect urban population centers with crop growing and animal husbandry. How can we better integrate farm animals, crop land, and humans to maximize the use of natural fertilizers and biological forms of pest control while ensuring that all humans are better connected to the land?

With energy, resource, waste, and toxic materials minimization and human comfort as primary objectives rather than minimizing economic costs as the bottom line, buildings can be retrofitted and beautiful new ones built. We need to take advantage of architectural design features for energy minimization and examine established techniques for limiting the need for external heating and cooling systems.

Utterly pointless industries producing useless things, advertising, marketing, and much of the packaging industry, along with the military, will be abolished. This will lead to huge energy and waste savings, not to mention reductions in all kinds of other social negatives. A lot of land previously off limits for military war games and weapons testing will be regained as wilderness or agricultural land. We can examine the practices of the Bolshevik ecologists as a starting point, along with all the more recent research, to rejuvenate over-grazed and otherwise degraded land to increase the carbon and nutrient content of soils.

No product will be made without its meeting the highest standards of use value—the questions will no longer be how quickly can it be made, at the lowest possible cost, and how quickly we can get it to wear out before someone has to buy a new one. Instead a whole set of new questions will be asked: what need does it serve, how little energy can it be made with, are the materials adapted to its purpose, how can it be made to last as long as possible, how much waste is produced in its manufacture and how we can best deal with this.

Recycling is pushed *not* because it's the most effective solution to the mountains of waste—indeed quite the opposite—it *justifies* waste as okay as long as we put it in the correct receptacle. One of the least likely phrases you'll ever hear from a capitalist is "please consume less." The problem of the generation of vast quantities of unnecessary industrial and commercial waste is shifted to the consumer and away from the producer. The idea is it's perfectly okay to generate all this waste if we just "recycle" it. The real solution is to reduce and reuse—a much more effective remedy that will be in full force in a sustainable democratic society based on production for need.

Agriculture is a huge topic by itself. Some general points: Capitalist agriculture is self-evidently not just bad for animals and humans, but it doesn't even do what it's supposed to— which is safely feed people. It is creating a homogenized and genetically impoverished world much more susceptible to super-bugs and epidemics of all kinds. There is only a single breed of pig used by all the industrialized farming corporations—apart from having massive haunches, which almost break their backs, they are now bred with only vestigial ears and tail because the animals are so distressed by being kept in such close proximity, wallowing in their own manure. They thrash around so much that not having ears and tails leaves them less damaged when they come to be culled. Whether they are sick or not, all are dosed with antibacterial agents. All these factors create the ideal incubator for the evolution of all kinds of new and more virulent strains of disease.[5]

More industries that we can essentially abolish or drastically reduce: the pesticide, herbicide, fungicide, and fertilizer industries. It wasn't science that drove the need for them, but the vast fields of monocultures required by capitalism. Agribusiness can cope with and indeed co-opt and buy out a niche organic movement—though note there are no real regulations on what "organic" really constitutes—but they cannot deal with going back to something as simple and effective as three-crop rotation cycles or growing legumes alongside non-nitrogen-fixing crops, having a diversity of crops, or pouring research funds into examining biological forms of pest control. It's far more profitable to apply fertilizers and pesticides to monocultures and let them run off into the rivers. We could feed all the people on the planet by practicing sustainable large- and small-scale agriculture. Currently we practice non-sustainable industrialized agriculture, which continually promises to feed all the people and yet doesn't. As several studies have shown, if all the produce of a small-scale sustainably managed farm is taken into account, it is more efficient than a field of monoculture.[6]

To move to sustainable agriculture means removing the triple metabolic rift that's been created between plants, varieties of plants, animals, and humans. Marx wrote at some length on the need to heal this metabolic rift in order to overcome the break in the nutrient cycle that transports all the goodness of the soil to the cities. It is complete insanity to have monocultures of one crop geographically separated from animals that could provide manure—and to have the crops and animals themselves geographically separated, by an average of a thousand miles or more, from the humans who are going to eat the crops and animals. Not only is there the huge waste and pollution as artificial fertilizers pour into our rivers and seas, not only is there the same thing going on with the pig and chicken waste in a different area of the country, but there is the enormous waste of all that excess transportation.

This is why we need to examine, apart from how we grow the crops and raise the animals, the location of crops, farm animals, and human population centers. The aim would be to decrease the separation of urban and rural humans and put people more in touch with the earth and where things come from as a way of healing the metabolic rift. As Marx remarked when commenting on this split, all the capitalists could think to do with the bodily excretions of four million Londoners was to poison the Thames.[7]

It also means examining what crops are grown where. Of the world's fresh water used by humans 70 percent is used for agriculture. Crops are no longer grown in a certain region based on climate or soil suitability, but purely on where the most profit can be made. Hence vast quantities of extra irrigation are needed in areas unfit for certain types of crops or in areas that lead to massive soil erosion, increased aquifer salinity and depletion, and accelerated deforestation and desertification.

Apart from the virtually unregulated and voracious logging industry, deforestation is further accelerated by forcing millions of landless peasants to constantly move to new plots of land, particularly marginal land, to clear-cut and farm.

Under socialism, no one would have the right to privately own pieces of the earth for their own private gain. There would be a rational plan for its sustainable use. This would have to be developed by and with the people who farm the land. Initially, land reform would mean giving the land to the peasants and farmers who grow the crops and raise the animals. This would immediately reduce deforestation and improve crop yields as technology is made freely available to do so. If the countryside in the developing world was no longer a place of extreme poverty, many millions living in the giant mega-slums in cities of the South would be encouraged to migrate back to the countryside to improve rural agriculture and return countries to food self-sufficiency.

Hundreds of millions of people still use wood and animal dung for heating, cooking, and lighting. India alone has four hundred million people who live without access to electricity. Poverty is a major part of the reason there is such vast deforestation in India, Africa, and parts of Asia. This also contributes to extremely poor air quality. Thousands die of smoke inhalation every year from inefficient indoor stoves burning biomass. Renewable electricity provision for the entire planet—and the eradication of poverty—would have to be part of any move to living sustainably with the earth.

It should be clear that there will no longer be nation-states after the abolition of the completely artificial lines on maps that we call borders. This will be necessary so that regional planning of resource use doesn't lead to the kind of international conflicts that characterize capitalist nations. Rational plans can be constructed for use of water resources that previously spanned multiple countries and led to friction between states using common water sources in Asia, Africa, and the Middle East. Rather than several countries battling over control of the life-giving waters of the Nile, for example, how can people of the region develop a rational plan for water conservation and use that ensures an adequate and sustainable supply for everyone and that doesn't degrade local ecosystems? There will be a true globalization—worldwide integration of natural and human resources in the interests of all life—human and non-human.

Under capitalism, it is entirely rational for individual fishermen and nationally based industrialized fishing fleets to try to catch the most fish in the shortest amount of time utilizing the most destructive fishing methods. In 1968 when Garrett Hardin wrote his infamous "Tragedy of the Commons" piece, he erroneously posited this as a reason everywhere had to be privatized, because any ecosystem that was public—such as the oceans—would be fished to the last fish by an ever-growing population. But it is the economic system that dictates that nonsustainability is rational, not people. Take away the dog-eat-dog, economic imperative of capitalism, and an international plan can be developed and implemented for replenishing declining fish stocks that doesn't depend on developing more industrial fish farms where all the fish are genetically altered and identical.

Socialist production for use, unlike production for profit, would allow for a calculation of the true costs of creating useful things and bringing them to the people who need them. To realign regions for growing different kinds of crops based on geographical and climate suitability is an extension of the idea that industry should be situated where it's needed, not wherever makes the most profit. Huge numbers of container ships now ply back and forth between continents; polluting the seas and the atmosphere, and introducing non-indigenous invasive species. The fact that the United States (along with other countries) has moved much of its heavy and light industry to China to keep down labor costs requires China to export all those manufactured goods right back. When those goods become obsolete or just break down after two years because they were crap, we dump it in Africa or re-export it to China.

Clearly there is a huge need for real development for countries of the Global South. They have the opportunity to leapfrog over the fossil-fuel age and move directly to clean energy. To do this, technological help, capital, and training will be required. One of the most urgent tasks of a new society will be to ensure that everyone is fed adequately, everyone receives health care and vaccinations, and massive infrastructure improvements are made to sanitation systems and for the provision of clean water. The UN estimates that around $25 billion per year for eight to ten years would be enough to provide clean water for all of the one billion people who currently don't have it. This is a tiny fraction of the world military or advertising budget. It's also far less than annual sales of bottled water at around $100 billion—$11 billion in the United States alone, which is another pointless and heavily polluting industry.[7]

The specific solutions to environmental challenges that will be found in a future society can't be enumerated with certainty here. This limit on our current vision comes in part from the limits that the profit system has put on investigation and even on our ways of thinking. The limit also comes from the squandering of ordinary people's abilities to contribute to solutions because they are weighed down with poverty and overwork. Freeing the minds of billions of people from the stress and degradation of unrelenting poverty and malnutrition will allow those minds to contribute productively to societal questions, facilitating a gigantic unleashing of human potential. The ideas and creativity of seven billion human brains actively and productively set to work represents an enormously expanded pool of collective knowledge and experience.

Mainstream attempts at conservation of endangered species and habitats have traditionally focused on setting aside natural preserves. This notion of small geographically isolated places where "nature" is set aside to try to eke out an existence in bio-diverse "hotspots," not in fact sustainable. Instead an ecologically rational society would expand wilderness areas and make them contiguous. Much more time and human resources would need to be devoted to understanding ecosystems, species interactions, and the closer examination of all aspects of the biosphere to enrich human understanding and appreciation for the natural world.

What will be required is an ecologically and culturally relevant diversity of agricultural, industrial, transportation, educational, and residential forms based on communal ownership and democratic control by the people themselves. Instead of passive consumers we will become active, educated, and involved participants in economic, cultural, and political life. Everyone will be involved in decisions about manufacturing methods, energy techniques, use of chemicals, and so on in order for the whole community to democratically decide the best alternative when toxin, resource, and energy minimization are the goals. Furthermore, with everyone productively engaged, the number of hours anyone works will be drastically reduced, leaving ample time for cultural and personal growth.

Things that are made by society will be valuable for their use to society, not for how much they can be exchanged for. How much more fulfilling will it be to design new materials not in order to maximize the shareholder profit of the company you work for, but to minimize resource use and waste production of a product that is socially beneficial?

Conclusion

> "The use-values, coat, linen, etc., i.e., the bodies of commodities, are combinations of two elements—matter and labour. If we take away the useful labour expended upon them, a material substratum is always left, which is furnished by Nature without the help of man. The latter can work only as Nature does, that is by changing the form of matter. Nay more, in this work of changing form he is constantly helped by natural forces. We see, then, that labour is not the only source of wealth. As William Petty puts it, labour is its father, and the earth its mother."
>
> —Karl Marx[1]

On the current path, at a time not too far distant, Homo sapiens will lose the ability to consciously and creatively direct our own destiny. We will have unleashed long-term planetary forces far beyond our control that will initiate a descent into a future that we thought we had escaped several thousand years ago. Natural forces will once again come to dominate and radically curtail social possibilities.

The rapacity of capitalism knows no bounds. Indeed, capitalism, by its very nature is "unbounded"—as soon as a limit or boundary is reached, it must be exceeded. Capitalism has reached a point in its development that it now threatens the basic biogeochemical processes of the planet as human civilization has come to know them. Ecological devastation is not an accidental outcome of capitalist development but an intrinsic element of the system, just as integral as class exploitation, poverty, racism, and war.

Capitalism forcibly alienates us both from ourselves and our own planet. The capitalist system effectively turns the planet into a giant machine for the manufacture and accumulation of larger and larger amounts of money. Raw materials, energy, and human workers are fed into the maw of this giant profit-making machine at ever-growing rates. The machine spews out money for a tiny minority along with truly gargantuan rivers of effluent, belching forth atmospheric toxins while tossing workers on the scrap heap after a lifetime of service.

The introduction of new technology on its own does not alter the nature of capitalism's treadmill of production, but merely serves to speed it up in new directions and enlarge the scale of the economy yet further. Capitalism's waste of resources and its sickening sense of priorities are plumbing new depths of absurdity and depravity. Apart from the $1 trillion spent annually on advertising and the $1.2 trillion on arms (with the United States accounting for more than half of what the world spends), import tariffs and subsidies in developed countries dictate that millions of European cows each get paid better for metabolizing grass than the one billion people living on less than $2 per day.[2]

Waste is not an accident; it is built into the structure of capitalism. In a world where almost one in every seven people goes hungry, including almost forty million in the richest country on the planet, easily the most despicable aspect of this waste is within the industrialized food industry. In the United States, the amount of food thrown away by supermarkets, restaurants, convenience stores, and consumers because of just-in-time production, a lack of time to cook or eat, the uniformity and inappropriate size of packaged food and portions, along with other aspects of mass-produced food controlled by a few giant food conglomerates, is enough to feed all one billion malnourished people *twice over*. If the waste food from the United States and the EU were combined, it could feed those billion people *three to seven times over*.[3]

The colossal negative effects of this wasted food don't stop with starving people; they also take away or poison our water supply. Wasting 25 percent of food around the globe effectively wastes 675 trillion liters of water used to grow it. That's enough water to supply the household needs of nine billion people at a generous 200 liters/day.[3] Then there is the land that was cleared to grow the crops and raise the animals that were wasted. If that land had instead been forested, or was reforested, it would cut down on anthropogenic global carbon emissions by significant percentages. Further, it has been estimated that industrialized agriculture uses ten calories of oil energy to produce one calorie of food—an enormous and criminal waste of energy that is highly polluting to extract and profitable enough to fight wars over. Finally, there is the habitat destruction and endangerment of wildlife and biodiversity from all the extra land clearance.

Aside from that, there is the waste of the stratospherically rich. As Eric Toussaint points out in *Your Money or Your Life*, 147 people on Forbes' 2002 list of the "World's Richest People" had a combined wealth of over $1 trillion dollars—equivalent to the combined income of half the planet's population.[5]

Capitalism creates and demands scarcity in order to facilitate competition and thus profit-taking. Where scarcity doesn't exist, it must be created. Because profit-taking is its raison d'être, in order to solve one problem—soil depletion for example, capitalism creates another—the fertilizer industry. In order to grow things as fast as possible for the greatest profit, monocultures are required, necessitating artificial pesticides rather than biological ones. The environmental "gains"of one country, say recycling, are often more about simply moving the problems somewhere else—in this case, to the developing world or underground where toxins from landfills leak back into the water supply. Capitalism is thus systematically driven toward the ruination of the planet and we underestimate how committed the system is to planetary ecocide at our peril. As stated above, ecological devastation is just as intrinsic to the operation of capitalism as is the exploitation of the vast majority of humans in the interests of a tiny minority, imperialism, and war.

Sustainability can't mean simply maintenance of the ecosystemic status quo as if that's stationary. Everything changes, evolves, and dies out, and new species come into being. However, to live sustainably must mean at the very least to attempt to maintain and stabilize current climatic conditions as human civilization has come to know them. We can achieve this in part by a necessary and urgent switch to renewable energy and through minimizing our use of resources and waste production based on the principle of a long-term view of interdependence with nature. I have shown how switching to renewable sources of energy is entirely possible.

A judicious, well-designed mix of solar, wind, wave, tidal, geothermal, existing hydroelectric, and energy storage mechanisms could supply the whole planet with carbon-free, clean energy. In the realm of preventing climate change, this is the single most urgent task. A clean energy future also holds the promise of creating millions of jobs around the world.

Abolishing capitalism will eliminate the production of useless products, services, and weapons and the corruption of humanity that comes with a thirst for commodities that stems from our own enforced alienation from nature and lack of control over our lives. Under capitalism, many of the most highly educated and creative minds are applied to designing more efficient weaponry to increase kill ratios or fathoming new and imaginative ways to market consumption. Under socialism, humanity's vast creativity and imagination would be put to socially useful pursuits and applied to reversing the earth's and our own degradation under capitalism. We want to develop alongside nature to leave the planet for future generations in an enhanced state of biodiversity, interacting with diverse landscapes and complex ecosystems. We can only do this if we collectively and democratically make all decisions based on human need not corporate profits.

I have attempted to show how capitalism relates to nature for to its overriding purpose: the production of greater and greater amounts of capital to reinvest in the next round of production. I have moved from there to explore how Marx and Engels saw our relationship to nature as something we are enmeshed within and an integral part of. Some will continue to argue that the quotes of Marx and Engels that highlight their commitment to ecological considerations are merely scattershot and judiciously chosen remarks separated from the main thrust of their socioeconomic analysis. It is difficult to maintain this position, however, when the Marxist concept of alienation is part of a *method* of analysis—a central theoretical component embedded within the philosophical framework of historical materialism. The historical materialism developed by Marx and Engels further lends itself to an ecological analysis by insisting on the inter-relationship and interdependence of all organisms set within their historical and natural development.

Moreover, the contributions to ecological thought made by socialists since Marx and Engels, a few of which I have highlighted, confirm the ongoing preoccupation that Marxists have had with conditions of environmental stability and human interaction with the earth. Despite the extremely unpropitious economic and material conditions existing immediately after the Russian Revolution, ecology was nevertheless a serious concern within the upper echelons of the Bolshevik Party and wider Soviet society as pioneering policies and research were implemented.

Capitalism has a basic and inbuilt antagonism to nature just as it does to the working class. Therefore, the transition to a production system free from wanton ecological degradation and crises must necessitate a struggle against capitalism—i.e., a struggle against the simultaneous commodification of humanity and nature. Today, the most successful popular movements for ecological gains are those based among the industrial and agricultural workers and peasants of the Global South—those most affected by ecological decay. We would do well to learn from them.

In the North, links must be forged between the social movements and the labor movement through a common focus and unified demands for the creation of millions of well-paid, skilled union jobs in the alternative energy, energy distribution and conservation, transportation, and building construction sectors of the economy. We need to argue that even if solar energy currently costs more than dirtier alternatives, it is the best solution and should be prioritized. Even though it's costlier, governing elites currently prioritize nuclear energy because of nuclear power's connection to Great Power status and the production of nuclear weapons. Our priorities are different, and these should be reflected in our choices, which cannot be limited by economic considerations, especially when the playing field is already so heavily tilted toward fossil fuels in the first place. This is why we also need to argue for a redirection of government subsidies and tax incentives away from conventional sources of energy and toward sources of renewable energy. And we need to forcefully argue that none of this is about sacrifice. On the contrary, we will be moving toward a much less polluted, much less alienated, and far higher quality of life.

Environmental activism, if it is to become reinvigorated and relevant, must engage just as much with questions of social justice as it does with ecology. And we cannot get side-tracked by questions of overpopulation, which places us on the same side as our own rulers and sets us against our natural allies—the workers and peasants of the developing world. It must become socio-ecologically radical because fighting for ecological and social justice are both urgent—and one cannot be won independently of the other. Real sustainable development must encompass social sustainability, equality, and justice as much as it does ecological concerns. This is only possible when the producers decide democratically and collectively how to allocate resources with the objective of meeting genuine human needs.

As stated earlier, this requires a pro-human and pro-nature re-definition of wealth based on a social union of the human producers and their existing "natural" conditions of production, a condition that is anathema to capitalism.

Ultimately, a necessary part of our self-emancipation will be to overcome the "metabolic rift" between us and the earth that is created by capitalism. It is telling that Marx, who had a classical education, chose this phrase to depict the change he saw as necessary in human relations with the earth. Metabolic was a new term in the scientific lexicon of the eighteenth century and derives from the Greek for "change." By one common definition, metabolism is the sum of the physical and chemical processes in an organism by which its material substance is produced, maintained, and transformed, and by which energy is made available. Here it is applied to a single cell or organism. What is revolutionary about the way Marx uses the term is that he sees it not in terms of a single organism, but as the way in which the *whole biosphere* should interact; that human society needed to overcome the metabolic rift between our species and the planet caused by an alienating and dysfunctional social system that drives a wedge between the two.

This will finally make it possible for us to live in harmony with the planet. This is not to say there will not be tension between human history and natural history, but humans will finally have both the chance to understand natural processes and a social structure that allows us to use this understanding to successfully direct our activity toward results we desire. We will finally be able to move toward that sustainable society—one we could bequeath to future generations in an improved state. I have outlined in broad strokes what some major aspects of that change would necessitate in areas of transportation, energy production, agriculture, housing, and production more generally. There is of course much more to say on this topic than the general outlines given above. The practical realization and detail of these plans must be voted for and carried out by the people. This will only happen once they are able to democratically and collectively decide their own destiny. Nothing short of a social revolution is required. To quote Marx on how we should envision a sustainable society from Volume III of *Capital*:

> The realm of freedom actually begins only where labour which is determined by necessity and mundane considerations ceases; thus in the very nature of things it lies beyond the sphere of actual material production...Freedom in this field can only consist in socialised man, the associated producers, rationally regulating their interchange with Nature, bringing it under their common control, instead of being ruled by it as by the blind forces of Nature; and achieving this with the least expenditure of energy and under conditions most favourable to, and worthy of, their human nature. But it nonetheless still remains a realm of necessity. Beyond it begins that development of human energy which is an end in itself, the true realm of freedom, which, however, can blossom forth only with this realm of necessity as its basis.[6]

There is a growing realization by some sections of the ruling class that they really do need to do something about climate change. We can use these splits of opinion at the top of society to push for reforms within the system that will slow down climate change and ecological degradation and develop our confidence and organization to push for more. When we fight for them, we can win meaningful victories under capitalism, and these are essential stepping stones on the path toward more victories. However, a massive redirection of wealth toward renewable energy runs directly counter to the deep-rooted self-interest and short-term profitability of the world's biggest and most powerful corporations. A recent poll of five hundred major businesses revealed that only one in ten regarded climate change as a priority.[6] The short-termism of capitalism and the gigantic size of the investments in fossil-fuel-related industries ultimately make any comprehensive solution within the system utopian, even as some valuable reforms will occur that we need to fight for. More fundamentally, as long as inter-imperial rivalry and military competition between states exists, it is impossible to speak seriously of a reduction in military spending or effective and rational international cooperation on the scale required.

The fact that some companies and world leaders have to at least pay lip service to making systemic changes is a reflection of the mounting pressure placed on them by people around the world genuinely concerned with pollution and climate change. This is where the hope lies. However, our vision needs to go much, much further than the changes so far on the table and incorporate activists not as consumers but where our real power resides—as producers. Apart from the tiny sliver of the population at the top of society hell-bent on accumulation and the continuation of business as usual—with the attendant war, racism, famine, and environmental degradation that that prospect necessarily entails—the rest of the population of the planet has a direct interest in ending this madness and has the means to do so.

Only a socialist future holds out the hope of a sustainable one for the planet. We need to build a global society in which production is democratically decided upon and centered round what nature and humanity collectively need. To do this means overthrowing capitalism and abolishing the "metabolic rift." There is simply no other alternative. However, time is short and because something is necessary does not make it inevitable. Organization lags behind the urgency of the need. The urban and rural working classes that make today's economy operate need to become organized into a political force that can take charge of the productive machinery and democratically redirect it toward the sustainable satisfaction of human need. Only by organizing and fighting for change on this class basis will the possible future become a real one.

Selected Bibliography and Resources

Angus, Ian, ed., *The Global Fight for Climate Justice: Anti-Capitalist Responses to Global Warming and Environmental Destruction* (London: Resistance Books, 2009)

Archer, David and Stefan Rahmsdorf, *The Climate Crisis: An Introductory Guide to Climate Change* (Cambridge: Cambridge University Press, 2010)

Arnove, Anthony et al., *Russia: From Workers' State to State Capitalism*, (Chicago: Haymarket Books, 2003)

Bellamy Foster, John, *The Vulnerable Planet: A Short Economic History of the Planet* (New York: Cornerstone Books, 1999)

——*Marx's Ecology: Materialism and Nature* (New York: Monthly Review Press, 2000)

——*Ecology Against Capitalism* (New York: Monthly Review Press, 2002)

——*The Ecological Revolution: Making Peace with the Planet* (New York: Monthly Review Press, 2009)

Bello, Walden, *The Food Wars* (London: Verso Books, 2009)

Benton, Ted, ed., *The Greening of Marxism* (New York: Guildford Press, 1996)

Broecker, Wallace and Robert Kunzig, *Fixing Climate: What Past Climate Changes Reveal about the Current Threat—and How to Counter It* (New York: Hill and Wang, 2008)

Brzezinski, Zbigniew, *The Grand Chessboard* (New York: Basic Books, 1997)

Burkett, Paul, *Marx and Nature: A Red and Green Perspective* (New York: Palgrave Macmillan, 1999)

——*Marxism and Ecological Economics: Toward a Red and Green Political Economy*

(Chicago: Haymarket Books, 2009)

Caldicott, Helen, *Nuclear Power Is Not the Answer* (New York: New Press, 2006)

Carson, Rachel, *Silent Spring* (New York: Mariner Books, 2002)

Chase, Allan, *The Legacy of Malthus* (Champaign, IL: University of Illinois Press, 1980)

Conor, Clifford, *A People's History of Science: Miners, Midwives, and "Low Mechanicks"* (New York: Nation Books, 2005)

Stan Cox, *Sick Planet: Corporate Food and Medicine* (London: Pluto Press, 2008)

Diamond, Jared, *Collapse: How Societies Choose to Fail or Succeed* (New York: Penguin Books, 2005)

Deffeyes, Kenneth, *Beyond Oil: The View from Hubbert's Peak* (New York: Hill and Wang, 2005)

Ehrlich, Paul, *The Population Bomb* (New York: Ballantine Books, 1968)

Engels, Frederick, *The Origin of the Family, Private Property and the State* (New York: International Publishers, 2007)

———*Anti-Dühring* (London: Lawrence and Wishart, 1934)

Environment, Capitalism and Socialism (Sydney: Resistance Books, 1999)

Evans, Robert L., *Fueling Our Future: An Introduction to Sustainable Energy* (Cambridge: Cambridge University Press, 2007)

Fagan, Brian, *The Long Summer: How Climate Changed Civilization* (New York: Basic Books, 2007)

———*The Great Warming: Climate Change and the Rise and Fall of Civilizations* (New York: Bloomsbury Press, 2008)

Goodall, Chris, *Ten Technologies to Save the Planet* (London: Profile Books, 2008)

Goodstein, David, *Out of Gas: The End of the Age of Oil* (New York: Norton, 2004)

Hamilton, Clive, *Growth Fetish* (London: Pluto Books, 2004)

Heinberg, Richard, *The Party's Over: Oil, War and Fate of Industrial Societies,* (Gabriola Island, British Columbia: New Society Publishers, 2003)

———*Power Down: Options and Actions for a Post-Carbon World* (Gabriola Island, British Columbia: New Society Publishers, 2004)

———*The Oil Depletion Protocol: A Plan to Avert Oil Wars, Terrorism and Economic Collapse* (Gabriola Island, British Columbia: New Society Publishers, 2006)

Hiro, Dilip, *Blood of the Earth: The Battle for the World's Vanishing Oil Resources* (New York: Nation Books, 2007)

Hoggan, James, *Climate Cover-Up: The Crusade to Deny Global Warming* (Vancouver: Greystone Books, 2009)

Holt-Jimenez, Eric, *Campesino a Campesino: Voices from Latin America's Farmer to Farmer Movement for Sustainable Agriculture* (Oakland: Food First Books, 2006)

Hughes, Jonathan, *Ecology and Historical Materialism* (Cambridge, England: Cambridge University Press, 2000)

Jorgenson, Andrew and Edward Kick, eds., *Globalization and the Environment* (Chicago: Haymarket Books, 2009)

Karliner, Joshua, *The Corporate Planet: Ecology and Politics in the Age of Globalization* (San Francisco: Sierra Club Books, 1997)

Keeping Things Whole: Readings in Environmental Science (Chicago: Great Books Foundation, 2003)

Kelly, Jane and Sheila Malone, eds., *Ecosocialism or Barbarism* (London, Socialist Resistance, 2006)

Kempf, Herve, *How the Rich Are Destroying the Earth* (White River Junction, VT: Chelsea Green Publishing, 2007)

Klare, Michael, *Resource Wars: The New Landscape of Global Conflict* (New York: Owl Books, 2002)

———*Rising Powers, Shrinking Planet: The New Geopolitics of Energy* (New York: Metropolitan Books, 2008)

Kolbert, Elizabeth, *Field Notes from a Catastrophe: Man, Nature and Climate Change* (New York: Bloomsbury, 2006)

Kovel, Joel, *The Enemy of Nature: The End of Capitalism or the End of the World?* (New York: Zed Books, 2007)

Lappé, Frances Moore et al., *World Hunger: 12 Myths* (New York: Grove Press, 1998)

Lawrence, Felicity, *Eat Your Heart Out: Why the Food Business Is Bad for the Planet and Your Health* (London: Penguin, 2008)

Lear, Linda, ed., *Lost Woods: The Discovered Writing of Rachel Carson* (Boston, MA: Beacon Press, 1998)

Leggett, Jeremy, *The Solar Century: The Past, Present and World-Changing Future of Solar Energy* (London: Profile Books, 2009)

Leonard, Annie, *The Story of Stuff: How our Obsession with Stuff Is Trashing the*

Planet, Our Communities, and Our Health—and a Vision for Change (New York: Free Press, 2010)

Lewontin, Richard and Richard Levins, *Biology under the Influence: Dialectical Essays on Ecology, Agriculture, and Health* (New York: Monthly Review Press, 2007)

Lovelock, James, *The Gaia Hypothesis* (New York: Oxford University Press, 2000)

——*The Revenge of Gaia: Earth's Climate Crisis and the Fate of Humanity* (New York: Basic Books, 2007)

Lynas, Mark, *Six Degrees: Our Future on a Hotter Planet* (London: Fourth Estate, 2007)

MacKay, David J. C., *Sustainable Energy—Without the Hot Air,* (UIT Cambridge: 2008)

Marx, Karl, *Grundrisse* (New York: Penguin, 1993)

——*Capital,* vol. I (New York: International Publishers, 1967)

——*Capital,* vol. II (New York: Penguin, 1992)

Maass, Peter, *Crude World: The Violent Twilight of Oil* (New York: Random House, 2009)

Merchant, Carolyn, *Key Concepts in Critical Theory: Ecology,* 2nd ed. (Amherst, NY: Humanity Books, 2008)

Molyneux, John, *What Is the Real Marxist Tradition* (Chicago: Haymarket Books, 2003)

Monbiot, George, *Heat: How to Stop the Planet from Burning* (Cambridge, MA: South End Press, 2007)

Neale, Jonathan, *Stop Global Warming: Change the World* (London: Bookmarks, 2008)

O'Connor, James, ed., *Is Capitalism Sustainable? Political Economy and the Politics of Ecology* (New York: Guildford Press, 1994)

——*Natural Causes: Essays in Ecological Marxism* (New York: Guildford Press, 1998)

Olivera, Oscar and Tom Lewis, ¡*Cochabamba!: Water War in Bolivia,* (Cambridge, MA: South End Press, 2004)

Parr, Adrian: *Hijacking Sustainability* (Cambridge, MA: MIT Press, 2009)

Parsons, Howard, *Marx and Engels on Ecology* (Westport, CT: Greenwood Press Inc., 1977)

Patel, Raj, *Stuffed and Starved: The Hidden Battle for the World Food System* (Brooklyn, NY: Melville House, 2007)

Pearce, Fred, *With Speed and Violence: Why Scientists Fear Tipping Points in Climate Change* (Boston: Beacon Press, 2007)

——*The Coming Population Crash and our Planet's Surprising Future* (Boston: Beacon Press, 2010)

Pepper, David, *Eco-Socialism: From Deep Ecology to Social Justice* (New York: Routledge, 1993)

——*Modern Environmentalism: An Introduction* (New York: Routledge, 1999)

Porritt, Jonathan, *Capitalism as If the World Matters* (London: Earthscan, 2007)

Ransom, David and Vanessa Baird, eds., *People First Economics* (Oxford: New Internationalist Publishing, 2009)

Roberts, Paul, *The End of Oil* (New York: Mariner Books, 2005)

Rogers, Heather, *Gone Tomorrow: The Hidden Life of Garbage* (New York: New Press, 2005)

——*Green Gone Wrong: How Our Economy is Undermining the Environmental Revolution* (New York: Scribner, 2010)

Romm, Joseph, *Hell and High Water: Global Warming—the Solution and the Politics—and What We Should Do* (New York: HarperCollins, 2007)

Ruddiman, William F., *Plows, Plagues and Petroleum* (Princeton, NJ: Princeton University Press, 2005)

Scientific American, Oil and the Future of Energy (Guildford, Conn.: Lyons Press, 2007)

Shiva, Vandana, *Earth Democracy: Justice, Sustainability, and Peace* (Cambridge, MA: South End Press, 2005)

——*Soil Not Oil: Environmental Justice in an Age of Climate Crisis,* (Cambridge, MA: South End Press, 2008)

Speth, James Gustave, *The Bridge at the End of the World: Capitalism, the Environment, and Crossing from Crisis to Sustainability* (New Haven: Yale University Press, 2008)

Stuart, Tristram, *Waste: Uncovering the Global Food Scandal* (New York: Norton, 2009)

Toulmin, Camilla, *Climate Change in Africa* (London, Zed Books, 2009)

Toussaint, Eric, *Your Money or Your Life: The Tyranny of Global Finance* (Chicago: Haymarket Books, 2005)

Trotsky, Leon, *Problems of Everyday Life* (New York: Pathfinder Press, 1973)

Tucker, Robert C., ed., *The Marx-Engels Reader* (New York: Norton, 1972)

Vernadsky, Vladimir, *The Biosphere* (New York: Copernicus, 1998)

Weart, Spencer, *The Discovery of Global Warming*, 2nd ed. (Cambridge, MA: Harvard University Press, 2008)

Weiner, Douglas R., *Models of Nature: Ecology, Conservation and Cultural Revolution in Soviet Russia* (Pittsburgh, PA: University of Pittsburgh Press, 2000)

Wilkinson, Richard and Kate Picket, *The Spirit Level: Why Equality is better for Everyone* (London: Penguin Books, 2009)

Yergin, Daniel, *The Prize: The Epic Quest for Oil, Money and Power* (New York: Free Press, 1992)

Useful Websites:

There are hundreds of useful sites. The *Guardian* and the *New York Times* both have extensive online environmental sections. Below are a few of the most authoritative sites providing the facts, figures, and science of climate change and other environmental issues:

Global Climate Change: NASA's Eyes on the Earth: http://climate.nasa.gov

Climate Progress: www.climateprogress.org

Environment 360: www.e360.yale.edu

Earth Trends: Environmental Information: www.earthtrends.wri.org

Energy Information Administration: www.eia.doe.gov

UN Food and Agriculture Organization: www.fao.org

Intergovernmental Panel on Climate Change: www.ipcc.ch

NOAA Global Warming FAQ: www.ncdc.noaa.gov/oa/climate/globalwarming.html

Nature Reports Climate Change: www.nature.com/climate

New Scientist environment web site: www.newscientist.com/section/environment

Real Climate: www.realclimate.org

Stockholm International Water Institute: www.siwi.org

Skeptical Science: www.skepticalscience.com

Union of Concerned Scientists: www.ucsusa.org

Sustainable Energy: Without the Hot Air: www.withouthotair.com

More political informational sites, campaigning, and activist sites (a very small selection):

Biofuelwatch: www.biofuelwatch.org.uk
Carbon Trade Watch: www.carbontradewatch.org
Climate and Capitalim: www.climateandcapitalism.com
Climate Ark: www.climateark.org
The Corner House: www.thecornerhouse.org.uk/subject/climate
Earth Justice: www.earthjustice.org
Food First: www.foodfirst.org
Grain: www.grain.org/front
Global Justice Ecology Project: www.globaljusticeecology.org
Green Left: www.greenleft.org.au
Indigenous Environmental Network: www.ienearth.org
International Rivers: www.internationalrivers.org
Oakland Institute: www.oaklandinstitute.org
Oil Sands Watch: www.oilsandswatch.org
Rainforest Action Network: www.ran.org

Documentaries worth watching (a small sample):

Blue Gold: World Water Wars
Crude Impact
Food Inc.
Flow: How Did a Handful of Corporations Steal Our Water?
The Future of Food
Global Warming: The Signs and the Science
Life and Debt
Who Killed the Electric Car?

Acknowledgments

Ever since childhood, which I spent largely up a tree or cavorting in and canoeing on the meandering River Avon, the beauty of water, land, and sky has always intrigued and thrilled me. Spending nights under canvas whenever I could, I've had a love for fresh air, the feel of tree bark beneath my fingers, the sight of sun-dappled water, the scent of freshly harvested fields, and the sound of the wind rifling through swaying poplar trees.

This book bears the imprint of all those days and everyone I've ever met, as my life, like that of all living beings, is a dynamic interaction of environment, organism, and genetic code. Naturally within that, some people deserve special mention for their impact in fostering a love for investigating the natural world and a keen desire to understand and change the social world. Geoff Petty, my former physics teacher at Worcester Technical College, ignited a love of science and education and most particularly clued me in to the fundamental importance of energy in our universe. Ultimately, this led me to pursue an undergraduate degree in physics and an MS in energy and the environment back in 1989, well before it became one of the central issues of our times.

Since then, an unpayable debt of gratitude exists toward a raft of people in Britain and the United States who have helped hone my politics, took the time to educate me in meetings, protests, and demonstrations and whose voices can be heard between the words. Without the prior scholarship of people like John Bellamy Foster and Paul Burkett, who have done so much to resurrect the Marxist approach to ecological questions, the necessary building blocks for my book would have been missing.

My thanks to countless comrades around the world who have contributed to meetings or raised prickly points in discussions and my students, past and present, who have kept me on my toes. While a full list would run to many hundreds, those who made this book far better as a collective project than had I been left to my own devices are David Whitehouse, for his untiring reading and comments on early drafts; Jonathan Neale, who took the time to meet with me and review my arguments; my friend Alex Nice; Paul D'Amato, for his editing and comments on previous articles in the International Socialist Review that formed the seed for this work; and Anthony Arnove, for pushing me to believe I could write a book.

Furthermore, Ecology and Socialism could not have seen the light of day without the indefatigable work and dedication of the people at Haymarket Books, especially Julie Fain and Rachel Cohen on the production side, and Dao X. Tran for copyediting and catching my errors. Any that remain are surely mine.

Notes

INTRODUCTION

1. Julio Godoy, "Pious Words Won't Save Endangered Species," Inter Press Service, January 12, 2010, www.ipsnews.net/news.asp?idnews=49948.

2. For a small taste of the wondrous diversity of life on our planet see the documentary *Planet Earth*, HD-DVD, narrated by David Attenborough (BBC Video, 2007).

3. J. Rockström et al., "Planetary Boundaries: Exploring the Safe Operating Space for Humanity," *Ecology and Society* 14, no. 2 (2009), www.ecologyandsociety.org/vol14/iss2/art32.

4. The Bulletin of the Atomic Scientists has assessed the risk as fluctuating over the years. For details see the "Doomsday Clock: Timeline," www.thebulletin.org/content/doomsday-clock/timeline.

5. For more details on where the earth is on a host of environmental and social problems see *Science* magazine's annual report, *State of the Planet* (Washington DC: Island Press, 2008).

6. For a great introduction to climate change and the science behind our knowledge of it, see David Archer and Stefan Rahmsdorf, *The Climate Crisis: An Introductory Guide to Climate Change* (Cambridge: Cambridge University Press, 2010).

7. David Adams, "Predictions Overtaken by Events," *Guardian*, October 23, 2007.

8. Hilary Osborne, "CO_2 Emissions Rise Outpaces Worst-Case Scenario," *Guardian*, May 22, 2007.

9. R. K. Pachauri and A. Reisinger, eds., *Climate Change 2007: Synthesis Report; Summary for Policy Makers,* www.ipcc.ch/pdf/assessment-report/ar4/syr/ar4_syr_spm.pdf.

10. OECD/International Energy Association, *World Energy Outlook 2008*, published online at www.worldenergyoutlook.org.

11. A. P. Sokolov et al., *Report 169: Probabilistic Forecast for 21st Century Climate Based on Uncertainties in Emissions (without Policy) and Climate Parameters*, Joint Program Report Series, The MIT Joint Program on Science and the Policy of Global Change, January 2009, http://globalchange.mit.edu/pubs/abstract.php?publication_id=990.

12. Johann Hari, "After the Catastrophe in Copenhagen, It's Up to Us," *Independent*, December 29, 2009.

13. Vandana Shiva, *Soil Not Oil: Environmental Justice in an Age of Climate Crisis*, (Cambridge, MA: South End Press, 2008), 44.

14. Ibid., 43.

15. This number given for food-borne illnesses is a Centers for Disease Control and Prevention average. With the dramatic reduction in food inspections by the FDA from 21,000 in 1981 to 5,000 in 1997, there is much uncertainty in the numbers. See Marian Burros, "The Debate over Merging Government Food Agencies," *New York Times*, April 9, 1997.

16. James Lovelock, *The Gaia Hypothesis* (New York: Oxford University Press, 2000) and *The Revenge of Gaia: Earth's Climate Crisis and the Fate of Humanity* (New York: Basic Books, 2007). Lovelock, incidentally, has been seduced by the dark side, and is now a strong advocate of nuclear power. See his website: www.ecolo.org/lovelock/lovebioen.htm.

17. "James Lovelock: 'Fudging Data Is a Sin against Science,'" interview by Leo Hickman, *Guardian*, March 29, 2010.

18. See Peter Schwartz and Doug Randall, "An Abrupt Climate Change Scenario and Its Implications for United States National Security," Pentagon Report, October 2003, Environmental Defense Fund, www.edf.org/documents/3566_AbruptClimateChange.pdf.

19. It is also the case that the UN's Food and Agricultural Organization (FAO) regularly reports that food production outstrips population growth. Given that most hunger is caused not by shortages but the inability of the poor to buy food, and that much agricultural land lies fallow or is swallowed up by unplanned development, there is no doubt that properly planned agriculture could feed even more people. See Frances Moore Lappé et al., *World Hunger: Twelve Myths* (New York: Grove Press, 1998).

20. Jonathan Neale, "Climate Politics after Copenhagen," *International Socialism* 126, April 2010.

CHAPTER ONE: THE SCIENCE OF CLIMATE CHANGE

1. Quoted in Fred Pearce, "Climate Change Special: State of Denial," *New Scientist*, November 4, 2006.

2. Mark Lynas, *Six Degrees: Our Future on a Hotter Planet* (London: Fourth Estate, 2007), 253–54.

3. "Global Warming Special Issue," *Time*, July 2007; "The Heat Is On: A Special Report on Climate Change," *Economist*, September 9–15, 2006; and "Special Issue: Surviving the Climate Crisis: What Must be Done?" *Nation*, May 7, 2007.

4. Schwartz and Randall, "Abrupt Climate Change Scenario."

5. The GCC was set up in 1997, operated until 2002, and was extremely successful in getting the media to present global warming as a debate around which there was no scientific consensus. It included such environmentally benign multinationals as ExxonMobil, Shell, Texaco, Ford, General Motors, and the American Petroleum Institute.

6. Union of Concerned Scientists, "Smoke, Mirrors and Hot Air: How ExxonMobil Uses Big Tobacco's Tactics to Manufacture Uncertainty on Climate Science," January 2007, www.ucsusa .org/assets/documents/global_warming/exxon_report.pdf.

7. Bob Ward, senior manager, policy communication, The Royal Society, letter to Nick Thomas, director, corporate affairs, Esso UK Limited, September 4, 2006, *Guardian*, http://image.guardian.co .uk/sysfiles/Guardian/documents/2006/09/19/LettertoNick.pdf.

8. For a full history of climate change science and when we knew what we knew, how it was discovered, and how predictions are made the American Institute of Physics has an up-to-date blog based on Spencer Weart's book *The Discovery of Global Warming*, 2nd ed. (Cambridge, MA: Harvard University Press, 2008). The entire book plus much more and lots of useful links can be found at www.aip.org/history/climate/index.html.

9. John Vidal, "U.S. Oil Company Donated Millions to Climate Sceptic Groups, Says Greenpeace," *Guardian*, March 30, 2010.

10. "Koch Industries: Secretly Funding Climate Denial Machine" (Washington, DC: Greenpeace, March 30, 2010), www.greenpeace .org/usa/campaigns/global-warming-and-energy/polluterwatch/ koch-industries.

11. James Hoggan, *Climate Cover-Up: The Crusade to Deny Global Warming* (Vancouver: Greystone Books, 2009).

12. Rachel Carson inspired the modern environmental movement and influenced a generation of activists with the release of *Silent Spring* in 1962. The book details the indiscriminate use of pesticides and their effect on the natural environment. Its central thesis is that pesticides (such as DDT) were developed with the profit motive as the first priority, human health a distant second, and the effects on the general environment entirely overlooked. As a predictable result, the book garnered a relentless assault from the chemical industry, which spent hundreds of thousands

of dollars on a campaign seeking to portray Carson as an over-
wrought, "bird and bunny loving," misinformed woman dab-
bling in science and overstepping the boundaries of her gender.
While the book led to congressional hearings and the eventual
banning of DDT (but not its export overseas) pesticide use has
skyrocketed in the forty-eight years since its first publication.
Rachel Carson, *Silent Spring* (New York: Mariner Books, 2002).
For more on Rachel Carson's legacy and radical politics, see
Sarah Grey, "In Defense of Rachel Carson," *International Socialist Review* 57, January–February 2008.

13. Every molecule has different wavelengths at which it will absorb or reflect energy. Among other things, this is how we know
the composition of our sun and the stars.

14. Robert L. Evans, *Fueling Our Future: An Introduction to Sustainable Energy* (Cambridge: Cambridge University Press,
2007), 46.

15. Pachauri and Reisinger, eds., *Climate Change 2007.*

16. Fred Pearce, *With Speed and Violence: Why Scientists Fear Tip-
ping Points in Climate Change* (Boston: Beacon Press, 2007) and
Brian Fagan, *The Long Summer: How Climate Changed Civiliza-
tion* (New York: Basic Books, 2007). See also Fagan's *The Great
Warming: Climate Change and the Rise and Fall of Civilizations*
(New York: Bloomsbury Press, 2008).

17. A graph that has come to be known as the "hockey stick" graph
for its shape shows that northern hemisphere temperatures
held steady up until industrialization took off with a vengeance
in the latter part of the twentieth century. Along with more recent refinements, it establishes beyond doubt that the planet is
warmer than at any time in the last thousand years and that the
vast majority of that warming coincided with massive societal increases in CO_2 production. Climate change deniers have focused much of their attacks on this influential graph, but it has

been fully corroborated by multiple sources. For a discussion of some of the controversies surrounding this graph and their refutation see *New Scientist*, "Climate Myths: The 'Hockey Stick' Graph Has Been Proven Wrong," September 4, 2009, www.newscientist .com/article/dn11646. For a full discussion of all climate change myths see *New Scientist*, "Climate Change: A Guide for the Perplexed," May 16, 2007.

18. Pachauri and Reisinger, eds., *Climate Change 2007*.

19. Joseph Romm, *Hell and High Water: Global Warming: The Solution and the Politics—and What We Should Do* (New York: HarperCollins Books, 2007), 21.

20. Pachauri and Reisinger, eds., *Climate Change 2007*.

21. Lynas, *Six Degrees*.

22. See Bill McKibben's website, www.350.org, for details on the significance of 350 and see Lynas, *Six Degrees* on the historical evidence for what can happen above 450.

23. See Lynas, *Six Degrees*, chapters five and six for details. Also see Minqi Li, "Climate Change, Limits to Growth, and the Imperative for Socialism," in *Monthly Review* 60, no. 3 (July–August 2008).

CHAPTER TWO: IS POPULATION THE PROBLEM?

1. Quoted in Walden Bello, *The Food Wars* (London: Verso Books, 2009), 76.

2. Lester R. Brown, "Could Food Shortages Bring Down Civilization?" *Scientific American* 300, no. 5 (May 2009).

3. Johann Hari, "Are There Just Too Many People in the World?" *Independent*, May 15, 2008.

4. "The Malthusian Question," editorial, *Guardian*, March 21, 2009.

5. Robert Engelman, "Population and Sustainability: Can We Avoid Limiting the Number of People?" *Scientific American Earth 3.0: Solutions for Sustainable Progress* (Summer 2009).

6. Frances Moore Lappé, "World Hunger: Its Roots and Remedies,"

A Sociology of Food and Nutrition (New York: Oxford University Press, 2009), 3.

7. Quoted in John Bellamy Foster, "Malthus' *Essay on Population* at Age 200: A Marxian View," *Monthly Review*, 50, no. 7 (December 1998) and appears revised in Bellamy Foster, *Marx's Materialism: Materialism and Nature* (New York: Monthly Review Press, 2000), chap. 3.

8. Karl Marx, *Grundrisse* (New York: Penguin Books, 1993), 605–606.

9. Ibid., 607.

10. Blue-green algae, a misleading name as it is a bacterium, is an ancient species still found all over the planet in aquatic and desert environments as primary photosynthetic producers.

11. Marx, *Grundrisse*, 607.

12. UN Food and Agriculture Organization, *World Agriculture: Towards 2015/2030; Summary Report* (Rome: UN FAO, 2002), www.fao.org/docrep/004/y3557e/y3557e00.htm.

13. Allan Chase, *The Legacy of Malthus* (Chicago: University of Illinois Press, 1980), 317–76.

14. Garrett Hardin, "The Tragedy of the Commons," *Science* 162, no. 3859 (December 13, 1968): 1,243–8.

15. In her essay, "No Tragedy of the Commons," Susan Jane Buck Cox examines the history of the common lands peasant communities managed collectively under English feudalism, and concludes: "Perhaps what existed in fact was not a 'tragedy of the commons' but rather a triumph: that for hundreds of years—and perhaps thousands, although written records do not exist to prove the longer era—land was managed successfully by communities." *Environmental Ethics* 7 (1985): 60.

16. George Monbiot, "The Tragedy of Enclosure," Monbiot.com, posted January 1, 1994, www.monbiot.com/archives/1994/01/01/the-tragedy-of-enclosure/.

17. Paul Burkett, *Marx and Nature: A Red and Green Perspective* (New York: Palgrave Macmillan, 1999), 83.

18. Garrett Hardin, "Lifeboat Ethics: the Case against Helping the Poor," *Psychology Today*, September 1974. More recently, Hardin's book *Living Within Limits: Ecology, Economics, and Population* (New York: Oxford, 1993) has a chapter entitled "The Necessity of Immigration Control" in which he writes: "To survive, rich nations must refuse immigration to people who are poor because their governments are unable or unwilling to stop population growth," 294.

19. Paul Ehrlich, *The Population Bomb* (New York: Ballantine Books, 1968).

20. Brendan O'Neill, "We've Got All the Space in the World," *Guardian*, June 13, 2009.

21. Randall Arnst, *Business as Usual: Responses within ASEAN to the Food Crisis*, a report for Focus on the Global South, Occasional Papers 4, February 2009, www.focusweb.org/pdf/occasionalpaper4.pdf.

22. World Bank, "Rising Food Prices: Policy Options and World Bank Response," http://siteresources.worldbank.org/NEWS/Resources/risingfoodprices_backgroundnote_apr08.pdf.

23. UN FAO, "Global Food Supply Gradually Steadying," UN FAO Media Center, www.fao.org/news/story/en/item/20351/icode/.

24. UN FAO, "Food Outlook, Global Market Analysis," FAO Corporate Document Repository, June 2009, www.fao.org/docrep/011/ai482e/ai482e00.htm.

25. UN FAO, "World Agriculture 2030: Main Findings," FAO Newsroom, www.fao.org/english/newsroom/news/2002/7833-en.html.

26. Ibid.

27. Cited in Ed Pilkington, "Population of Older People Set to Surpass Number of Children, Report Finds," *Guardian*, July 20, 2009.

28. Figures on population in this section are taken from Fred Pearce, *The Coming Population Crash and Our Planet's Surpris-*

ing Future (Boston, MA: Beacon Press, 2010).

29. Fred Pearce, "The Population Crash," *Guardian*, February 1, 2010.

30. Jack A. Goldstone, "The New Population Bomb: The Four Megatrends That Will Change the World," *Foreign Affairs* 89, no. 1 (January/February 2010): 37.

31. Walden Bello and Marva Baviera, "Food Wars," *Monthly Review*, 61, no. 3 (July–August 2009): 17.

32. Martin Khor, "Obama, Africa and Food Security," *The Star* (Malaysia), July 13, 2009.

33. Philip McMichael, "The World Food Crisis in Historical Perspective," *Monthly Review* 61, No. 3 (July–August 2009): 32.

34. For analysis of how Haiti came to be in the same predicament, see "Inside USA: The Politics of Rice, Part 1," (Al Jazeera, July 2008), 17 min., 17 sec., video, GRAIN.org, www.grain.org/videos/?id=191.

35. Human Development Reports, UN Development Program, Statistics, http://hdr.undp.org/en/statistics/.

36. Quoted in UN FAO, "Number of Hungry People Rises to 963 Million," FAO Newsroom, December 9, 2008, www.fao.org/news/story/en/item/8836/icode/.

37. Lappé, "World Hunger: Its Roots and Remedies."

38. Aditya Chakrabortty, "Secret Report: Biofuel Caused Food Crisis," *Guardian*, July 3, 2008.

39. For more details on the short- and long-term causes of the food crisis see the July–August 2009 special edition of *Monthly Review*, "Agriculture and Food in Crisis: Conflict, Resistance, and Renewal."

40. Matthew Bigg and Tim Gaynor, "Downturn Forces More in U.S. to Rely on Free Food," Reuters, June 5, 2008.

41. Bellamy Foster, "Malthus' *Essay on Population*."

42. Carson, *Silent Spring*.

43. Quoted in John Bellamy Foster, *The Ecological Revolution: Making Peace with the Planet* (New York: Monthly Review Press, 2009), 67.

44. Quoted in Burkett, *Marx and Nature*, 131.

45. Ibid., 77.

46. J. Lundqvist, C. de Fraiture, and D. Molden, "Saving Water: From Field to Fork—Curbing Losses and Wastage in the Food Chain," SIWI Policy Brief, Stockholm International Water Institute, 2008, www.siwi.org/documents/.../PB_From_Filed_to_Fork_2008.pdf.

47. Ibid.

48. Leslie Kaufman, "Greening the Herds: A New Diet to Cap Gas," *New York Times*, June 4, 2009. In this example, cows are switched back to eating grasses, with a demonstrable decrease in methane emissions and healthier cows.

49. Felicity Lawrence, *Eat Your Heart Out: Why the Food Business Is Bad for the Planet and Your Health* (London: Penguin Books, 2008), chap. 2.

50. Jeff Tietz, "Pork's Dirty Secret: The Nation's Top Hog Producer Is Also One of America's Worst Polluters," *Rolling Stone*, December 14, 2006.

51. Lawrence, *Eat Your Heart,* chap. 4.

52. Doreen Carvajal and Stephen Castle, "A U.S. Hog Giant Transforms Eastern Europe," *New York Times*, May 5, 2009.

53. *Scientific American Earth 3.0*, 12.

54. Elisabeth Rosenthal, "Environmental Cost of Shipping Groceries Around the World," *New York Times*, April 26, 2008.

55. "About the Issues," Hungry for Change website for the film *Food Inc.*, www.foodincmovie.com/about-the-issues.php.

56. Cited in Lawrence, *Eat Your Heart,* chap. 6.

57. "Falling Fertility," *Economist*, October 29, 2009.

58. Engels, "The Housing Question," *Marx-Engels Collected Works*, vol. 23 (Moscow: Progress Publishers, 1988), 324–25.

59. Miguel A. Altieri, "Agroecology, Small Farms, and Food Sovereignty," *Monthly Review* 61, no. 3 (July–August 2009): 102.

60. See the Hungry for Change website for a list of small companies now bought out and owned by multinationals.

61. Brian Halweil, "Can Organic Farming Feed Us All?" WorldWatch Institute, April 16, 2006, www.worldwatch.org/node/4060.

62. Ibid.

63. Ibid. For further details, see *Monthly Review*'s special issue on Agriculture, July/August 2009.

64. Frederick Engels, *The Condition of the Working Class in England* (London: Penguin Books, 1987).

65. Ian Taylor, "Population Overload," BBC *Focus*, Issue 207 (September 2009): 32.

66. Ibid., 31.

CHAPTER THREE: WHY CAPITALISM CANNOT SOLVE THE PROBLEM

1. James Gustave Speth, *The Bridge at the End of the World: Capitalism, the Environment, and Crossing from Crisis to Sustainability* (New Haven, CT: Yale University Press, 2008), 63.

2. This figure depends on when we start. The sooner things begin, the more room we have for maneuver later. Either way, countries in the North would have to aim for a higher percentage than countries of the South.

3. Karl Marx, Abstract from the Preface of *A Contribution to the Critique of Political Economy* (Chicago: Charles Kerr and Company, 1911).

4. Dilip Hiro, *Blood of the Earth: The Battle for the World's Vanishing Oil Resources* (New York: Nation Books, 2007), 304.

5. Quoted in John Broder, "Industry Flexes Muscle, a Weaker Energy Bill Passes," *New York Times*, December 14, 2007.

6. Quoted in Nancy Pelosi, "Pelosi on Energy Bill: 'This Is a

Choice Between Yesterday and Tomorrow," press release, December 18, 2007, www.house.gov/pelosi/press/releases/Dec07/energyindependence.html.

7.   Quoted in Broder, "Industry Flexes Muscle."

8.   Juliette Jowit, "Biofuels Do 'More Harm Than Good,'" *Guardian*, January 20, 2008.

9.   Nigel Hunt, "FACTBOX: World Biofuels Production and Its Impact," Reuters, June 3, 2008, www.reuters.com/article/GCA-Agflation/idU.S.PAR34047820080603.

10. Ben Webster, "Green Fuels Cause More Harm Than Fossil Fuels, According to Report," *Times* (London), March 1, 2010.

11. Evans, *Fueling Our Future*, 103.

12. "Some Biofuels Are Worse Environmentally Than Fossil Fuels, Analysis Shows," Science Daily, January 7, 2008, www.sciencedaily.com/releases/2008/01/080103144404.htm.

13. Chakrabortty, "Secret Report: Biofuel."

14. For details on the campaign against biofuels and biochar and why they are absolutely not the answer to climate change, see www.biofulewatch.org.uk.

15. Pelosi, "Pelosi on Energy Bill."

16. *Scientific American Earth 3.0* 18, no. 4 (2008): 19.

17. For more details on the EV1 story, see *Who Killed the Electric Car?* www.sonyclassics.com/whokilledtheelectriccar/; and the "EV1 White Paper," www.cleanup-gm.com/ev1.html. For discussion of Chevron's role in killing the EV1 car, see www.ev1.org/chevron.htm. On California's ZEV mandate, see Chuck Squatriglia, "California Cuts ZEV Mandate in Favor of Plug-In Hybrids," Wired, March 27, 2008, http://blog.wired.com/cars/2008/03/the-california.html.

18. The whole ACES Bill, HR 2454 (at 932 pages) is available here: Committee on Energy and Commerce, publications, http://energycommerce.house.gov/press_111/20090515/hr2454.pdf.

For a more digestible summary see Kate Shepherd, "Every-thing You Always Wanted to Know About the Waxman-Markey Energy/Climate Bill—in Bullet Points," Grist.org, June 3, 2009, www.grist.org/article/2009-06-03-waxman-markey--bill -breakdown. For an extensive breakdown of the bill by the Pew Center, see www.pewclimate.org/acesa. Bill Meyer, "Oil Indus-try Floods Money into Lobbying Effort to Keep U.S. Using Fos-sil Fuels, Protect Profits," www.Cleveland.com, June 18, 2009, www.cleveland.com/nation/index.ssf/2009/06/oil_industry _floods_money_into.html.

19. Anne C. Mulkern, "Oil and Gas Interests Set Spending Record in 2009," Greenwire, www.EENews.net (subscription required), January 2, 2010.

20. Iain Murray, "Keep the Lights On!" The Corner blog, National Review Online, posted June 23, 2009.

21. Moshea Oinounou, "In Alternte Energy Plan, GOP Calls for 100 New Nuclear Plants in 20 Years," Foxnews.com, June 10, 2009, www.foxnews.com/politics/2009/06/10/Alternate-energy-plan -GOP-Calls-New-Nuclear-Plants-years/.

22. Dara Colwell, "Creating a 'Pollution Casino': Why the Energy Bill May End Up a Boon for Our Dirtiest Industries," AlterNet, June 24, 2009, www.alternet.org/environment/140884.

23. Government Account Office Report, "International Climate Change Programs: Lessons Learned from the European Union's Emissions Trading Scheme and the Kyoto Protocol's Clean Devel-opment Mechanism," GAO-09-151, November 18, 2008, www.gao .gov/new.items/d09151.pdf.

24. James Kanter, "Obama Beware: Brinksmanship Over Carbon Trading in Europe," *New York Times*, December 8, 2008.

25. Quoted in Colwell, "Creating a 'Pollution Casino.'"

26. Cited in ibid.

27. Cited in Friends of the Earth, "Take Action: Tell Congress It

Must Do Better," action alert, http://action.foe.org/t/8815/p/dia/action/public/?action_KEY=1117.

28. Ibid.

29. Eric Etheridge, "Waxman-Markey: As Good as It Gets," Opinionator blog, nytimes.com, June 24, 2009.

30. Text of President Obama's State of the Union Address is available at www.whitehouse.gov/the-press-office/remarks-president-state-union-address.

31. Quoted in Katherine Ling, "What Does $36 Billion Buy Democrats?" E&E News, February 2, 2010, www.eenews.net/public/EEDaily/2010/02/09/1.

32. Quoted in Darren Samuelsohn, "Obama Says He'll Meet Republicans 'Halfway' on Energy," E&E News (subscription required), February 9, 2010.

33. Barack Obama and Joe Biden, "New Energy for America," campaign statement on energy, http://my.barackobama.com/page/content/newenergy.

34. Stephen Ansolabehere et al., *The Future of Coal: Options for a Carbon-Constrained World* (Cambridge, MA: Massachusetts Institute of Technology, 2007), http://web.mit.edu/coal/.

35. Lynas, *Six Degrees*, 249.

36. Fred Pearce, "Time to Bury the 'Clean Coal' Myth," *Guardian*, October 30, 2008.

37. Quoted in Clifford Krauss, "Energy Research on a Shoestring," *New York Times*, January 25, 2007.

38. Christa Marshall, "'Coal Country' Poses the Biggest Obstacle in Senate Climate Debate," Climatewire, E&E News, November 2, 2009, www.eenews.net/public/climatewire/2009/11/02/1.

39. Khwaja Salim, letters, *Guardian*, March 26, 2010.

40. "Further Signs of Stress in Canada's Oil Sands," Associated Press, November 17, 2008.

41. Kenneth Deffeyes, *Beyond Oil: The View from Hubbert's Peak*

(New York: Hill and Wang, 2005), chaps. 6 and 7.

42. Cahal Milmo, "Biggest Environmental Crime in History," *Independent*, December 10, 2007.

43. Quoted in Mark Milner, "BP to Pump Billions into Oil Sands Despite Green Worries and High Costs," *Guardian*, December 6, 2007.

44. Quoted in Terry Macalister, "Big Oil Lets Sun Set on Renewables," *Guardian*, December 11, 2007.

45. Ibid.

46. Fred Pearce, "Green Wash: BP and the Myth of a World 'Beyond Petroleum,'" *Guardian*, November 20, 2008.

47. Gareth Dale, "'On the Menu or at the Table': Corporations and Climate Change," *International Socialism* 116 (Autumn 2007): 119.

48. Krauss, "Energy Research on a Shoestring."

49. Andrew Revkin, "Budgets Falling in Race to Fight Global Warming," *New York Times*, October 30, 2009.

50. Quoted in Mike Soraghan, "Shale Plays Create 'New World' for Energy Industry," E&E News, March 11, 2010, www.eenews.net/public/Greenwire/2010/03/11/1.

51. Professor Robert W. Howarth, "Preliminary Assessment of the Greenhouse Gas Emissions from Natural Gas Obtained by Hydraulic Fracturing," Cornell University, March 17, 2010, draft, www.eeb.cornell.edu/howarth/GHG%20emissions%20from%20Marcellus%20Shale%20—%20with%20figure%20—%203.17.2010%20draft.doc.pdf.

52. Jad Mouawad and Cliffford Krauss, "Dark Side of Natural Gas Boom," *New York Times*, December 7, 2009; Mike Soraghan, "Oilfield Company Failed to Report Fracking Violations to EPA—Documents," E&E News, March 23, 2010, www.eenews.net/public/Greenwire/2010/03/23/1.

53. Anne Mulkern, "Industry Targets 'Hydraulic Fracturing' Bill," *New York Times*, May 7, 2009.

54. Mike Soraghan, "Industry Supports Push against Hydraulic Fracturing Regs," E&E News (subscription required), March 24, 2010. Energy in Depth is a group of independent drilling organizations led by the Independent Petroleum Association of America.

55. Paul Roberts, *The End of Oil* (New York: Mariner Books, 2005). See also Deffeyes, *Beyond Oil*.

56. Ian Sample, "Oil Shock—the Real Crisis Has Yet to Hit," *New Scientist*, June 28–July 4, 2008, 34.

57. Terry Macalister, "Shell's Record Profits Branded 'Obscene,'" *Guardian*, January 31, 2008.

58. Michael Klare, *Rising Powers, Shrinking Planet: The New Geopolitics of Energy* (New York: Metropolitan Books, 2008), 60.

59. Julian Borger, "Closed Door Arctic Deal Denounced as 'Carve Up,'" *Guardian*, May 28, 2008.

60. Robin McKie, "Arctic Thaw Opens Up Fabled Trade Route," *Guardian*, September 16, 2007.

61. Daniel Yergin, *The Prize: The Epic Quest for Oil, Money and Power* (New York: Free Press, 1992), 183.

62. See Klare, *Rising Power, Shrinking Planet*.

63. Klare, *Resource Wars: The New Landscape of Global Conflict* (New York: Owl Books, 2002). For more details on the implications of the rise of China, India, and Russia for geopolitical conflict over diminishing resources, see Klare, *Rising Power, Shrinking Planet*.

64. Brown, "Could Food Shortages."

65. For details see Barnett R. Rubin, "The Political Economy of War and Peace in Afghanistan," *World Development* 28, no. 10 (2000), http://pdfcast.org/pdf/the-political-economy-of-war-and-peace -in-afghanistan.

66. From 2004 to 08 the United States supplied 31 percent of world arms, compared to 25 percent for Russia. See Mark Bromley et al., "Recent Trends in the Arms Trade," Stockholm International Peace Research Institute (SIPRI) Background Paper, April 2009,

http://books.sipri.org/files/misc/SIPRIBP0904a.pdf. According to a report in the *Boston Globe*, in 2006 the United States supplied almost half of all conventional weapons sales to developing countries. Brian Bender, "US Is Top Purveyor on Weapons Sales List: Shipments Grow to Unstable Areas," *Boston Globe*, November 13, 2006. For data on the United States as the biggest market for illicit drugs, see Oriana Zill and Lowell Bergman, "Do the Math: Why the Illegal Drug Market Is Big Business," *Frontline* Special Report: Drug Wars, WGBH Educational Foundation, www.pbs.org/wgbh/pages/frontline/shows/drugs/special/math.html.

67. Darren Samuelsohn, "No 'Pass' for Developing Countries in Next Treaty—Stern," Greenwire, E&E Newst, December 12, 2009, www.eenews.net/public/Greenwire/2009/12/09/1.

68. David Smith, "Africa May Have Lost £1tn in Illegal Flows of Money, Researchers Say," *Guardian*, April 1, 2010.

69. Brown, "Could Food Shortages."

CHAPTER FOUR: FALSE SOLUTIONS FAVORED BY THE SYSTEM

1. Quoted in Darren Samuelsohn, "House Panels Seek to Limit Effect of Cap and Trade on Nation's Pocketbook," E&E Daily, March 9, 2009, http://www.eenews.net/public/EEDaily/2009/03/09/1.

2. For the official text and specifics of targets of the 1997 Kyoto Protocol, how they would be achieved, and differentiating targets between countries at differing levels of economic development, see the UN-FCCC Report on Kyoto, available for download at: http://unfccc.int/kyoto_protocol/items/2830.php. A summary report and analysis of the estimated economic impact is available at the U.S. government's International Energy Agency: www.eia.doe.gov/oiaf/kyoto/execsum.html. For a political analysis of

the failings of Kyoto and how the treaty introduced the concept of cap and trade, see Larry Lohman, "The Kyoto Protocol: Neocolonialism and Fraud," The Corner House, April 2002, www.thecornerhouse.org.uk/item.shtml?x=52199.

3. Steve Connor, "Britain's Carbon Strategy 'Up in Smoke,'" *Independent*, December 17, 2007.

4. James Hansen, "Coal-Fired Power Stations Are Death Factories. Close Them," *Observer*, February 15, 2009.

5. Ben Stewart, "Kingsnorth Climbdown Is the British Climate Movement's Biggest Victory," *Guardian*, October 8, 2009.

6. Michael McCarthy, "Cleared: Jury Decides that Threat of Global Warming Justifies Breaking the Law," *Independent*, September 11, 2008.

7. David Adam, "Analysis: Has the Kyoto Protocol Worked?" *Guardian*, December 8, 2008. Quoted in the article is Yvo de Boer, former executive secretary of the UN climate secretariat of the IPCC, who is pretty straightforward about the outcome of Kyoto when asked whether it worked: "In terms of emission reductions achieved, the answer would be no."

8. Evans, *Fueling Our Future*, 33.

9. George Monbiot, "We've Been Suckered Again by the U.S. So Far the Bali Deal Is Worse Than Kyoto," *Guardian*, December 17, 2007.

10. Alex Kaplun, "Energy Industry Dollars Increasingly Fill Democratic Coffers," E&E News (subscription required), July 28, 2009.

11. Quoted in "Deal Agreed in Bali Climate Talks," *Guardian*, December 15, 2007.

12. Lynas, *Six Degrees*, 264.

13. Michael A. Levi, "Copenhagen's Inconvenient Truth," *Foreign Affairs* 88, no. 5. (September/October 2009): 92–93.

14. Ibid.

15. Shiva, *Soil Not Oil*, 24.

16. John Broder, "Many Goals Remain Unmet in 5 Nations' Climate Deal," *New York Times*, December 18, 2009.

17. Richard S. Chang, "Tata Nano: The World's Cheapest Car," *New York Times*, January 10, 2008.

18. Quoted in Suzanne Goldenberg, "Copenhagen Climate Change Talks Must Fail, Says Top Scientist," *Guardian*, December 2, 2009.

19. See Herman Daly's extensive writings on ecological economics for details.

20. Nick Davies, "Power Firms Accused of Emissions Trade Cheating," *Guardian*, December 7, 2007. According to a report by International Rivers and cited in the *Guardian* article, the UN's Clean Development Mechanism "allows organizations in richer countries to emit extra greenhouse gases by paying for carbon credits to fund schemes in poorer countries that cut emissions"—when, in fact, many of these projects do not appear to be contributing to a lowering of emissions.

21. Fiona Harvey and Stephen Fidler, "Industry Caught in Carbon 'Smokescreen,'" *Financial Times,* April 25, 2007.

22. Mark Shapiro, "Conning the Climate: Inside the Carbon-Trading Shell Game," *Harper's*, February 2010.

23. Stephen Castle, "EU Carbon Trading Scheme Failing to Curb Emissions from Big Polluters," *Guardian*, April 3, 2007.

24. Danny Forston, "Power Firms to Pocket 6bn from Carbon 'Handouts' in New Emissions Regime," *Independent*, January 2, 2008.

25. Faisal Islam, "CO_2nering the Market," *Ecologist*, June 2008.

26. Dan Milmo, "We'll Fight You All the Way, Airlines Warn EU Over Carbon Trading Plans," *Guardian*, November 19, 2007.

27. Quoted in Dale, "On the Menu or at the Table."

28. Heather Rogers, *Gone Tomorrow: The Hidden Life of Garbage* (New York: The New Press, 2005), 97.

29. Ibid.

30. Ibid., 123.

31. Ibid., 114.

32. Marx, *Capital,* vol. 2 (New York: Penguin, 1992), 391.

33. Hamilton, *Growth Fetish*, 84.

34. Rogers, *Gone Tomorrow,* 6.

35. James Gibson, *The Perfect War: Technowar in Vietnam* (New York: Atlantic Monthly Press, 1986), 319.

36. Quoted in Rogers, *Gone Tomorrow*, 132.

37. Keep America Beautiful (KAB) was founded in 1956. According to its website, it continues to receive major funding from corporations such as Philip Morris USA, PepsiCo, Waste Management Inc., and the Aluminum Association among many other organizations with a history of opposing bottle returns. In the 1970s KAB ran the now infamous ads of the Native American canoeing through a river littered with waste as a single tear trickled down his face. For a list of KAB's corporate donors, see their website: www.kab.org/site/PageServer?pagename=Corporate_contributors. On the American Can Corporation, see Louis Blumberg and Robert Gottlieb, *War on Waste: Can America Win Its Battle with Garbage?* (Washington, DC: Island Press, 1989), 19.

38. Rogers, *Gone Tomorrow,* 4.

39. Ibid., 158.

40. Consumers International Report, "E-Waste: West Africa Continues to Drown in the Rich World's Obsolete Electronics," August 21, 2008. See the Consumers International website at www.consumersinternational.org/therealdeal.

41. Cited in Fred Pearce, "Greenwash: E-waste Trade Is the Unacceptable Face of Recycling," *Guardian*, May 28, 2009.

42. Sohbet Karbuz, U.S. Military Energy Consumption—Facts and Figures," at the Energy Bulletin, www.energybulletin.net/node/29925.

43. Peter Atherton et al., *New Nuclear: The Economics Say No*, November 9, 2009, Citi Global Markets report, www.citigroupgeo

.com/pdf/SEU27102.pdf.

44. Julio Godoy, "Nuclear Does Not Make Economic Sense Say Studies," Inter Press Service, February 12, 2010, www.ipsnews .net/news.asp?idnews=50308.

45. Quoted in Ling, "What Does $36 Billion Buy."

46. Quoted in Brendan Borrell, "Nuclear Power Could Cost Trillions over Renewable," *Scientific American*, June 19, 2009.

47. David Biello, "Will the Nuclear Power 'Renaissance' Ever Reach Critical Mass?" *Scientific American*, May 21, 2009.

48. Amory Lovins, "'New' Nuclear Reactors, Same Old Story," *Solutions*, Spring 2009.

49. Biello, "Will Nuclear Power."

50. Godoy, "Nuclear Does Not."

51. Dilip Hiro, *Blood of the Earth: The Battle for the World's Vanishing Oil Resources* (New York: Nation Books, 2007), 255.

52. Helen Caldicott, *Nuclear Power Is Not the Answer* (New York: New Press, 2006), 6.

53. Shiva, *Soil Not Oil*, 26.

54. Greenpeace/European Renewable Energy Council, *Energy [R]evolution: A Blueprint for Solving Global Warming*, January 2007, 15, www.energyblueprint.info. A report specific to the United States that illustrates how the United States could move to a fossil-fuel-free future without nuclear power is available at www.energyblueprint.info/65.0.html.

55. David J. C. MacKay, *Sustainable Energy—Without the Hot Air,"* (Cambridge: UIT Cambridge Ltd., 2008), 100.

56. Sharon Squassoni, "Hanging Questions," *IAEA Bulletin* 50–52, (May 2009): 54.

CHAPTER FIVE: REAL SOLUTIONS RIGHT NOW: WHAT WE NEED TO FIGHT FOR

1. Hari, "After Catastrophe in Copenhagen."

2.   "Beyond Carbon," *Scientific American* 295, no. 3, special issue (September 2006).

3.   Quoted in Penny Cole and Philip Wade, *Running a Temperature: An Action Plan for the Eco-Crisis* (London: Lupus Books, 2007). Williams Hoagland, "Solar Energy: Technology Will Allow Radiation from the Sun to Provide Non-polluting and Cheap Fuels, as Well as Electricity," in *Oil and the Future of Energy* (Guildford, CT: Lyons Press, 2007).

4.   George Monbiot, *Heat: How to Stop the Planet from Burning* (Cambridge, MA: South End Press, 2007).

5.   Linda J. Blimes and Joseph Stiglitz, "The Iraq War Will Cost Us $3 Trillion, and Much More," *Washington Post*, March 9, 2008.

6.   Williams Hoagland, "Solar Energy: Technology Will Allow Radiation from the Sun to Provide Non-polluting and Cheap Fuels, as Well as Electricity," in *Oil and the Future of Energy* (Guildford, CT: Lyons Press, 2007).

7.   Vasilis Fthwenakis, James Mason, and Ken Zweibel, "A Solar Grand Plan," *Scientific American*, January 2008.

8.   Christopher Flavin, *Low-Carbon Energy: A Roadmap*, Worldwatch Institute, Report 178, 2008, 22, www.worldwatch.org/node/5945.

9.   Mark Jacobson and Mark Delucchi, "A Path to Sustainable Energy by 2030," *Scientific American*, November 2009, 58.

10.   MacKay, *Sustainable Energy*, 236.

11.   Caldicott, *Nuclear Power Is Not the Answer*, 168.

12.   Fthwenakis, Mason, and Zweibel, "Solar Grand Plan."

13.   The Royal Society, *Philosophical Transactions A: Mathematical, Physical, and Engineering Sciences* 365 (2007), 1,057–94.

14.   American Lung Association, "State of the Air Report," May 1, 2008, www.lungusa.org/assets/documents/publications/state-of-the-air/state-of-the-air-report-2008.pdf.

15.   Ibid.

16. Ibid.

17. James Gustave Speth, *The Bridge at the End of the World: Capitalism, the Environment, and Crossing from Crisis to Sustainability* (New Haven: Yale University Press, 2008), 35.

18. "Reduced Fertility Linked to Flame Retardant Exposure," Science Daily, February 10, 2010, www.sciencedaily.com/releases /2010/01/100126123208.htm.

19. Sara Goodman, "Human Testing at Heart of Debate over U.S. Toxics Law," E&E News, February 15, 2010, www.eenews.net/ public/Greenwire/2010/02/15/4.

20. Goodman, "EPA Oversight of New Substances Fails to Protect Human Health," E&E News, February 19, 2010, www.eenews .net/public/Greenwire/2010/02/19/18.

21. "Chemical Controls," editorial, *Scientific American*, April 2010.

22. Monbiot, *Heat*, 65.

23. Chris Goodall, *Ten Technologies to Save the Planet* (London: Profile Books, 2008), 121.

24. Adenike Adeyeye et al., *Estimating U.S. Government Subsidies to Energy Sources: 2002–2008*, Environmental Law Institute report, September 2009.

25. "Declining Defense: Obama's Budget Does Cut on Federal Department," *Wall Street Journal Review and Outlook*, March 2, 2009; "China's Defense Budget to Grow 7.5% in 2010: Spokesman," *China Daily*, May 13, 2010.

26. David Ransom and Vanessa Baird, eds., *People First Economics* (New Internationalist Publishing: Oxford, 2009), 116.

27. Nelson Schwartz and Lisa Story, "Pay of Hedge Fund Managers Roared Back Last Year," *New York Times*, March 31, 2010.

28. Oscar Olivera and Tom Lewis, *¡Cochabamba!: Water War in Bolivia* (Cambridge, MA: South End Press, 2004).

29. Hiro, *Blood of the Earth*, 333.

CHAPTER SIX: MARXISM AND THE ENVIRONMENT

1. Frederick Engels, *Socialism: Utopian and Scientific* (Chicago: Charles H. Kerr and Company, 1910) chap. 2.

2. See John Bellamy Foster, *Marx's Ecology: Materialism and Nature* (New York: Monthly Review Press, 2000); Paul Burkett, *Marx and Nature*; and Burkett, *Marxism and Ecological Economics: Toward a Red and Green Political Economy* (Chicago: Haymarket Books, 2009).

3. For details on how Marxism became distorted by states calling themselves socialist and how the Soviet Union decayed into a state-run dictatorship of extreme exploitation and oppression see John Molyneux, *What Is the Real Marxist Tradition?* (Chicago: Haymarket Books, 2003) and Anthony Arnove et al., *Russia: From Workers' State to State Capitalism* (Chicago: Haymarket Books, 2003).

4. "We are fifty to a hundred years behind the advanced countries. We have to make good this distance in ten years. Either we do this or they crush us." Quoted in J. Miller, "A Political Economy of Socialism in the Making," *Soviet Studies* 4, no. 4 (April 1953): 418.

5. Frederick Engels, "The Part Played by Labor in the Transition from Ape to Man," in *The Origin of the Family, Private Property and the State* (New York: International Publishers, 2007), 260–61.

6. Ibid.

7. Leon Trotsky, *Problems of Everyday Life* (New York: Pathfinder Press, 1973), 317.

8. Quoted in Foster, *Marx's Ecology*, 132.

9. Quoted in Speth, *Bridge at the End of the World*, 56.

10. Karl Marx, *Capital*, vol. 1 (New York: International Publishers, 1967), 505–07.

11. Quoted in Bellamy Foster, *Marx's Ecology*, 72.

12. Ibid., 112.

13. Engels, "Part Played by Labor."

14. Vladimir Vernadsky, *The Biosphere* (New York: Nevraumont Publishing Company, 1998), 57.

15. Trofim Lysenko was the director of the Lenin All-Union Academy of Agricultural Sciences under Stalin. His theories of vernalization backed the disproven ideas of Lamarck concerning acquired characteristics. Lysenkoism has become synonymous with the idea of science and scientists backing certain scientific ideas based on their political expediency rather than their scientific rigor.

16. Douglas Weiner, *Models of Nature: Ecology, Conservation and Cultural Revolution in Soviet Russia* (Pittsburgh, PA: University of Pittsburgh, 2000), 27. Information in this section, including the Podiapolsky quote, is taken from here.

17. Ibid. 169.

18. A. G. Tansley, "The Ecosystem," reprinted in *Keeping Things Whole: Readings in Environmental Science* (Chicago: Great Books Foundation, 2003), 191.

19. Quoted in Bellamy Foster, *Ecological Revolution*, 159.

20. Ibid., 181.

CHAPTER SEVEN: FROM CAPITALIST CRISIS TO SOCIALIST SUSTAINABILITY

1. G. Brundtland, ed., "From One Earth to One World," in *Our Common Future: Report of the World Commission on Environment and Development*, part IV (A Call for Action), 3, 1987, www.un-documents.net/wced-ocf.htm.

2. U.S. General Services Administration, "Strengthening Federal Environmental, Energy, and Transportation Management," Executive Order 13423, January 2, 2007.

3. Cargill, Inc., Statement on the Environment, www.cargill.com/commitments/environment/index.jsp.

4. Adrian Parr, *Hijacking Sustainability* (Cambridge, MA: MIT

Press, 2009).

5. Lauren Morello, "Navy and Marines Aim for a Leaner, Greener Fighting Machine," *E&E News*, March 25, 2010, http://www.eenews.net/public/climatewire/2010/03/25/3.

6. "Towards Sustainable Development," *Our Common Future*, chap. 2.

7. The definition was criticized by indigenous groups who have argued that there is a fourth component to sustainability: culture.

8. Burkett, *Marx and Nature*, 88.

9. Quoted in Eric Ruder, "What Is Socialism?" *International Socialist Review* 65, May–June 2009.

10. Quoted in Foster, *Ecological Revolution*, 24.

11. OECD Environment Program, "Indicators to Measure Decoupling of Environmental Pressure from Economic Growth," Executive Summary, May 16, 2002, www.oecd.org/dataoecd/0/52/1933638.pdf.

12. Richard York, Brett Clark, and John Bellamy Foster, "Capitalism in Wonderland," *Monthly Review* 61, no. 1 (May 2009).

13. Foster, *Ecological Revolution*, chap. 6.

14. Quoted in "Energy for Tomorrow: Repowering the Planet," *National Geographic* special issue, May 2009, 52.

15. Quoted in Foster, *Ecological Revolution*, 22.

16. Burkett, *Marx and Nature*, 139.

17. Ibid., 89.

18. Quoted in Joel Kovel, *The Enemy of Nature: The End of Capitalism or the End of the World?* (New York: Zed Books, 2007), 60.

19. Karl Marx, "Speech at the Anniversary of the *People's Paper* (1856)" in Robert C. Tucker, *The Marx-Engels Reader* (New York: W. W. Norton, 1978), 427.

20. Quoted in Clifford Connor, *A People's History of Science: Miners, Midwives, and "Low Mechanicks"* (New York: Nation Books, 2005), 364.

21. Marx, *Grundrisse*, 409–10.

22. Karl Marx, "Estranged Labor," in *Economic and Philosophic Manuscripts of 1844* (Amherst, NY: Prometheus Books, 1988), 75–76.

23. "To make the earth an object of huckstering—the earth which is our one and all, the first condition of our existence—was the last step towards making oneself an object of huckstering. It was and is to this very day an immorality surpassed only by the immorality of self-alienation. And the original appropriation—the monopolization of the earth by a few, the exclusion of the rest from that which is the condition of their life—yields nothing in immorality to the subsequent huckstering of the earth." Frederick Engels, "Outlines of a Critique of Political Economy," appendix to Marx, *Economic and Philosophic Manuscripts*, 185.

24. Barry Commoner's Four Laws of Ecology (the fourth one not mentioned is nature knows best) were formulated in his book *The Closing Circle: Nature, Man, and Technology* (New York: Knopf, 1971).

25. Quoted in Hamilton, *Growth Fetish*, 14.

26. Ibid., 83.

27. Karl Marx and Frederick Engels, Phil Gasper, ed., *The Communist Manifesto: A Road Map to the History's Most Important Political Document* (Chicago: Haymarket Books, 2005), 43.

28. Karl Marx, *Capital,* vol. 1 (New York: International Publishers, 1967), 264–65.

29. Marx, *Grundrisse*, 409.

CHAPTER EIGHT: WHAT WOULD A SUSTAINABLE SOCIETY LOOK LIKE?

1. "All progress in capitalistic agriculture is a progress in the art, not only of robbing the labourer, but of robbing the soil; all progress in increasing the fertility of the soil for a given time, is a

progress towards ruining the lasting sources of that fertility. The more a country starts its development on the foundation of modern industry, like the United States, for example, the more rapid is this process of destruction. Capitalist production, therefore, develops technology, and the coming together of various processes into a social whole, only by sapping the original sources of all wealth—the soil and the labourer," in Marx, *Capital*, vol. 1, 506.

2.   Juliette Jowit, "World's Top Firms Cause $2.2tn of Environmental Damage, Report Estimates," *Guardian*, February 18, 2010.

3.   David Adam, "50 Billion Pound of European Investment Needed to Kick-Start Saharan Solar Plan," *Guardian*, March 11, 2009.

4.   MacKay, "*Sustainable Energy*," 120.

5.   See Lawrence, "Pigs," *Eat Your Heart Out,* chap. 4.

6.   For more details on how sustainable agriculture is more productive—and an awful lot less polluting—than agribusiness, see the July–August 2009 special edition of *Monthly Review*.

7.   Quoted in Foster, *Ecological Revolution*, 180.

8.   Stan Cox, *Sick Planet: Corporate Food and Medicine* (London: Pluto Press, 2008), 62.

CONCLUSION

1.   Marx, *Capital*, vol. 1 (New York: International Publishers, 1967), 43.

2.   Larry Elliott, "Subsidising Cows While Milking the Poor," *Guardian*, October 17, 2005.

3.   See chaps. 5 and 6 of Tristram Stuart, *Waste: Uncovering the Global Food Scandal* (New York: Norton, 2009). The whole book is a gruesome and devastating indictment of the capitalist agricultural system.

4.   Ibid.

5.   Eric Toussaint, *Your Money or Your Life: The Tyranny of Global Finance* (Chicago: Haymarket Books, 2005), 34. By 2008, it was

the top thirty-nine billionaires on Forbes' list whose combined net worth topped $1 trillion. See Forbes, www.forbes.com/2007/03/07/billionaires-worldsrichest_07billionaires_cz_lk_af_0308billie_land.html.

6. Karl Marx, *Capital*, vol. 3 (New York: International Publishers, 1977), 820.

7. Tricia Holly Davis, Geoffrey Lean, and Susie Mesure, "Big Business Says Addressing Climate Change 'Rates Very Low on Agenda,'" *Independent*, January 28, 2008.

Index

Black Liberation and Socialism

Ahmed Shawki • A sharp and insightful analysis of historic movements against racism in the United States—from the separatism of Marcus Garvey, to the militancy of Malcolm X and the Black Panther Party, to the eloquence of Martin Luther King Jr., and much more—with essential lessons for today's struggles. • ISBN 9781931859264

Sexuality and Socialism: History, Theory, and Politics of LGBT Liberation

Sherry Wolf • *Sexuality and Socialism* is a remarkably accessible analysis of many of the most challenging questions for those concerned with full equality for lesbian, gay, bisexual, and transgender (LGBT) people. Sherry Wolf analyzes different theories about oppression—including those of Marxism, postmodernism, identity politics, and queer theory—and challenges myths about genes, gender, and sexuality. • ISBN 9781931859790

Women and Socialism

Sharon Smith • Thirty years have passed since the heyday of the women's liberation struggle, yet women remain second-class citizens. Feminism has shifted steadily rightward since the 1960s. This collection of essays examines these issues from a Marxist perspective, badly needed today. • ISBN 9781931859110

The Meaning of Marxism

Paul D'Amato • This book is a lively and accessible introduction to the ideas of Karl Marx, as well as other key Marxists, with historical and contemporary examples. The Meaning of Marxism shows that a "radical, fundamental transformation of existing society" is not only possible, but urgently necessary. • ISBN 9781931859295

ABOUT HAYMARKET BOOKS

Haymarket Books is a nonprofit, progressive book distributor and publisher, a project of the Center for Economic Research and Social Change. We believe that activists need to take ideas, history, and politics into the many struggles for social justice today. Learning the lessons of past victories, as well as defeats, can arm a new generation of fighters for a better world. As Karl Marx said, "The philosophers have merely interpreted the world; the point, however, is to change it."

We take inspiration and courage from our namesakes, the Haymarket Martyrs, who gave their lives fighting for a better world. Their 1886 struggle for the eight-hour day, which gave us May Day, the international workers' holiday, reminds workers around the world that ordinary people can organize and struggle for their own liberation. These struggles continue today across the globe—struggles against oppression, exploitation, hunger, and poverty.

It was August Spies, one of the Martyrs targeted for being an immigrant and an anarchist, who predicted the battles being fought to this day. "If you think that by hanging us you can stamp out the labor movement," Spies told the judge, "then hang us. Here you will tread upon a spark, but here, and there, and behind you, and in front of you, and everywhere, the flames will blaze up. It is a subterranean fire. You cannot put it out. The ground is on fire upon which you stand."

We could not succeed in our publishing efforts without the generous financial support of our readers. Many people contribute to our project through the Haymarket Sustainers program, where donors receive free books in return for their monetary support. If you would like to be a part of this program, please contact us at info@haymarketbooks.org.

Shop our full catalog online at www.haymarketbooks.org or call 773-583-7884 to order.